D0455612

CALGARY PUBLIC LIBRARY

JUL   2018

Should the Tent Be Burning Like That?

Also by Bill Heavey

If You Didn't Bring Jerky, What Did I Just Eat?

It's Only Slow Food Until You Try to Eat It

You're Not Lost if You Can Still See the Truck

Should the Tent Be Burning Like That?

A Professional Amateur's Guide
to the Outdoors

BILL HEAVEY

Atlantic Monthly Press
New York

Copyright © 2017 by Bill Heavey

All rights reserved. No part of this book may be reproduced in any form or by any electronic or mechanical means, including information storage and retrieval systems, without permission in writing from the publisher, except by a reviewer, who may quote brief passages in a review. Scanning, uploading, and electronic distribution of this book or the facilitation of such without the permission of the publisher is prohibited. Please purchase only authorized electronic editions, and do not participate in or encourage electronic piracy of copyrighted materials. Your support of the author's rights is appreciated. Any member of educational institutions wishing to photocopy part or all of the work for classroom use, or anthology, should send inquiries to Grove Atlantic, 154 West 14th Street, New York, NY 10011 or permissions@groveatlantic.com.

This book is published by arrangement with *Field & Stream* magazine. All of the pieces in this collection were originally published in *Field & Stream*, except for "The South's Top Gun," which first appeared in *Garden & Gun* (June/July 2015), and "Point Well Taken," which first appeared in the *Washington Post* (June 1996).

FIRST EDITION

Published simultaneously in Canada
Printed in the United States of America

First Grove Atlantic hardcover edition: December 2017

ISBN 978-0-8021-2710-5
eISBN 978-0-8021-8927-1

Library of Congress Cataloging-in-Publication data is available for this title.

Atlantic Monthly Press
an imprint of Grove Atlantic
154 West 14th Street
New York, NY 10011

Distributed by Publishers Group West

groveatlantic.com

17 18 19 20   10 9 8 7 6 5 4 3 2 1

To Emma

Fail. Fail again. Fail better.
                    —Samuel Beckett (1906–1989)

Contents

Contents

Contents

PART III

Contents

PART IV

Contents

Should the Tent
Be Burning
Like That?

Introduction

The important things to know about this book are that it is crammed with the kind of practical advice* that you will never use and that it contains about sixty short works (most from *Field & Stream*, but also from the *Washington Post* and some magazines) that can be read in any order. These pieces have been known to make people laugh, cry, or curse, often in their bathrooms, since that is where many people prefer to read my stuff.

Once, asked to define my job as a writer, I replied with the following anecdote: I used to spend a lot of time at a friend's farm, where I killed my first deer and caught my first big largemouth bass. My friend employed a number of locals to help manage the place. One, he said,

---

* On second thought, there are occasions when the knowledge in these pages could prove invaluable. This book will show you why it is sometimes necessary to shoot a hunting arrow into your motel room's phone book. Why you'll never be a good bird hunter if you aim your shotgun and why—if you absolutely cannot stop yourself from aiming—you will never hit anything unless you aim at empty air. You will learn why putting a boy on his first bluegill is as high an honor as a man can aspire to in this life and that the secret to success in this is—contrary to everything you've been told—to forget about using a bobber. Why William Faulkner's "The Bear" may be the best thing ever written about hunting. Why, when your heart has been crushed in love or by the death of a friend, the proper response is to go fishing. Why, when it comes to exacting revenge, the mafia have nothing on your teenage daughter. Why, if you are riding a horse for five hours up into the mountains on a weeklong trout expedition, pantyhose is essential. (And, if you are male, not to let the lady at the lingerie counter jerk you around. What you want is size XL, taupe, opaque rather than sheer, and regular rather than control top. Be firm about this. Otherwise, you'll look unmanly.) Finally, never shy away from having your picture taken because you don't like how you look at this age. Right now you look better than you ever will again.

was a fan of my writing in *Field & Stream* and wanted to meet me. I agreed immediately, feeling the warmth that comes from having your efforts appreciated. "I should probably tell you a few things about Doug," my friend said. "Guy's about seventy, has been divorced three times, and lives in a trailer. He's broke, has a bad leg, but refuses to see a doctor about it." I said that sounded rough but that I didn't see how it mattered. I'll take an admirer wherever I can find one. Just then, Doug came limping into the paddock. Introductions were made. We shook hands. "I really enjoy your stuff, Bill," he said. "I really do." I thanked him and told him I appreciated it. Then came silence. It stretched out for a good while. Doug's features creased into a kind of perplexed and agitated state. He had something else to say but wasn't sure whether he should. Finally, he plunged ahead. "I just gotta tell you this, man. Sometimes I read your stories and, well, I just feel so *sorry* for you." I laughed and assured him it was fine. Which was true.

When I first started writing for *Field & Stream*, I saw that the expert end of its masthead was overpopulated. The other end—a place for amateurs with more passion than proficiency, for guys who fail more often than they succeed—was wide open. It was here that by inclination and experience I planted my flag. I confess that Doug's remark captured what I do in a way I hadn't heard before, but in time I came to see it as an affirmation and compliment. At its best, my writing makes people whom the world often judges as failures feel better about themselves. I think there's a certain nobility in that.

I

Chasing the Chrome

When the steelhead are running, nothing else matters to Mikey Dvorak. Not money, not manners, not even where he's going to sleep at night. What matters is finding a biting steelie somewhere, anywhere, on the West Coast. We went along for the ride.

The first time I met Mikey Dvorak, he asked if he could borrow fifty bucks.

At the time I thought he was a bum. I still think he's a bum, but in the same way that an itinerant Buddhist monk is a bum. Except Mikey's spiritual path was chasing steelhead.

I met Mikey through Kirk Lombard, a hard-core angler in San Francisco, who told me that if I really wanted to meet a "true fishing nomad" I should meet Mikey, a steelhead addict who had no fixed address and never seemed to have more than a few bucks on him. But it didn't seem to bother him. "All he cares about is being where the fish are," Kirk said. That's why Mikey often slept in his truck—not on a pad in the back so he could stretch out, but upright in the driver's seat because the rest of the truck was too full of gear. "And he's such a maniac that he sleeps on the ramp."

"I'm afraid I don't follow."

"When Mikey's steelhead fishing, he wants to be the first guy on the river. So, the night before, he backs his drift boat down the ramp, puts the truck in park, and conks out. The next morning, the first guy at the ramp finds Mikey there. The guy is pissed and bangs on Mikey's window to wake him up. At which point Mikey wakes, apologizes, and launches. So he's on the river ahead of anybody else."

I had to meet this guy.

A few days later the three of us headed down the California coast to chase white sea bass, a highly mobile fish that migrates up from Baja, California, as the ocean warms in spring. We hoped to intercept some around Monterey. I dug myself a hole in the backseat of Mikey's truck, which was crammed to the roof with fishing and camping gear, as well as a great deal of stuff that should have been in a landfill. Mikey said that the police had recently stopped him on this very stretch of road because his truck fit the profile of a meth user's vehicle. The cops had searched it thoroughly. Actually, Mikey said, the stop had been a good thing. The cops turned up tackle that he'd given up for lost.

I was already captivated by the guy. He named every bird we saw at surprising distances, and when I asked how, he explained that he was doing it by the birds' flight characteristics, which were generally more distinctive than markings. He talked about all kinds of fish, their life cycles, what biologists knew and what they still hadn't figured out.

It was just outside Monterey that he asked for the fifty bucks. I gave him the money, but I also pointed out that I was leaving in three days and asked how he proposed to pay me back. "No problem," he said. "I just need a battery for the boat."

"You're losing me, Mikey."

"Oh, right," he said, as if the connection were so obvious that he hadn't bothered to explain. "We need the battery. So we buy one, fish for two days, and then return it for the refund." In my world, owning a motorboat implied that you also owned the battery needed to start the motor. In Mikey's world, I soon realized, only the present mattered. The past was done, the future abstract. If you live in the moment and care about fishing, there are only two important questions. Where are the fish? What do I need to go fishing for them right now?

In a way, I admired that Mikey had freed himself from the unproductive worries that so often kept me, like most people, from being fully present in the moment. Mikey, Kirk had said, was a barely legal walking disaster in the real world. He had a cell phone only because his sister, frustrated at never knowing where he was, bought him one. He forgot things, lost things, routinely showed up late or not at all, and failed to follow through on promises. But put him around a fish and he became focused, intent, and tireless.

For the next two days, the three of us and our new battery bobbed around on six-foot swells in the Pacific in a fourteen-foot skiff, jigging our brains out. The only other boats we saw were tankers and container ships on the horizon. Just half a mile away, waves that had traveled thousands of miles across the ocean hurtled against the coastal cliffs with thunderous claps. At some point I realized that we had nothing but life jackets if anything were to happen. And no safe beach to swim to. I didn't want to think about this too hard, so I asked Mikey what it was about steelhead for him. He shrugged, as if to say that the answer was ineffable, but he gave it a try. "They're the most mysterious, smartest, toughest fish I've ever seen.

"Think about it. A steelhead gets born in a particular patch of gravel in the river, spends a couple of years growing, and then decides to head down to the ocean. Which is not a safe place for a smolt. Everything out there wants to eat it. It spends a couple of years fattening up at sea, maybe swims halfway around the world. Then—if it's the one or two fish in a hundred that make it—it'll beat its brains out to return to the same patch of gravel. To the same square foot of gravel, you know? Amazing. And you don't know when or if they're gonna show up. They're just really tough, smart fish."

Over the years, he'd had steelhead strike so viciously that they yanked rods out of the holders on his drift boat. "Three times that's happened. Right outta something designed to hold your rod no matter what. And they were good outfits—five-hundred-dollar ones, Loomis and Lamiglas rods with Shimano Calcutta reels. How can you not love a fish that wild, with that much heart?"

We fished hard for two whole days and never got a bite. By the time I left, however, I'd vowed that if I ever got the chance to go steelheading with Mikey Dvorak, I'd jump on it. The season along the California coast usually ran from late December or January through March, he said. It all hinged on getting enough rain to raise the rivers so the fish could get over the bar and swim up.

The call came two years later.

Hot Pursuit

It had been an unusually dry year, Mikey told me, but the rains had finally come in mid-February. The fishing was fantastic.

By the time I booked a flight, however, there had been too much of a good thing. The rivers were unfishable—high, fast, and muddy. I delayed my departure a week. As I was checking in at the airport, Mikey called again to ask if I could delay for two more days. I couldn't.

"What the hell," he said, "we'll just have to do the best we can."

I was standing outside baggage claim at the San Jose airport when he drove up. There's something about guys like Mikey that threatens certain types of people. I could see every cop within sight eyeballing the truck, driver, and trailered drift boat as if all three might blow up. "Mikey," I asked, sliding into the passenger seat, "what is it about you that freaks everybody out?"

"Beats me, man." I got the feeling that Mikey was so accustomed to this phenomenon that it hardly registered anymore.

It was late. We'd sleep that night on the forty-four-foot boat he kept in a marina near Half Moon Bay, then drive north tomorrow, looking for whichever steelhead river would clear up first. Mikey said the boat was a 1949 naval rescue vessel that he'd bought at auction, along with the commercial ocean salmon fishing license attached to it. It had seemed like a way to make some money. In fact, he'd had a remarkably good first year, bringing in 23,000 pounds of salmon, worth more than $100,000.

Mikey's boat was a floating version of his truck, the hands-down winner of any Most Derelict Vessel contest in the large marina. I suspected that Mikey was less than an authority on seamanship, and I damn sure knew the boat would have failed any inspection. And yet

Mikey had somehow succeeded in a very competitive industry. As long as fish were involved, Mikey found a way.

I bunked that night on a narrow bench in the wheelhouse. Mikey bid me good night and disappeared into the hold. Presumably he had a bed down there somewhere. In a way, it was a shame the harbor police didn't have a profile of a meth user's boat. A good search was exactly what that boat needed.

The next morning we rolled north. "We're chasing the chrome," Mikey said, referring to the silvery appearance of a steelhead fresh from the ocean. The longer the fish stayed in the river, the more they reverted to rainbow trout colors. Fifty miles north of San Francisco was like being in another state. Everything changed. The towns were small, and each was smaller than the one before. It was redwood country; trees with tops you couldn't see growing on steep, rugged mountains. Mikey started making phone calls to half a dozen guiding buddies. All the steelhead rivers—the Napa, Russian, Noyo, Eel, Van Duzen, Trinity, Mad, Klamath, and Smith—were blown out. "We're probably screwed for the next two days wherever we go," he said.

Which river would clear first depended on a multitude of factors: today's level; how much rain had fallen and how much more might come; the extent to which degradation from lumbering, mining, and the cultivation of grapes and marijuana increased the river's runoff; and the river's record of recovery after rains in recent years. There were so many factors in play that it was impossible to take them all into account. Mikey sifted the data and decided to bet on the Smith, one of the most intact river systems in the state. It had received the least rain and had the most favorable forecast, at that moment anyway. It was also 350 miles north. Off we went. As we drove, I asked Mikey if this was the same Pathfinder we'd driven in two years ago to chase white sea bass. "No, this is the second I've had since then." Mikey, I was to learn, bought Pathfinders exclusively, never paid more than a grand, and drove them until the wheels came off. "But only the first generation, '85 to '95. Those were tanks, man. After '96, they got all round and fruity-looking. Stopped being a truck, you know?" This was his sixth. He'd bought it a year ago, with 200,000 miles on it. He'd put on 66,000 since then. I asked what he'd paid. "Seven hundred and twenty-two bucks," he said. And smiled.

"Sounds like you've got the truck thing down," I said.

"Yeah, but I got a problem with boats."

"How so?"

"I can't get rid of 'em. I've got six right now." These included the 17-foot drift boat we were towing, a 9-foot Avon inflatable, a 14-foot Wahoo, a 16-foot Wellcraft ("in a marina in Alameda"), a 20-foot Mako, and the 44-foot salmon boat. This inconsistency—the way he could be brutally practical about trucks and completely sentimental about boats—was typical Mikey. "It's hard to explain," he said. "But a boat, it becomes, I don't know, *who I am*. And they're not all great boats. But there are things about my own personality that I don't like, okay? But I'm stuck with them. I can't disown them. Does that make sense?" Of course it didn't. But I understood it.

Racing the Rain

We found a motel in Crescent City, close to the river, and woke the next morning to light rain. By now, having discovered that my phone could get on the Internet, Mikey was borrowing it every hour. The reports he was looking at said the rain might stop. It didn't. Soon it was raining hard. Mikey decided we should head up into Oregon and check the Chetco. "It's on the other side of a ridge that sometimes splits weather systems," he explained. This seemed like a fool's errand. An unrelenting downpour like this one was anything but localized. But we went anyway. It was raining just as hard in Oregon.

Mikey didn't despair. The thing, it seemed, was to maintain momentum, keep chasing. He took me to the house of a guiding buddy in the area, Jim Burn. Jim knew the Smith as well as anybody. The two of them sat in front of Jim's computer for the next several hours, poring over water levels and weather reports while I played with Jim's dog.

The guides were as different as two guys could be and still share the same passion for steelhead. Mikey's boat, for example, while neater than his truck, was still pretty funky. Jim's boat was spotless. He even had a "bra" to protect it from debris when towed.

Eventually they concluded that there was no use even trying to fish the river until the next day. They adjourned to Jim's garage and spent the next two hours in what seemed to be a long-standing ritual, in which each showed off his newest lures while energetically insulting the other's. Each had hundreds of steelhead plugs, the most prized of which were "pre-Rapala" Storm Wiggle Warts, Magnum Warts, Wee Warts, and PeeWee Warts. After Rapala acquired Storm in the late 1990s, I was told, they destroyed the original Storm molds and moved production to China. The new ones had lost the distinctive "hunting" action of the best Storms. They had steel rattles rather than lead, which resulted in a harsher sound. The plastic was different. They were disasters. Now, they told me, old Storm lures in rare or desirable patterns went for as much as a hundred dollars on eBay. Mikey showed Jim one of his favorites, a pearl-colored PeeWee Wart that he'd recently bought for fifty dollars from a seller called Plugwhore. It was a tiny thing, but Mikey maintained that its action was fantastic. "Oh, yeah, I've bought from Plugwhore," Jim said, then explained in detail why Mikey's lures, both in general and individually, sucked. Mikey returned the favor.

While the finer points escaped me, I did learn a bit of plug terminology. A light-colored lure with a red back was said to have a "rash." Black glitter was a "Michael Jackson." Black-and-white was a "cop." Silver-and-black was an "Oakland Raider." And chrome pink with a black bill was a "Dr. Death."

It wasn't until the next day, the fourth of the trip, that we finally threw a line in the water. And that was bank fishing, throwing weighted clusters of salmon roe rolled in borax, the better to make the eggs adhere to one another, into the Smith. I think Mikey and Jim knew the river was too high, that the fish were hunkered down until the water cleared. But maybe fishing when you knew damn well it was pointless was an act of faith, a demonstration of your humility to the river gods.

The Smith dropped a foot over the course of that day (we marked the changing levels with branches stuck into the bank), but in eight hours of fishing, not one of our three rods got so much as a bump. A few people stopped by to chat with Jim and ask about the river. By this time, Mikey had tired of telling people I was an outdoor writer. His new story was that, despite looking like a middle-aged bald guy, I was actually a Make-A-Wish kid with one of those premature aging diseases who wanted to catch a steelhead before what would be his eleventh and, tragically, final birthday. Mikey said that it was his mission to make that happen.

We tried again for a few hours the next morning in a deep gorge of the river, the descent into which required holding my rod in my mouth so I could use all four limbs. The Smith is a gorgeous river, but parts of it were just plain scary. Fall off your rock where we were, for example, and you wouldn't be coming up anytime soon. Back at the truck, Mikey decided our last, best shot was a small river 150 miles south, which he forbade me to name. I didn't question his choice. Neither did Jim, who followed us.

Steeling Secrets

When we left the coastal highway, it was like finding another world inside another world, one even more remote and beautiful. We crossed a range of mountains, corkscrewing our way up over dirt roads through country where you'd go for miles without seeing a house. We rounded a bend and were looking at miles of undeveloped coastline, rocks the size of houses in the surf, which broke hundreds of yards offshore. "Wow, Mikey, this is incredible," I said.

"My happy place," he said. "It's known but not really known. I mean people know it's here, but most of them think it's just another steelhead river." I didn't. I thought we had landed in paradise.

We got to the river itself an hour before sunset. Mikey wanted to back the boat in and throw plugs from it for a while, get reacquainted with the water, maybe catch a fish. Jim countered that Mikey, as usual, had everything ass-backward.

"Look, we don't know where we're staying. We don't know where we're going to eat tonight. The way to do this is get squared away tonight and do it right first thing in the morning."

"C'mon, Jim," Mikey coaxed. "For once in your life just relax and go with it. Fish for half an hour and then we'll go figure all that out. There's still time."

For the next half hour, they argued. Jim was by the book, linear, logical. Mikey was seat-of-the-pants, intuitive, eccentric. It was like listening to the two halves of my brain fight each other. By the time they finished, my head hurt and it was too late to fish.

Since it was all coming down to the next day, Mikey wanted to see if he could get some local intel. About 9 p.m., he swung the truck into a mostly deserted campground. When he saw a drift boat by one of the occupied sites, he made a beeline for it. "We come in peace!" Mikey bellowed. The boat belonged to an elderly couple, who had evidently just finished dinner and were talking quietly by the light of a kerosene lantern, their dishes stacked before them. It was hard to tell what they made of the little dude with a full beard and a bush of hair tucked up into a wool hat. But they smiled as if nothing was out of place.

They listened as Mikey told them the Make-A-Wish story. They knew he was full of it but didn't seem to mind. At a certain moment, however, the woman looked at Mikey curiously, cocked her head, and said, "Why, don't you know that you can't *plan* to catch a steelhead? Goodness! Everybody knows that. All you can do is go someplace where the fish might be, wait until the water looks right, fish it hard, and hope you get lucky."

"Absolutely!" Mikey agreed.

No one had bothered to tell me this, the first principle of steelhead fishing. Maybe, to guys like Mikey and Jim, it's so obvious that it doesn't bear mentioning. I'd slowly been making my way toward this fact on my own, but it was striking to hear it confirmed by a third party.

The man said that he hadn't even put the boat in today. Tomorrow would be a little better, but the river needed at least two rainless days to fish well. Back at the truck, Mikey announced that he'd figured it out. If we were to have any chance on the river, it was essential that I ride in the trailered boat, drink deeply of whiskey, and savor the soft night air rushing by. "You need to do this, dude," Mikey declared. "Trust me. The river needs to know you're here. Plus, it's just awesome."

Mikey went on for a bit, making it sound like a carnival ride one moment, a solemn duty the next. It was, of course, an idiotic thing to do. But something had changed. We were chasing the chrome and I was in the grips of the chase. Mikey had sucked me into his world. What we were doing had become a pilgrimage, a quest. And although I still wanted terribly to catch a steelhead, I wanted even more to be true to the spirit of the trip, which meant giving it everything I had.

Thirty seconds later, I was sitting in the boat's front chair, a rope in one hand, a bottle of bourbon in the other, both feet braced against the front rail, the liquor burning in my throat as I howled at the moon. I rode the trailered boat over bumps and potholes, around curves and plunging down straightaways. It was, on the one hand, a moron's steeplechase, requiring nothing more than a total lack of common sense. But it was also glorious, flying through the night air with only the stars above and the river somewhere close. I realized that whatever happened tomorrow, everything would turn out fine. I had, unbeknownst to myself, entered Mikey's world, the eternal present. The future would bring whatever it brought. The important thing was *now*. And no matter how it turned out, I was now taking one hell of a ride.

A few minutes of this turned out to be about all I really needed. I jarred my back pretty hard a few times. Through the back window, I could see Mikey and Jim, gesturing to each other. They had resumed their argument. It had become quite animated. They weren't looking back and couldn't hear no matter how loudly I shouted. There wasn't anything in the boat I could throw onto the roof of the truck except my shoe, which I couldn't really get to because I needed both feet to brace myself. It was another five miles before Mikey finally decided to check on me, at which point I told him to stop the damn truck.

Back at the little cottage we'd rented for the night, Mikey and Jim continued arguing. It was like listening to an old married couple rehash the same feud endlessly. Then, just before lights-out, I heard Jim's voice from the other room. It sounded different, almost plaintive. "Mikey, you think the river might drop eighteen inches overnight?"

"Yeah, maybe."

"And maybe it'll even get another six inches of visibility?"

"Yeah, could be," Mikey said. He sounded like a parent reassuring a child that there was indeed a Santa Claus.

"Okay. Good night."

The next day, we set out early. Mikey was at the oars, while Jim and I were plugging, in which you let out line fifteen, maybe twenty yards, engage your reel, and let the current impart action to your lure. Meanwhile, the guide rows to counteract the current and put your plug in the spots that might hold fish. In essence, it's the guide rowing the boat who does the fishing. "It's not the most romantic way to fish," Mikey said. "But in this kind of water, it's your best bet."

Just then, Jim's rod arced. "Fish on!" he cried, letting the fish fully take the plug before setting the hook. He passed the rod to me. I suddenly felt like the Make-A-Wish kid Mikey had made me out to be. I'd done nothing to catch this fish. But I dutifully reeled it in anyway. It fought hard, but not remarkably so, and within a minute or two I'd landed what both guides deemed an 11-pound hen, her sides bright. Both guides were adamant about releasing the fish quickly, and did so.

We were pumped at having hooked a fish so soon after launching. As time went by without another hookup, we began to despair of the quick-fish curse, that peculiar deal in which the omen of all-day success turns out to be false. We changed lures. Since we weren't finding fish in the fishy spots, Mikey began fishing unconventional ones. That didn't work, either.

Jim hooked another fish late in the float and again handed me the rod. I'm still not sure what I did wrong. Maybe I pressed it too hard. Maybe Jim should have cut more of his line off after the first fish. I saw the fish leap once in fast water, then the lure was gone.

It was over. It was late afternoon, and Mikey and I had 250 miles to cover to get back to the marina. My plane was leaving at seven the next morning.

An Unstoppable Force

As we drove south, I tried to sort through what I was feeling. There was some disappointment, but I was surprised at how insignificant it seemed. I would have liked to have caught more fish, but we had succeeded. We'd chased the chrome and landed one freshie. I was tired, but it was the pleasant fatigue of having done everything you could. I had no regrets.

About 150 miles north of San Francisco, Mikey left the highway. Within minutes we were bombing down dirt roads on which we saw almost no other vehicles. "Mikey, what's up?" I asked.

"This is one of the forks of the Eel," he said. "Got one last spot we gotta try. We'll get back later, but you can sleep on the plane."

I smiled. *How,* I wondered, *could you not love a guy like Mikey?*

We arrived at a small house, a little ranch, at the bottom of a dead-end road. "I know these folks," he said. "Good people."

It felt to me as if we'd just bailed out of the highway arbitrarily and driven down an anonymous dirt road. "What do you mean, you know these people?" I asked. "There must be hundreds of roads just like this one up and down the coast. What'd you do, drive down every one and ask if you could fish?"

Mikey looked at me. "Pretty much," he said, "if it bordered a steelhead river. Most of these people have let me park on their land and sleep in the truck at one time or another." He parked, left me in the truck while he went to have a word with the owners, and returned to tell me everything was cool.

There was maybe an hour of light left. We rigged up quickly, tying on sacks of red roe and slinky sinkers beneath slip bobbers on spinning rods, and headed for the water. The bushes were so thick that there were only a couple of places you could cast from. It had been a long shot from the start, but I cast to a pool on the far side and drifted my bait through it half a dozen times. Then I moved to another spot, which involved climbing a boulder, and threw again. And then it was dark. We'd fished the sun all the way down. We'd given it everything we had. I felt a tremendous exhilaration.

As we drove back toward the highway, Mikey was already talking about how I'd have to come back next year, how we'd nail it. We stopped for gas. Mikey asked if he could borrow a few bucks. I said yes.

Adventures of a Deer Bum

A lone trek to a trophy buck factory reveals amazing local grace, shot-up phone books, and a hardscrabble land where wall-hangers skulk and prowl.

At the moment I am parked outside a strip-mall laundromat at 10 p.m. on a Tuesday in Jackson, Ohio, a working-class town of ten thousand. Most of the locals are in bed by this hour. Not me. Four days into my hunt, I'm as hyper as Paris Hilton on an unescorted visit to a boys' prep school. By the green glow of my Streamlight headlamp, I am shuffling through six adjoining topo quads spread out over the dashboard, scarfing down an eighteen-hour-old sausage biscuit and a twenty-ounce Pabst (discovered while Dumpster diving in my own backseat), and madly scanning the radio for a weather fix. Inside the establishment, my ScentLok is tumbling around in a dryer hot enough to cook pizza, and my other hunting duds are swishing through a final rinse of Sport-Wash. By forgoing a real dinner, I can do a total scent overhaul and still make it back to my motel for five hours of rack time. At 4:30 a.m., my nervous system will go off automatically, sending me afield again for a chance at an Ohio bighead.

Meanwhile, I'm poring over the dog-eared topos, pressing them for the secrets only they can impart. After hours of agony, I have whittled the Miss Stand Site contestants down to two finalists for tomorrow morning: a shapely little ridge finger near Blue Hollow on the Pedro

Quad and a perky bench along the stream in Pokepatch Hollow on the Gallia Quad. My whole world depends on the wind, and I'm endlessly scanning the radio for a weather report. But the night airwaves here have been seized by Bible study insurgents.

I note a faint odor of decay in the car and wonder if an unfinished sandwich from the recent past is out for revenge. A Jackson Township police cruiser rolls past, the cop slowing to eyeball me. As always, any distraction from my quest fills me with indignation. Yes, I am sitting in a parked car at night wearing long underwear with a green light on my forehead. You got a problem with that? Evidently I look too whacked to be a real criminal, and the cruiser rolls on.

Searching for the source of the stench, I am drawn to my feet. I take off my shoes and socks and resist the impulse to scream aloud. I have a case of athlete's foot that would look at home in a leper colony. But there's no time to deal with that now. My immediate task is to figure out where I can put an arrow into a giant whitetail tomorrow in the Wayne National Forest.

Big Deer . . .

I discovered the Wayne last year, when I was looking for a place to bowhunt trophy bucks without having to pay a guide, an outfitter, or a lease fee. A review process including examination of QDMA maps of record-book deer and deer densities, state website inventories of public lands and hunting pressure, and the brain of every hunting buddy I could find soon had me leaning here: huge acreage, low pressure, and challenging terrain.

There be monsters here. Ohio is archery-only for most of November, so mature bucks enjoy high survival rates. On opening day of the 2005 season, a hunter named Mike Rex killed a deer in nearby Athens County with antlers so big that he thought at first that he was looking at two bucks standing right behind each other. For the number Nazis: Think 6-by-5 main frame and 13-inch brow tines.

. . . Big Land

A convergence of conditions natural and man-made make this part of southeastern Ohio a heaven for bowhunters with big dreams and little wallets. Most of the wooded country in Ohio is leased up by guys with more money than you, especially in the northwestern Corn Belt. The standout exception is the southeastern quadrant, Ohio's hardscrabble Appalachian counties.

The glaciers that smoothed the rough edges of the land and dropped their load of rich topsoil during the last ice age never made it here. Geologically, it's part of the Unglaciated Allegheny Plateau, an elevated arc of shale, sandstone, and thin soils extending around southeastern Ohio into western Pennsylvania and the West Virginia panhandle. If you were a pioneer looking for prime farmland, you would probably have sifted the dirt through your fingers, said, "I didn't come all this way for this," and kept going. Deer, however, have always liked the rugged forests—oak, ash, hickory, and beech—just fine. The double bonus is that the three Wayne National Forest districts contain more than 237,000 acres of land—a lifetime's worth of country where a guy with a little grit can hunt until he either succeeds, has to go back to work and family, or loses his mind.

A bunch of guys from states near and far are already making the annual pilgrimage to this part of the Buckeye State. In the motel, I ran into Ricky Quaue, who comes up from Mississippi with friends to hunt. "I can drive up, go on a weeklong hunt, and have a chance of getting a monster for five hundred dollars," he said. "Best so far this year is a fifteen-inch spread, but a boy from Hattiesburg killed a whopper." James Smith, from Tennessee, has been coming for years with five first cousins. "Big deer, nice folks, what's not to like?"

The hitch is that it's big-woods hunting. You know those neat little diagrams of imaginary hunting grounds in magazines that show ambush points along fence lines, brush funnels, and power-line crossings? Forget 'em. This is subtler terrain. You will have to take your game to the next level to play here. The deer are more difficult, too, harder to pattern, seminomadic, and extremely wary. Spook one and he'll be gone for good before you ever lay eyes on him. And this year features a special wrinkle: a bumper crop of mast exceeding any in local memory, acorns and nuts two layers thick even in town parking lots. A deer can feed all day and scarcely have to turn its head. No matter. I am possessed of an attribute that surpasses all others: deranged perseverance.

First Day, First Bucks

By 5:22 the first morning, my car is parked at a trailhead, and I am climbing through the darkness along Blue Hollow to a ridgeline at 900 feet that broadens into a mini-plateau, ridge fingers running northwest to southeast. Acorns and nuts crunch under my boots at every step. I have picked my stand site too well and can hear deer running as I near the faint saddle in the ridge. I'm pleased at having my topo instincts verified and kicking myself for not trusting them enough to have set up farther off. The invisible bolting deer don't snort—a good sign—then bail off the ridge and out of earshot almost immediately. It's so steep that it's hard to say if they went one hundred yards and stopped or are headed for the next county.

A climbable tree is silhouetted against the false dawn fifty yards downwind. I stalk it at glacial speed, set out some estrous scent, and settle in twenty-five feet up. As morning replants the last of the darkness into the ground, faint trails appear crisscrossing the leaves. All bear evidence of recent use, but none is a main route. Maybe there is no main route.

Just past 8 a.m., a 6-pointer with no brow tines pops over the notch from the opposite side, walking fast and purposefully. He passes fifty yards off, ignoring my scent wicks, grunt tube, even the bleat can. I wait five minutes and rattle lightly for thirty seconds—just casual sparring.

Twenty minutes later the buck climbs back up, accompanied by a smaller 6, this one limping slightly. The two of them work the wicks' scent stream and pass thirty yards below my stand. I draw, but only for practice, and am pleased that they don't pick up the movement. They seem less pressured than deer around home. But I didn't come all this way for a one-and-a-half-year-old 6.

At noon, having seen only a couple of does feeding slowly along the hillside seventy yards below me, I descend and hike farther up the path, both to scout and to stop by the office of Dean State Forest (a pocket park surrounded by Wayne National Forest lands), seeking local intelligence. Here I run into Tim Boggs and two other equipment operators for the state Forestry Division. Boggs says he saw my car parked this morning, and I tell him about the 6-pointers.

"There are some pigs here all right. But they're tough deer. I rifle hunted three days a week in season for six years before I took my first buck as a kid." He and the other workers were all born within four hundred yards of one another, not far from here. I'm expecting resentment at an out-of-stater horning in on hallowed local ground, but soon he's drawing on my topos, showing me the places he mowed recently, which often attract deer. Then he taps a spot where a creek he would prefer I not name runs through a deep hollow.

"They pull a couple of one-fifty-class bucks out of there most years," he says. He writes down the name of a cousin who works just up the road for Wayne National Forest (who took a nice 10-pointer a few weeks earlier on public land). He even gives me the name of a retired farmer with land adjoining the secret creek and recommends I ask nicely for permission to hunt there, or at least to access the creek across his land. As if this isn't enough, he gives me a lift back to my car. I'm from the East, and anytime a stranger is this accommodating, I'm expecting to be assaulted, robbed, or carjacked. But he shakes my hand, wishes me well, and drives off. I stand there, wondering what the hell is wrong with the guy.

The cascade of inexplicable goodwill continues. Twenty minutes later, at the Wayne headquarters, Boggs's cousin shows me a picture of his buck, points out a few productive spots he has hunted over the years, and marks individual pear and persimmon trees on my maps that are worth scouting. An hour later, I'm buying meatball subs for the retired farmer, Coleman, and his friend, Pete, at a cafe in Oak Hill. Again, these are seriously ill men: friendly, content with their lives, and thoroughly decent.

Both are in their eighties and eat lunch together more days than not. When Pete excuses himself for a moment, Coleman confides, "Pete's wife died a couple years ago, and if I don't get him outta the house, he just sits there. I tell him, 'Pete, you're getting grouchy.'" When Coleman makes a trip to the men's room, it's Pete's turn. "Coleman's more like my brother than anything else. He's eighty-seven, but he won't tell you that. I worry about him. His brother died last year, and now his nephew owns half the farm." I ask what the nephew is like. "He's a butthead," says Pete.

Coleman returns. Soon they're finishing each other's sentences while telling me the one from forty years ago when they were bringing a 60-inch moose home from Canada strapped onto the body of a '51 Cadillac. "Broke down with a vapor lock right in downtown Columbus," Coleman says. "Remember that, Pete? Jeez, we drew a crowd that day."

Coleman, naturally, gives permission to cross his land to get to the creek I want to hunt. I find a trail crossing three-quarters of the way up the hillside overlooking the creek, an area made almost impenetrable by trees felled in an ice storm two years back. It's noisy walking, and it's nearly 70 degrees. I sit for four hours. I sit until dark-dark, until even the bone-white sycamores are swallowed up in the blackness. Then, out of sheer cussedness, I sit some more. At last I hear the tentative sounds in the leaves—not crunching, more like a gentle sweeping—of deer. They pass somewhere below me toward the farmer's fields. They're here all right. They just don't much feel like getting killed.

Madness as a Way of Life

My days fall into a kind of routinized frenzy, fueled by deer adrenaline and cans of Starbucks DoubleShot espresso. By dawn I am high in my trusty Lone Wolf sit-and-climb, which has yet to squeak in six years

23

of use. From about 11 to 1:30, I'm a road warrior, speed-scouting as many as six locations and making notes on the topos. From two until dark I'm back in the air, sometimes higher up than a lone guy should be in a place where cell phone reception is spotty at best.

I've yet to see the town of Jackson or the Comfort Inn where I'm staying by daylight. Totally consumed by the hunt, I am insatiable for the next new piece of ground, knowing that it's only a matter of time before a shower of antlered glory descends on my humble head. Daytime highs have been in the 70s for the past four days, well above the average of 50. It's not exactly a deer aphrodisiac. All I need is a drop in the temperature to pump up the rut or a hot doe to lure a buck past my stand. A tobacco farmer I run across while driving one afternoon confirms my fears. When I stop to ask if I might hunt his land, he answers the door still in camo from his own morning hunt. "They're just not moving till after dark. I hear them every morning underneath me. I just can't see them. I know they're chasing." I set up on a beaver dam deep in a heavily wooded bottom near his place along trails showing the hardest use I've seen so far. Three o'clock turns to four. Sunset turns to twilight; twilight fades until the brighter stars come out. Still I sit. Finally, there comes a gentle but regular sloshing in the water. I strain my eyes but can see nothing. For dumb animals, they sure are elusive.

Coming out, I get more than a little turned around. A creek I don't remember crossing blocks my way, and I fall off a log into the waist-deep water when a vine snags the stand on my back. Another step and I'm up to my chest. I claw my way across and up the bank and wait until the noise of an engine indicates the direction of the road. By the time I finally make the car, I'm sweating from more than exertion.

The fact is, revving this high for this long has begun to degrade my finely honed mental edge. Example: Unwilling to burn a moment of daylight to practice good shooting form, it has seemed like a good idea to shoot a single arrow each night in my room. Turning on the shower, TV, and radio for covering noise, I screw on a blunt tip, muffled with foam rubber and electrical tape, and take one point-blank shot at the Yellow Pages. The blunt penetrates all the way to page 358,

"KITCHEN CABINET—REFACING & REFINISHING." Each day, the cleaning people replace the phone book.

I have taken to downing three or four Starbucks DoubleShot espressos before lunch and a couple more in the afternoon. Though tired, I have no desire to rest. Not while it's legal to be up in a tree with a bow.

One afternoon, bombing down State Route 141 in Gallia County after scouting a ridge studded with crab apples, their fruit spread on the ground in perfect drip lines around the trunks, I pass a cornfield where a combine is harvesting. Three or four men are leaning on the guardrail in the shade, watching.

A mile later, I come to my senses and pull a U-turn. "Any way a guy could bowhunt any of that corn?" I ask. A fellow about my age walks over and says that it's his land and he keeps the hunting on the farm itself for friends and family. "But there is a monstrous big buck running that ridge up behind you. He comes down just about every evening to get to it. You set up there long enough and you can kill him. I'll show you." He hops on a four-wheeler and leads the way, indicating with a flick of his hand where to park. "He's a pig, two fifty, three hundred pounds," he whispers, pointing out a trail up to the saddle. "I've killed tons of deer right up there. I'd be hunting him myself 'cept I got cancer and had to do chemo." He lifts his hat to reveal a bald head. "Hell, I just thought you were good looking," I answer.

I see a basket 8-point, well inside the ears, waltzing carelessly down the trail half an hour before sunset. My heart leaps. The big guy can't be far behind. Except he is. It's the same old story. Half an hour after dark, I hear deer come sneaking down the ridge in ones and twos for the better part of an hour, maybe a dozen deer in all. In the morning, when it is still black dark, they do the same thing returning from the corn. They repeat the pattern the next evening and the next morning.

Last Shot at Glory

Time is running out, and the daytime highs are still hitting the seventies. As November 10—my last day—approaches, I find that my writer's luck is holding firm. The temperature is forecast to drop 25 degrees, and I can hunt the entire morning before I have to catch my flight home.

I decide to go back to the secret creek and its ice-storm blowdowns. In darkness I climb a poplar tree a quarter of the way down from the top of the ridge on a bench where several trails intersect. It is deliciously cold, in the 40s at dawn, with a light northerly breeze. The squirrels are out in force. I see a hawk hunting from a tremendous dead hickory that somehow is still upright. The hours pass with nary a hoofed quadruped to be seen.

At noon, I climb down with just enough time to haul ass to the airport. My disappointment is not as bitter as you might imagine. Bowhunting for whitetails is dicey under the best of circumstances. It is almost a relief to have the enforced deadline of a departing flight. Otherwise, I would keep at it until success or the calendar forced me to stop. I point the car west, pop a last can of double espresso, and feel a strange weight gradually lift from my body. I have no regrets. I hunted as hard as I could. I wasn't defeated, I just ran out of time. I would go again in a heartbeat.

Running dangerously late to the regional airport, I stop in front of the terminal, throw all my gear onto the sidewalk, and change out of my camo right there. Unbeknownst to me, the security guys have been observing the unshaven, distracted guy who just took all his clothes off out front. They wave me through the metal detector and immediately pull me over for a search. "How'd you do?" asks one, obviously a bowhunter himself. "No luck," I tell him. I sit and remove my shoes for inspection. My long-neglected athlete's foot makes him recoil as if hit with a stun gun. "Might want to see a doc about that," he says.

"I'm going to," I say. "Just as soon as rifle season ends."

Angler's Paradise

Whenever I walk into a big-box sporting-goods store, it feels like a camera locks on to my wallet, looking for ways to drain it. You want a nice compound bow, a two-man fully enclosed blind, a fishing kayak? Right this way. But the low-dollar stuff you actually need—a tube of string wax, a dozen field points—is almost always sold out.

Naturally, my force field was up when, killing time in downtown Baltimore, I saw a neon largemouth bass sign and walked into Tochterman's Tackle for some hooks. There was gear from floor to ceiling, much of it the little stuff you can't do without. They had, for instance, what looked like four hundred kinds of snap-swivels. These guys seemed to know their onions.

I overheard a customer talking to a salesman. He didn't fish, but a buddy had invited him to go after croakers. He'd use his friend's gear but didn't want to show up empty-handed. "Take a bottom rig," the salesman suggested. "And call me Tony." I watched from a distance as Tony explained the rig, the snap at the bottom for sinkers, how you stick the loop of a snelled hook through the end of the wire arm, then pass the hook through the loop. "Hey, that's slick," the guy said. Tony did one hook and had the customer do the other.

You could sell a guy like that a $9,000 teak fighting chair, a $3,500 fishfinder preloaded with maps of the Martian canals, and a pair of alligator "croaker shoes." Instead, Tony was selling maybe four dollars of terminal tackle and teaching the guy something. *Noble gesture*, I thought. But this place had to be circling the drain.

As he rang up the sale, Tony said, "Listen, I gotta ask: Do you know how to tie the line to the rig?" The guy admitted that he didn't. Tony showed him. It looked like a uni, the simplest of all fishing knots. The only thing cashiers ask me these days is for my e-mail address and whether they can sign me up for the bonus club. What was this place, a living museum? "Hope you catch some fish," Tony said. The guy left with a bounce in his step.

I looked back at the counter, where another salesman was smiling as if he'd read my mind. Rich Holewinski, a former ironworker, has worked here six years and has known Tony Tochterman for forty. "That's Tony all over," he said. "I've seen guys barge in here with busted-up tackle claiming it's defective. No receipt, sometimes stuff we don't even carry. Tony helps them. They come in angry, but they leave smiling. Because that's what Tony does." Bragging on your boss—how weird was that? "Another time," Rich continued, "guy's brother died, left him some old reels. He asks Tony to buy 'em for thirty dollars. Tony goes in the back and comes back with a two-hundred-dollar check. Tells the guy, 'If I bought them for thirty dollars, it'd be stealing.'"

Time for a reality check: How's business under a softie like that?

"Great. We're the oldest family-run tackle store in the country. Started right here in 1916. Ninety-eight years. Three generations. There was the grandfather. Then Tony's father, Thomas Jr., took over in 1936. Tony took over in 1981. We have people who came here as kids, then brought their kids. Now those kids are bringing theirs. There's no other place like this that I've ever seen."

I had to talk to the boss. His story wasn't complicated. Tony and his wife, Dee, never had kids. Their house was right across the street. He told me they "did the country club thing" for a few years but decided it wasn't for them. "We walk the dog, have a beer now and then, grow tomatoes. We're not flashy people." They own both the shop and the house free and clear. They're in here seven days a week.

Why? "Because I'd rather be here than anywhere else. It's like a garden or something. After you build it, you want to sit in it and enjoy it."

I asked if he fishes. "Sure, but not that much. I listen to my customers' stories about catching fish. To me, that's better than any fish I could ever catch."

He was unlike any salesman I'd ever met. I didn't understand what made him tick. Then it hit me. Tony loves his store the way I love fishing. It is a business and he is a businessman. But he is playing the long game. He doesn't just want to sell you something today; he wants you as a customer for life. He wants you to succeed. Because that means he has contributed to your success. And that gives him something you can't buy or sell—a purpose, a sense of connection. Pride is involved, of course. But it isn't the look-at-me kind. It's about running things the way his father and grandfather had, not just profitably but well, aiming higher than the bottom line. It is about honor.

I suddenly realized I was late and left. Later I remembered I'd forgotten the hooks. That was okay. I had a hunch I'd be back.

No Pain, No Elk

Eating an early dinner in the cook tent the evening before firearms season opens, we hear distant bugling, and all nine of us hit the tent flap like frat boys who've just heard the words "free beer."

Just five hundred yards across the creek, grazing through a series of hillside parks, is the jackpot we've all gambled a few grand on: elk. There must be forty of them—great yellow-brown beasts with chocolate heads and chests. The scene is so stunning it looks fake, like a hokey wildlife painting. Meanwhile, all three guides produce binoculars out of thin air and start calling targets. "Legal bull. Looks like a four-by-five, three o'clock low, right-hand clearing," says one. "Legal bull. Walking, ah, left to right. Lower end of the other clearing," calls another.

"Legal bull, one o'clock high, half in the timber. Four points visible on the left side," reports the third. And then, like the finale of the Super Bowl halftime show, the herd bull, a shaggy 6-by-6 so big and distinct you can see him without optics, calmly steps out of the black timber and into the open for our viewing pleasure.

"Dibs!" I shout, almost before the thought is fully formed in my head. The guides, still glued to their glasses, all crack up. As if anything in this harsh country—least of all a herd of bull elk that has probably made it through four hunting seasons—plays by the rules of the schoolyard.

"There are a hell of a lot of elk in this country," the outfitter tells us that first night. "But there's a hell of a lot of country, too. You need to think real hard about what kind of bull you'll settle for." Prior to

30

showing up here, I thought I was ready. I'd run, lifted, and crunched myself into the best physical shape of my life. Armed with a scoped Gamo pellet rifle that cost nearly as much as my .30/06, I practiced shooting daily in my backyard. And I showed up thinking I wouldn't be satisfied with anything less than a trophy bull. Now, at ten thousand feet, in some of the roughest country I've ever seen, I'm gasping like a fish and having second thoughts.

Great gym shape doesn't cut it here. What elk country calls for is someone like my guide, Mark Nichols. At fifty-three, he is still as lean and tough as jerky, a tall, salt-cured strip of a man. One-eighth Blackfoot Indian, he takes your measure through watery blue eyes beneath a sweat-stained black hat with a hank of horsehair stuck in the band. He has a fairly typical elk guide background. He grew up on a farm in Missouri, was orphaned at nine when his father died in a tractor accident, and spent eleven years wrestling steers on the pro rodeo circuit. A mishandled rope led to an accidental head-butting contest with his horse. The horse won. At the Mayo Clinic they reconstructed a large portion of his face with titanium. When the light hits him at a certain angle, you can see where the bone stops and the metal begins. At such moments he looks like the Terminator, a machine that has assumed human form. Personal habits reinforce the image. He sleeps four hours a night, appears impervious to pain or fatigue, and never gets upset. I find him very likable and a little terrifying.

Here, the elk camp is typical. Get up well before light, eat, retrieve your rifle from the latrine tent, and ride out. Return exhausted well after dark, belt down a drink, eat, and fall unconscious into your sleeping bag for what feels like fifteen minutes before it's time to do it again.

If I could find a bull with his lungs in his hindquarters, I'd make a damn fine hunter. So far, I've had only fleeting glimpses of disappearing bulls. In two days, this country has taken me down a few pegs. I've quietly told Nichols I'll be happy with any legal bull. We spent sundown today overlooking a grassy bowl with snow still lingering in the shadows of the trees while a beaver pulled a V of cold water across a pond he'd built. It was a perfect place for elk, but none showed.

Now it's dark again, and we're on the long, cold ride back to camp. In the timber, I can't even see my horse's mane, much less the trail. There's no option but to surrender, sit back, and trust him. At last we come out into open country under a dome of stars so clean and sharp they almost hurt to look at. In three days—elk or no elk—I'll head back to a smaller life, to the world of telephones, shaving cream, and worry. But for the moment, this country has stripped the scab of daily existence clean, leaving just the core of what it is to be alive. What I know is that I'm exhausted, sore, almost numb with cold, and strangely happy. I only know that we are headed for camp and the promise of a drink, a hot meal, and a warm sleeping bag, all just a few miles ahead, somewhere below the lowest star in the Big Dipper.

The South's Top Gun

If you want to learn the art of British driven shooting—and shotgun shooting in general—there's no one better to see in the States than Chris Batha. Just don't let him catch you aiming.

Shooting a shotgun accurately is the easiest thing in the world if you remember two things. First, you must never "aim" the gun. You especially shouldn't look at the bead at the end of the barrel, which was apparently put there to tempt you into using it. Nothing makes you miss so predictably as aiming. Second—to the extent that you do aim, which, as you know, you shouldn't—it's paramount that you try to miss the target. Unless you are shooting at empty air, you'll never hit anything.

After explaining these principles, Chris Batha, acknowledged to be one of the world's best and most experienced shooting coaches, looks around the table for questions. He's a big, friendly bear of a man who has been in love with shotguns and shooting all his life. He's usually smiling, as if after thirty years he still can't quite believe that he gets to shoot and hunt, teach shooting, and mess around generally with shotguns for a living. He seems to have every certification possible for a shotgun instructor—right up to the Olympic level—and is a master gun fitter for E. J. Churchill guns. He has shot game birds on three continents and in fourteen countries. He shot competitively—and successfully—for years and still does when he has the time, which is never. He represents a number of fine gun companies and owns one himself, Charles Boswell. He designs sporting clay courses and is a noted authority on fine guns. He is one of seven people in the world who have qualified at all three levels of the British City & Guilds program. If it involves a shotgun, Batha is your man.

At twelve he was already shooting birds and selling them to local butchers. At fifteen he joined the Merchant Navy. He became a London firefighter, which required that he be able to carry someone of his own weight across his shoulders. Only a small percentage of such candidates were accepted into the London Fire Brigade. He became a London taxi driver, the exam for which is regarded as the world's single most difficult geography test, entailing the memorization of twenty-five thousand streets and twenty thousand landmarks. He studied catering and once owned two pubs. He was shooting competitively, instructing, and hunting at the same time. He considers one of his highest accolades that he is a member of the Worshipful Company of Gunmakers—a great title for a prayer breakfast—which was founded by royal charter in 1637.

And, yes, I actually do have a question for Chris Batha. I'd like to know which brand of dog food he's been smoking. But I don't ask because none of the seven students in his two-day British Driven Game Shooting Academy look at all perplexed. It's clear both that they have heard this before and that they take it as gospel. I can't decide whether I'm nuts or simply out of my depth. The class is at the Dorchester Shooting Preserve, outside of Savannah, Georgia, and students have come from as far away as Colorado and Wisconsin. Some have hunted previously in the United Kingdom and just want to brush up on their shooting skills. Others want to learn the vocabulary and the right fork to pick up if they ever do go. There's a lady in smart tweeds and what are evidently the right kind of purple socks, which have tassels at the top, and a feathered hat to match. She has brought a number of guns in cases made of animal hides that still have the hair on them and undoubtedly cost more than my Remington 11-87, which I had the sense to leave home. Her bespoke Purdey 20-gauge, I was discreetly told, cost between $85,000 and $100,000. A number of these folks have already signed up for four days of shooting with Batha in

Scotland in November (at $13,864 plus airfare, it's on the low end of such hunts). I'm here for two reasons. One is to get a jump on the lifestyle I intend to bear-hug after I win the lottery. And while I have shot poorly for so long that improvement seems unlikely, I would like to miss with a bit more style.

Right, then, Batha says, moving on to the finer points of shooting. The way you mount the gun to your shoulder and eye is everything. You want it to be automatic, so deeply grooved in the brain that it becomes instinctive. This is a simple matter of practicing the mount ten thousand times before a mirror, your gun empty, your eye focused on itself in the glass. He makes this sound like a minor detail, easily accomplished in just over three months. "You do five repetitions of ten mounts in the morning, five reps of ten in the evening, and then you've got it." Onward. The moment you see the bird (clay or feathered), you point at it with your leading hand (the one holding the forend, the wooden grip below the barrel) and track its line of flight with the leading hand and muzzle. Many people grip with the index finger pointing straight down the forend so that you really are pointing at the bird. As you track its line of flight, you bring the gun up and into your shoulder so that your cheek presses into the comb (the top edge of the stock) and your eye aligns with the barrel. Which you never look at, of course. You're accelerating the speed of your swing as you do all this. As the gun touches shoulder and cheek, you accelerate the swing even more so that the gun moves ahead of the bird. You want to fire into empty space ahead of it. "They do not fly backwards!" Batha says. You pull the trigger and continue the swing through the shot, just as you would with a golf club or a tennis racket. And, depending on the composition of the bird, you have just transformed it into a little cloud of black dust or an inert feathered object even now plummeting from the sky.

And not for an instant have you either aimed your shotgun or shot it at the bird itself.

We will be not aiming and intentionally missing a lot very soon. At which point I'll confirm both that I'm by far the worst shot in the group and that the cocktail of pleasurable neurotransmitters released when you do happen to make a shot is so pleasurable as to be addictive.

First, however, a bit of history. The French nobility of the seventeenth century were evidently the first to shoot birds on the wing for sport, walking in step with a line of "beaters" to drive the birds into flight. In 1660, when Charles II returned from France after his unfortunate exile (which we shan't discuss here), he ignited a passion for the sport in England. It was soon found to be more effective to have the line of beaters driving birds toward a line of hunters, or "guns," as they are called. Further, a line of pickers-up positioned forty yards or so behind the guns was a handy thing, saving you from finding and retrieving the birds yourself.

In the mid-nineteenth century, the English gentry had a great deal of money and very little to do. Wing shooting—which required considerable outlays of cash, time, and work, done by other people, naturally—was the ideal outlet. The upper class became passionate and competitive devotees of the sport. They competed to see which estate could shoot the most birds, the tally being published in London newspapers. They competed to see who could acquire the best grouse moors, which was a particular coup (pheasant and partridge can be raised in captivity, grouse can't). As tweed clothing became popular, estate owners went to great lengths to commission "estate" tweeds, patterns unique to a given property. Many aristocrats did little but hunt, becoming, in effect, professional shots. Their insistence on the best-quality guns drove the development of the modern shotgun, which needed to handle the hundreds or thousands of cartridges shot over a day's hunt without malfunction.

It took a few seconds to load any gun after it had fired its two shots, so the hunter who went afield with three shotguns and two loaders—and rotated guns continuously—could shoot without ever taking his eyes off the sky. Lord Ripon, the Earl de Grey, was a particularly keen hunter and considered one of the best shots of his era. Over his lifetime, he recorded taking 552,813 furred and feathered game. He dropped dead on the grouse moor after a successful day's hunt in 1923. A photo from the period shows him with his loaders and guns as he shoots directly overhead. You can't see much of the earl's face except the underside of his chin. Even while downing birds at a furious pace, he was relaxed enough to have a pipe between his teeth. He once shot twenty-eight pheasant in sixty seconds as a guest on the Sandringham House estate.

Driven shooting is nearly the opposite of American "shoe leather" hunting. We generally "walk up" birds behind dogs, which then point and flush them from cover, offering low and straightaway shots. The classic setup in driven game shooting—especially with pheasant and partridge—has beaters driving the birds from one hilltop to another, with the line of guns positioned in the valley between. These days, Batha tells us, "the true sportsman is measured by the difficulty of the shots he makes, not the number of birds killed." A sportsman allows low, easily shot birds to pass, opting instead for the more challenging high birds. Since these birds may be 150 feet up, they are best shot when nearest, just as they pass overhead. What you want to be doing, Batha tells us, is acquiring the bird at ten o'clock and shooting in front of it at eleven thirty or so. "You make a good shot on a difficult bird," he says, "and you fall asleep reliving it, thinking, Gosh, I really did something there." It's obvious that to Batha, nothing on earth compares with this feeling.

The enormous manpower involved is what makes driven game shooting so spendy. "It's like putting on a play," Batha says. "All the audience sees are the actors, but it takes a host of people backstage to pull the thing off." In addition to the beaters, pickers-up, and loaders, there are flankers, also known as flaggers, positioned to discourage birds from sneaking out the sides of the advancing line of beaters. The gamekeeper manages the estate's operation, from selecting cover crops to raising birds to discouraging poachers. There are guides, who know the land, the birds, and how to fix a gun.

Before the hunt, each gun draws a numbered "peg" to establish his or her position in the line. The pegs may be actual ivory or steel pegs or playing cards. A line of guns usually includes up to ten people, spaced between ten yards and forty yards apart, depending on terrain.

Often the pegs at the ends have the most action, which is why pegs are rotated two or more spaces between drives. "There will be drives when you might be almost a spectator," Batha tells us. "And others when you can't believe the number of birds flying over." No matter the circumstances, it's bad form to shoot birds that are flying over your neighbor's head. When someone does this to you, it's called "taking a bird off your barrel." If, however, your neighbor has fired both barrels and missed, you may attempt to "wipe your eye" with a follow-up shot. It's considered very bad form to shoot others, whether a neighboring gun, beater, or picker-up. For this reason you want to establish safe "arcs of fire" and never take a shot less than 45 degrees up. "The only safe bird to shoot is one that has blue sky all around it," Batha tells us. Although he confides that he has seen men squat down in order to get a blue-sky shot. Also bad form.

After a light lunch, we take golf carts to an open field. Sixty yards away and forty-five feet up a rented cherry picker are machines that zing out orange clays in all directions, all of which are up. We've broken into two groups. I'm in the one overseen by Batha's assistant for the class, Elizabeth Lanier, a charming top-tier shooting instructor from Richmond, Virginia, and the founder of GRITS—Girls Really Into Shooting—an organization that encourages women's participation in the shotgun sports. I'm doing my best not to aim and to miss each bird, and damned if I'm not succeeding at it as bird after bird floats unbroken to the ground. On the other hand, I've got a nice rhythm going: swing, mount, miss. "You're behind it," a voice says. It's Lanier, standing eighteen inches behind me. "And right. Try shutting your left eye when you shoot." I tell her I'm already shutting my left eye, which is what my last shooting instructor advised. She shrugs. "So try shutting it earlier, while you're bringing your gun up to your eye."

I try this and turn the next bird to black dust, which bathes my brain in the wonderful chemicals. "That's it!" Lanier exclaims and actually does a little shimmy. "Do it again." I do. Twice.

"Oh yeah! Flight canceled!" she crows, actually hopping from one foot to another. She's not faking it. She gets genuinely excited when a student succeeds. I do another, transforming this one into a particularly fine dust cloud. "We call that Alabama talcum powder!" she says. "You're nailing them!"

This kind of success is evidently more than I can take, so I start to miss again. "You're cocking your head," she says. "Think about keeping your eyes level the whole time." This is a new concept. The clays start dusting again. Then they don't.

"You're losing your lead," Lanier says. "Pretend you're holding a garden hose and spraying the target." This is a concept I can grasp. I start breaking them again. Lanier crows again. The woman is amazing. You can't fake this kind of excitement. You'd die of exhaustion in a couple of hours. I break six of the next eight with my garden hose. It feels fantastic.

I overhear Batha instructing a student in the other group, a trim fellow and excellent shot with his Perazzi, which has long barrels, thirty-four inches, often favored by trapshooters. But even he misses occasionally. "You're trying to be too precise," Batha says. "You're shooting a rifle. What do you do for a living?"

"I'm a surgeon," the man says.

"Well, there's your trouble right there, innit?" Batha says. "It needs to be quick—touch and go. You're staying in the gun too long. You're starting to think. And then you're done."

Batha strolls over to watch me. "You're shooting well now, but then you do this weird Magic Johnson flourish with your barrels at the end. So then you're not ready for the next shot, are you?" I've been told I sometimes fail to swing through the shot, so I've been trying to do that. But Magic Johnson flourish? Where did that come from? "Yeah," Batha says, finger-scribing an elaborate squiggle in the air. (Does Magic Johnson decorate cakes?) Not sure how Magic got here, but I resolve to stop doing his flourish.

Next Batha has us work as two-person teams, a gun and a loader. Fine shotguns are all double-barreled guns, and opening the action ejects the two spent shells, which you replace with two new cartridges. The instant the gun fires his second shot, he opens the action. The loader quickly inserts the cartridges and calls "Close," the moment his hands are clear. This allows the shooter to keep his eyes skyward, and he may be swinging on a bird he sighted while you were loading the moment he hears "Close." I'm surprised at how much I enjoy being a loader. It's a skill. "Oh, a good loader is worth his weight in gold," I remember Batha saying earlier. The task rewards dexterity and focus. It's like being a one-man pit crew.

To end the class, Batha announces that each group will get a few "hundred-bird flurries," a bunch of birds coming in large groups at unpredictable intervals. It's a scenario you'd never see in American sporting clays, where the maximum number of birds in the air at any one time is two. And it's where I do my best shooting of the whole course. There are so many birds zipping by that I don't have time to think. I'm just reacting, reaching out at bird after bird, pointing the gun out and up, swinging and shooting. For a time I'm unaware of anything else, completely lost in the moment, dusting birds left and right. It's bliss. And then the machines are done, out of birds.

"Excellent!" Batha says, clapping me on the shoulder. "I'd hardly guess that you're a writer."

Back at the lodge over a cocktail, I find myself talking to Jim, a farm boy turned lawyer in Midland, Texas, who has already signed up for the November trip. "I'm not the world's most live-on-the-edge guy, but I've really enjoyed this," he says. "I know that in one sense it's kind of ridiculous, kind of extravagant. But I grew up in cotton fields and now I'm gonna be shooting birds near a castle in Scotland." He isn't even trying to disguise a happy, what-the-hell smile. It's clear that he can't wait for November.

Fifty Shades of Green

When a man orders himself some new camo in one of the "scientifically based" patterns—which are way better than the "musically based" or "Italian Renaissance–painter based" patterns of just a few years ago—he expects to be the object of envy among his friends. This, after all, is why we buy camo. Just kidding. We hunters are results-oriented guys. We want evidence that a given technology works before we pull out our wallets. And research has shown that when deer are intrigued by a new pattern, they often stop and approach a hunter to learn more about it. Still kidding. The truth is that we buy the latest pattern because, well, it looks cool. Possession of something cool turns your brain into an endorphin-filled Jacuzzi. It's like when you order a twelve-ounce draft and the bartender brings you a pint. Or when you blow into a grunt tube at a buck and—despite the fact that it sounds like someone with big hands is choking a bunch of mice—the deer changes course and comes your way. That is an amazing feeling and one I hope to experience someday.

But there's a fly in the ointment of the new camo–endorphin connection. Until recently, most camo has been designed to be effective— by which I mean effective at making you want to buy it—at "retail distance," which is less than thirty inches. We are just now discovering that a terrific retail-distance pattern may not be the optimum choice for fooling a deer's eye at eighty yards. Fortunately, camo designers are responding nimbly to this new information. They're not changing the patterns, but they are changing the way they *market* them. So every pattern out there is now the best possible choice for concealing you at every possible distance from deer. The new patterns will also do anything else you need your camo to do, including clean the gutters.

Confused? You've got company. Even the U.S. military—run by some of the smartest people ever to be homeschooled by chimpanzees—can't make up its mind. In 2005, they began outfitting soldiers in Afghanistan with new uniforms in Universal Camouflage Pattern (UCP). The new pattern was said to be effective in "all environments." This, of course, is code for "all environments except the one you happen to be in right now." Soldiers pointed out that in Afghanistan pretty much everything—not just the mountains and valleys, but the lettuce, all flavors of ice cream, and everybody's lawn—is brown. And while the UCP had a very cool pixel look, it contained no brown whatsoever. Soldiers dismissed the new pattern for the flimsiest of reasons—that it didn't work. They said it made them more visible rather than less. And that this was bad because the people who could now see them better would sometimes shoot bullets and other stuff at them. I guess you can't please everybody.

What does this mean to you as a hunter? Well, say you're just getting started hunting and want some appropriate clothing. You go to the Web page of a popular outfitter—whose name, incidentally, can be rearranged to spell Abs Lace—and find its camo buyer's guide. "Got questions about camo patterns?" it asks. "We have the answers." The answer is to show you eighty-three patterns, each of which is the most advanced, realistic, and versatile ever devised. And yet the patterns are becoming more specialized rather than less. There are patterns for river-bottom/deciduous trees and ones for conifer forests. For western/open country and snow/winter. There are two completely different-looking patterns, each of which claims to be the first of its kind, *specifically designed to be worn inside a ground blind*. That's right. And here I thought the whole purpose of a ground blind was to provide a darkened shelter that would keep the animal you're hunting from seeing you regardless of your clothes. I understand a ground blind might not be the place to wear my white sequined Elvis jumpsuit. But buying special camo to wear inside one? That's like saying you should buy different cars for different trips. You know, one for grocery shopping, another for taking shoes in to be resoled, another to buy more cars if you take up badminton or darts.

What's next? Camo stickers for your teeth. I can't tell you how many big bucks I've spooked just before closing the deal because the sunlight glinted off my dazzling smile. Or a pill you could take that would instantly make your face break out into True Timber XD3 for twelve hours.

All this camo overload sends me back to the basic rules of hunting, the oldest of which is that making like a statue is the best concealment. Don't move and you're unlikely to get busted. Move and you likely will. No matter whose camo you're wearing. And the only reason you don't hear much about that is that nobody has figured out how to make a quick buck off the best things a hunter can take into the woods, things for which no substitute has been or ever will be found—patience and skill.

The Making of a Stand Hunter

Four million years ago on the African savanna, a few of the more adventurous primates climbed down from the trees, stood up on two legs, and, at a crucial moment in evolutionary history, were eaten by giant hyenas. Sadly, the genetic material of those brave hominids (Greek for "appetizers") is lost to us. The remaining proto-humans spent a terrorized night listening to the cracking of bones and murmuring to each other, "Let's hang out here awhile longer."

Every fall, in response to a primal tug in the blood that we can neither fathom nor control, millions of modern whitetail hunters go back to the trees. Some of us carry two-way radios. About 11 a.m. on opening day, whispered conversations take place in tree stands all over the United States.

"You see anything?"

"Zip. You?"

"Nothing."

"You wanna go?"

Long, thoughtful silence.

"Let's hang out here awhile longer."

"Okay."

You see how far we've come.

But that, of course, is the beauty of hunting. It allows us to reconnect with our primordial selves and the eons of genetic hardwiring that have enabled us to survive predators, diseases, and telemarketing. Think about it. It has only been in the past eleven thousand years that humans turned to domesticating animals and planting seeds to get food. Before that, for more than 99 percent of our time as a race on earth, we hunted. That means none of us, from the members of the World Wrestling Federation to the PETA board of directors, would be here today if a few thousand generations of our forebears hadn't been incredibly proficient at bringing home meat.

Even among hunters, however, those of us who pursue our quarry from above are a different breed. We're not like the quail and grouse guys, who unload a dog they could have sworn was trained and watch as it takes off like a bullet through miles of briers and thickets. We're not like turkey hunters, sprinting breathlessly through the woods with foam cushions bouncing silently against their butts as they try to head off a gobbler. We don't lug our hearts up to ten thousand feet like elk hunters just to see whether they'll explode in the thin mountain air.

No. Our particular madness is more finely honed. What we do, after a bit of scientific observation, a little gut feeling, and untold mental agony, is select a single tree in a place we believe the deer will show up. Then we climb that tree, set up a stand, and sit quietly until a deer comes by or the season runs out. In a world whose only quarrel with instant gratification is that it takes too long, we are practitioners of a dying art: waiting. This is both simple and immensely hard, not unlike quitting drinking.

In his apprenticeship stage, the stand hunter has trouble changing mindsets from clock time to woods time. After half an hour on stand his butt is numb, his nose itches, and his last good pee seems an early childhood memory. Further, he has a nearly uncontrollable urge to tap his fingers against his gun or bow, or his feet against the stand. He is bored. There is nothing happening. If there are squirrels crashing about in the leaves, he is sure that each is a deer. An endless squirrel-induced cycle of expectation and disappointment sets in, which, unchecked, can lead to institutionalization.

I remember my own progression vividly. At first, I really only wanted to subject myself to the misery of four straight hours of stand hunting when the odds of success were best: the rut. Even then I required a paperback and candy bars to balance against the long hours of inactivity. The next year, something had shifted. I had a mild hankering to be on stand for the opening of bow season in mid-September. My body had changed, relaxed. It was possible to sit quietly for longer periods. And there was something about the woods at that time of year that sucked me in: an air of expectation, of possibility. Even the trees were working harder now, as if they knew this was the homestretch of photosynthesis. I heard the first acorns dripping through the leaves, a hopeful sound, a rain of fat and protein. My mind had begun to sort itself out. Twenty feet up, waiting for deer to arrive, was not a bad seat in which to find oneself.

I took a big doe at twenty-seven yards one afternoon as she bent to feed on the acorns of a white oak. The arrow passed directly through her and stuck in the ground. She ran less than forty yards. I lay a hand on her flank, felt self-conscious asking her forgiveness for taking her life, did it anyway. It became a ritual I perform for every deer now. The next afternoon, on my way to setting up, I passed by the spot where I'd field-dressed her. Everything—heart, liver, lungs, and intestines—was gone. The forest had already turned her remains into new forms of energy. Only a few bloodstained leaves marked where she'd fallen.

During the October lull, I found a strange pleasure in witnessing the leaves one by one make a break for it after seven months of indecision and take their annual joyride down. I was no longer an outsider in my woods; I had become as much a part of them as any fox, sycamore, or woodpecker. My ears wised up, learning to distinguish squirrel from deer almost subconsciously. I began to think of the hyperactive little rodents as my straight men, helping me convey to passing deer that all was well. One November morning a red fox walked beneath my stand to roll luxuriously around on a cotton ball soaked with Trail's End #407 that had fallen off the branch I had placed it on. Two minutes later, it trotted off with its tail held a little straighter, delighted with its new and seductive cologne.

I glassed my surroundings endlessly for the flick of an ear or the shift of a haunch. I tried to imagine where I would see deer next and was almost always wrong. I'd see ten deer for every one that came within bow range. And the ones that did come within range either wouldn't stop, halted instinctively in places no arrow could penetrate, or stood obligingly in my shooting lanes but facing the wrong way. On those days, I was grateful there was no one waiting back at the cave for me to bring home supper.

It was the decoy that turned the tide for me just before gun season opened. Wearing rubber gloves, I set up a freshly de-scented Flambeau CommanDoe twenty yards upwind and sprinkled some estrous-doe urine on the ground beneath it. At around 8 a.m., I saw a small brown piston firing in the underbrush just beyond. At first I thought it was a squirrel doing his morning jumping jacks. Then it turned into the foreleg of a small doe trying to goad the frozen deer into acknowledging her. This went on for ten minutes before she snorted and left the area. An hour later, a good 6-pointer with no brow tines cruised boldly in, head down and sniffing. The deke wasn't the most animated girl he'd ever been with, but she more than made up for this in availability. I had plenty of time to calm down before taking the shot. My heart rate was probably no more than 170 beats per minute. This deer went to Hunters for the Hungry. The guy at the processor was happy to saw the antlers off for me to use as rattlers.

With two down, I thought I was through with deer for the year. The deer had other ideas. They still ran through my dreams all night. I succumbed to the pull of December. Explaining to editors that I was under a mountain of work, I left for the woods at noon every day. Wearing two pairs of wool long underwear under my hunting clothes, I kept coming after the holidays. The odds of seeing a shooter buck in January are about the same as for seeing Bigfoot, but I couldn't help myself. I was the worst kind of addict, the one who falls for the hunt itself rather than the results. I rode the sun down each evening from my stand, driving home strangely happy for a guy who'd been skunked.

47

Like all seasons, this one finally came to an end. I readjusted to the rhythms of working life. One morning, waiting for my computer to boot up, I idly pulled out the topos for my woods and noticed a spot I'd overlooked. It was a tiny bench above a dry streambed, perfect for the prevailing northwest winds. Suddenly I felt more focused, more alive. I knew exactly where I'd be hanging out come September.

My Gun Guru

David E. Petzal scares me a little. In a good way. Mostly. His unsurpassed knowledge of all things firearms is a given. But it's the man himself that you remember—a peerless malcontent of the old school, opinionated, cynical, incorruptible, allergic to fluff, intolerant of fools, and someone who doesn't give a rat's ass whether you like it or not. Why, one reader asked in the March 2013 "Ask Petzal" column, such a curmudgeon? "Because I've had the opportunity to observe human beings for seven decades, and if you do it for that long and don't have a foul disposition, either you're simple or you haven't been paying attention."

Questions, anyone?

Dave writes as he talks, in complete paragraphs. His online review of my book was more penetrating than any other. In it, he called me a "strange and repellent character." He worked in references to Shakespeare, Robert Ruark, and Bill Tarrant. In 223 words. Michelle bristled at "strange and repellent character." I waved her off. "Babe, from Petzal that's practically a love tap."

Recently, I took a notion to get myself a .22 pistol. I'd just weathered one of those birthdays where people give you what they would have liked. From my mom, a lumbar support pad. From the kids, a kickball, a Wiffle ball and bat, and a Nerf football.

I opted for a well-known gun brand that is highly rated on a bunch of shooters' forums. Torn about which model to get, I screwed up my courage and e-mailed the man who made Antonin Scalia look like Peter Pan. Dave's reply didn't even deign to mention the gun I'd named.

Instead came words that, in their Petzal-ness and innate authority, might have been incised on a stone tablet. "Get a Smith & Wesson Model 41 with the longest barrel you can find. Length of barrel does not make a handgun more accurate, but it increases the sight radius and cuts down on aiming error."

The 41 was double the cost of the gun I'd asked about. But there are people with whom one does not argue. David Petzal is one of them. I took the hit, got my hands on a newish Model 41 with a 7-inch barrel, and fell in love as soon as I hefted the thing. The gun's open sights and middle-aged eyes, however, do not make a happy marriage. I could focus on the sights or the target, not both. I hiked back up the mountain and e-mailed D.E.P. again. First things first, he replied. Were there "four small but attractive filler screws" atop the pistol's slide?

"Present and accounted for," I wrote back.

"Then our job just got a $#*+load easier." I was directed to midwayusa.com to acquire a red-dot sight and a base on which to mount it. "The UltraDot 30mm. The original model. Get it in black. It comes with rings." As for the rail, I wanted a "Weigand one-piece Weaver-style base." The specificity of sight and mount both impressed and enraged me. The UltraDot was $204.99. Other red-dot sights started at $30. There was one for $99.50 that had earned a four-and-a-half-star rating from sixty-six satisfied reviewers. Wasn't that good enough? And what was with the Weigand mount at $32.99—four times the price of other compatible mounts?

But I'd asked the man for his expertise and he'd given it freely. And, once again, there was that Petzal-esque authority to contend with. Could I assemble a cheaper pistol? Undoubtedly. But a pistol built to D.E.P. specs would be a noble thing, impeccable, immune to regret. I dug another trench in my wallet and reported back.

"Now you have a fundamental choice: Install the thing yourself, or find a gunsmith to do it. The job is so simple that it almost seems criminal to pay to have it done." Dave knows that I have the technical prowess of a sock puppet. Was he baiting me for his own entertainment or genuinely urging me to stretch my boundaries? Either way, I had to see this through. Something "so simple it almost seems criminal" took me three days and eighteen e-mails to Dave, many with photos. I made every mistake possible and invented a few new ones. But when it was over, I had a .22 pistol for the ages. Largely because Dave walked me through each detail without the slightest hint of exasperation or mockery.

But do me a favor. Keep this good deed under your hat. He'd be furious if the truth ever got out.

Castaway in Deer Paradise

With 120,000 whitetails, and ideal conditions for still-hunting, Anticosti Island is the ultimate destination for deer hunters. Just forget everything you know about stand hunting, and prepare to be humbled by your guide every ten minutes.

Stalking along a hillside of broken conifers behind my guide, Michel Quévillon, on the first day of the hunt, I'm playing a high-stakes version of *Dancing with the Stars*. Maintaining my interval of exactly two steps behind, I mirror his every move—Ginger Rogers with a .270 and Muck boots trying to keep up with this Fred Astaire, a Québécois whose English sounds like it has just gone through a garbage disposal. Not that he speaks much. My job is to avoid costing us points with the judges, who are wearing antlers and will vanish at the first misstep. When Quévillon steps, I step. When he slows, I slow. When he stops, I stop. And I hardly dare breathe until he is moving again. I've done this dance many times over the years, but I've never felt such urgency to get it right—nor such dread about missing a step.

I can't yet put my finger on what it is about this guy that ups the ante. We are a few miles from the southeast coast of Canada's Anticosti Island—three thousand square miles of essentially uninhabited sub-boreal forest in the Gulf of St. Lawrence. Visibility at the moment ranges from ten yards to more than one hundred, and the yellow grass in the conifer forest's understory is loaded with beds and piled droppings. I don't know what these deer are eating, but they are processing large quantities of it. We've already bumped a few, which fled without snorting—their white flags erased in midair on the second or third leap, as if sponged up by the forest. I couldn't say whether they were buck or doe, but all looked uncommonly round and sleek. Not that it matters now.

Quévillon and I have not spoken in forty minutes, but he did shoot me a momentary glance awhile back that spoke volumes. The uppers of my boots had brushed each other midstep, sending out the faintest whistle of faced neoprene. Quévillon turned and cocked an eyebrow, prompting me to fall to my knees and roll my pants legs outside my boots, the way he wears his. I vowed never to make that mistake again. The problem right now, however, is that my arms are killing me. Somewhere down on my body—dangling from a pack strap, binoc harness, or belt—is some loose plastic snap or buckle that keeps hitting my rifle. I compensate by extending my arms, carrying it farther out. Felt gun weight naturally increases proportionally to the gun's distance from your core, however, so my Model 70 Featherweight .270 now feels like pig iron. I'd be perfectly happy to stop for the twenty seconds it would take me to find and fix the problem. But I've already used up one stop to fix my pants legs. I'm not about to stop for a second wardrobe malfunction.

Keeping my interval and focusing on Quévillon's boots, I become aware of the force field of energy he emits: a combination of mental focus, physical awareness, and sheer predatory determination. He seems to intuit the presence of deer before his physical senses have located them. When this happens, he suddenly stops midstride and simply waits for his eyes or ears to confirm what he already believes. As he stands there, hands motionless at his sides, his concentration is such that the tips of his fingers twitch involuntarily, as if that much electrical current must find an outlet. I recognize that I'm in the presence of an increasingly rare phenomenon in the modern world: a man making a living at a task he seems born to be doing. And it makes me redouble my efforts to win his approval, even as it triples my dread at disappointing him.

Beach Bums

I've come to Anticosti Island after a couple's therapist advised that my tree stand and I ought to see other people. Like nine out of ten American deer hunters, I do my field work twenty feet up, where I sit motionless for hours on end—a lawn dwarf in a Lone Wolf. Lately, I've found myself lusting after something more physical: an old-fashioned, boots-on-the-ground whitetail hunt. A little research revealed that Anticosti, where a hunter can take two deer of either sex, is arguably the best place in North America for that.

I glommed on to a party already booked for a five-day hunt that included Ric Riccardi, brothers Jack and Paul Reilly, and Steve Burnett. I met Burnett, my entrée to the group, through David E. Petzal.

"Heavey," Petzal told me, "he's the only human I know of even half as strange as you. I think you two would hit it off." The hell of it is that Petzal was right. Burnett and I have become fast friends.

Riccardi has come to Anticosti camps run by Cerf-Sau Outfitters for twenty-two of the past twenty-six years. "Three things make this place special," he tells me. "The ground here is quiet enough to make still-hunting effective. I mean, if you're walking in Rice Krispies, you're not going to see much. Second, it's the only place I know of where I can walk all day and never see another hunter. Third, every time you take another step, there's the chance you'll see a shooter buck."

Cerf-Sau has camps in the Bell River and Chaloupe River territories, with a combined area of 425 square miles on the southeastern part of the island. We're staying at the Chaloupe River camp, where we settle into a roomy cabin with hot water, electricity, and a woodstove. We take meals and pick up boxed lunches in the main building with other hunters, almost all of whom are American. The Reilly brothers are sharing another guide, François. Riccardi, the veteran, knows the island so well that he prefers to hunt solo. Burnett and I, the Anticosti newbies, are hunting with Quévillon.

We've been warned by the others in our party that Quévillon is a hellacious guide.

"The best I've ever seen at spotting whitetails," says Riccardi.

"He doesn't talk much," says Jack Reilly. "But everybody around here listens when he does."

Paul nods. "He wants you to get a deer even more than you do."

A Shot of Relief

On this, our first day, Burnett had Quévillon in the morning, and I got him after lunch. When I asked how the morning had gone, Burnett piped up, "Good!" Then he added, "And sort of humbling. He's a great guy. It's just that he's so damn competent you feel like a moron. Don't even take your binocs. They're just extra weight."

At a certain moment on the hillside where Quévillon has stopped, seeking confirmation of his deer intuition, his fingertips cease twitching. Then two fingers of his right hand gesture me forward.

"Dere's a good buck in dot ticket," he whispers. "See his hantler?"

Quévillon points toward a clump of stunted firs full of the swaying antler-colored grass that so often fools the novice into thinking the grass holds a buck. The difference this time is that hidden in this yellow clump there actually *is* a pair of swaying deer antlers, and they belong to a buck. He's feeding calmly, facing away and nearly screened by brush. I mirror Quévillon as he takes a half step to the right, which reveals a small window to the buck. We wait. The deer is quartering away sharply, but if he will stay put and turn our way just a few inches, a shot almost behind his ribs will take out the opposite shoulder.

"Now," Quévillon says at last.

The shot is only seventy yards, but my rifle and scope choose this moment to transform from pig iron to rubber. Quévillon moves in front of me, squats slightly, and taps his left shoulder. My first thought is that this is a totally inappropriate time to indicate his desire to deepen our relationship. Then I understand that he's offering a rest, so I place the forend on his shoulder. He inserts fingers into his ears. When the crosshairs settle on the buck's flank, I press the trigger.

The blood trail is heavy and short. Seventy yards into it, as we search for the next splotch of red, Quévillon grunts. Not four feet away, in the middle of a bush, lies my buck—a 7-pointer with a kicker on the left side.

"His hantlers looked bigger when first I saw," says Quévillon apologetically. "From de light on dem. But you make de good shot. Both lungs."

He shakes my hand, and a wave of something washes over me. It takes me a moment to sort out my feelings. I'm elated to have taken a buck, of course, and I'm greedy to devour my guide's compliment. Beneath that, however, lies a stronger emotion: relief. The thrill of victory is sweet, but it's the tip of the iceberg. The real adrenaline rush is in having escaped the agony of defeat.

By the time I've retrieved my knife and a Butt Out from my pack, Quévillon has finished field-dressing the buck with a small blade. He cuts slits in the hocks and inserts the front legs through them. Then he binds the arrangement with twine, kneels, and asks that I give him a hand both for support as he rises and to keep the buck's antlers from poking him in the head. With a practiced motion similar to that of lifting a canoe, he rolls the deer onto his back, grabs my hand, and stands. Then he's off and striding down the hillside toward the road, stepping over fallen trees and plowing right over everything else. Stumbling to keep up with a guy hauling 120 pounds of dead deer on his back, I feel both proud and slightly foolish. It's as if I've just won the trophy for Most Promising Hunter, 12-and-Under Division.

The Anticosti Experiment

For thousands of years before chartered airplanes began ferrying American hunters here from Montreal, Anticosti was a hunting ground visited by native peoples living on the mainland. The Innu, for example, called it Notiskuan ("where bears are hunted"). Accounts from as early as 1542 note the abundance of black bears; in 1797, one Thomas Wright, who spent a winter on the island, reported that bears were "extremely numerous: 53 were killed within six weeks and many more were seen." The island went through a number of hands before being sold in 1895 to chocolate maker Henri Menier, who promptly set about creating a private game preserve, importing buffalo, elk, caribou, moose, foxes, and 220 whitetail deer. The big winners in this zoological version of *Survivor* were—drum roll, please—the deer. Within fifty years they had grazed the native black bear population into extinction—a rare documented instance of a prey species killing off a whole class of predators.

Today, there are a few moose on the island and a great many foxes (red, black, and hybridized), but none of the other introduced critters could keep up with the whitetail eating machine. The deer population fluctuates, but the absence of nonhuman predators and the relatively mild maritime climate (cool summers and long but generally mild winters) has resulted in a herd that numbers around 120,000. That's about 40 deer per square mile. At that density, of course, you aren't breeding monsters. In fact, biologists say the average size of an Anticosti whitetail has decreased over the past twenty-five years as the deer do to their preferred forage what they did to the black bear. But the deer are sleek and round and fun to hunt, and Cerf-Sau claims that success rates on two deer run about 85 percent (exclusive of outdoor writers, of course). Further, the venison is uncommonly tasty, perhaps because some of the deer feed on seaweed that washes up on the beaches, in effect pre-brining themselves. While big racks are not the norm, they do exist.

Island Monster

By the end of the third day, our group has only two bucks hanging in the meat house, an unusually poor showing, according to Riccardi. "It's partly the weather," he tells me. "We're still in the forties and fifties in late October, which is not normal. I've never seen so few deer moving up here."

On the next-to-last morning, Quévillon and I are once again stalking, this time in open country studded with patches of evergreens along a stream valley. It's windy enough that the deer don't hear us, and they're feeding so intently that several times we come upon animals ten yards away with their heads in the grass. I put one rounded, sway-backed body in my scope, waiting for what I'm sure will be an antlered head when it finally looks up. It turns out to be a big doe. We pull this trick three times—all does. At lunch we switch, Burnett and Quévillon circling back toward the road one way and me the other. Having absorbed something of the rhythm and rhyme of this kind of hunting, I'm pleased at being able to stumble on a few deer on my own. Once again, however, they're all does. I'm waiting at the truck when Quévillon and Burnett show up. Up the road, we stop for Riccardi, who hasn't seen a buck all day.

"See anything?" he asks Burnett.

Burnett, who has what I take to be the same tired, slightly dazed look that I imagine I'm wearing, shrugs. "Killed a nine-pointer," he says in a monotone. "Biggest deer of my life. Too far to drag him out, though. They'll have to get him with the four-wheeler later."

Riccardi and I exchange irritated looks. We're all beat, and Burnett thinks it's a good time to jerk our chains? Quévillon's expression looks the same as always, so there's no information to be gleaned there. Burnett, I notice, is in an uncharacteristically good mood during cocktails. Then, halfway through dinner, when we hear the crunch of truck tires on gravel outside, he rises from his seat and murmurs, "That's probably my buck."

A truck backs up to the meat house. In the bed is a four-wheeler and, overhanging both sides, a very long buck with a heavy 9-point rack. It's a beast, requiring two men to wrestle it onto the scales, where it clocks in at about 185 pounds. Burnett's own body seems to go slack as heavy slaps of congratulations rain down upon him.

This buck is a honker. The rack, typical of Anticosti bucks, while not especially long tined, is impressively thick. The tines are fat as Vienna sausages and taper to sharp points. It's all business, this rack, like a compact .45, and there's no doubt that it could hurt you. The guides all say it's the highest-scoring rack of the year so far and likely as not to remain that way.

Back in the cabin, the tale unravels. Burnett is now openly giddy but confides that he almost blew his chance at this trophy. He and Quévillon were skirting the edge of an open area when they saw the buck chasing after two does.

"'It's big' is all Michel said," Burnett begins. "Then he dropped to all fours and started, like, running after it. Like a dog, man! Booking. I'm doing my best to keep up, but I can't. Meanwhile, my gun is whacking me in the shoulders and face at every step." *They stalk to within 250 yards and Burnett misses it—twice.* "By then I couldn't even look at him. I just wanted to crawl into a hole. I couldn't even think." *Quévillon sees that the buck is so preoccupied with mating that it moves off only a short distance.* "Michel sort of shook me and said, 'He didn't leave.'" *The guide just motors forward again on all fours and Burnett follows as best as he can.* "So I'm still whacking myself with my own gun as I crawl—on hands and knees—soaked and scraped up and just scared to death. I've screwed it up twice, and now I'm going to get to put the final nail in my coffin. And when I finally get to where Michel is, the buck is still there." *Quévillon has Burnett use his back as a rest.* "I'm working at ten percent of brain capacity now. I'm flooded with shame and fear and adrenaline." *At 125 yards Burnett gets the buck in his crosshairs and pulls the trigger.* "All I heard Michel say was 'He's down.' By then I was afraid to believe him. And that's how it happened. I hit him in the neck and dropped him in his tracks. Obviously, I shouldn't have taken those first shots, but you see a buck like that, and it just fries your mind. You can't think straight. And once I'd missed, all I could think about was having to drive back in the truck, because having Michel sore at you is just the worst thing in the world, and—"

"Wait," I interrupt. "It's not the *worst* thing in the world."

Paul Reilly, who has been listening the whole time without saying a word, weighs in: "Oh yeah? Up here it is."

The Odd Couple

He drew me wearing pantyhose, in a yellow medieval fool's costume, with icicles hanging from my nostrils. With a pig's nose, straitjacketed on a psychiatrist's couch, sporting antlers and red high heels. He always gave me a big red nose and vacant, yellow, bloodshot eyes that couldn't quite focus on the same point and therefore looked crazed. And I would have done anything for the guy.

It's fitting that the last time I saw illustrator Jack Unruh, I was modeling a hot pink bra as he took pictures to sketch from. I'd come to Dallas as soon as I could after hearing that he had cancer. He was finally home from the hospital. That meant Jack could draw, which was better for him than any drug. I'd written a column about dumb survival hacks, one of which touted what great "debris masks" you could make from the cups of a padded bra. Jack's idea was to draw me in a bra for the illustration. This wasn't what I'd had in mind, but I'd learned the hard way that protest just meant I'd look worse in the final image. I drove to the nearest Walmart. I bought the bra.

Jack posed me bending forward as if I were trying to undo the clasp while a mushroom cloud rose in the distance. "Look to your left like you've just seen the cloud," he said. "Look terrified." Click. "Okay, astonished." Click. "Close your mouth," he said, choking back the laugh rising in his throat because it hurt. "You look like an idiot with your mouth open."

"I'm half-naked in women's underwear in your kitchen," I pointed out, "but I *don't* look like an idiot when my mouth's closed?" He shrugged. Dignity was irrelevant. We were professionals.

The Odd Couple

I met Jack around 2003, when I was given my column on a trial basis (I think it's still on a trial basis) and he was hired to illustrate. One of the first recounted how I'd gone to Brazil to fish for peacock bass but ended up so propulsively sick that I never left my hotel and was lucky to fly home alive four days later. The guy in his drawing was me all right. But me as a man who, after a life of unspeakable depravity, was now dying—deservedly—of some Ebola-like illness. He drew me sitting bolt upright in bed, rivulets of sweat running down my face. Purple and gray skin was stretched tight over my skull and I already had the red nose that would be there for thirteen years. Three fish swam over my bed blowing little bubbles. The image was disturbing, twisted, and striking. It was brilliant.

My mother was not amused. "You're a good-looking boy," she protested—I was in my late forties at the time. "Why is that man so mean to you?" I explained that it was because he liked me, that you couldn't make somebody look that awful unless you had some affection for him. Mom didn't buy it. I had already decided that anybody with an imagination this bent and strange was somebody I would get along with.

For the next dozen years we took hunting and fishing trips all over the country, often bamboozling this magazine into funding them. Jack outfished and outshot me, but he was such a gentleman about it that it never stung. He had twenty years on me, but I never thought of him as old. He was vigorous and from long-lived people. Subconsciously, I was banking on his being around a long time.

Outwardly, we were an unlikely pair. I go through life expecting to be fired, audited, or arrested for crimes I don't remember committing but probably did anyway. Jack was an optimist. He never lost a sense of gratitude and wonder that he made a living "doodling"—despite being sought out by magazines from *National Geographic* to *Rolling Stone*, *Time* to *Sports Illustrated*. He was never happier or more himself than when drawing.

You never really understand why you love someone. Different as we were, each of us recognized something in the other—some spark,

61

some sense of the divine absurdity of life. We never spoke of this. The closest we ever came was once when having a cocktail on our motel beds after pheasant hunting in South Dakota. Jack always brought better whiskey, so I saw to it that we drank his first, and I generally poured my drink taller than his. Being a gentleman, he waited years to say anything. "It's because you're an optimist and I'm a cynic," I said airily. "When a cynic's glass gets below half-full, it's kind of critical. He's worried that there might not be any more coming. Whereas you're pretty sure there will be."

"Heavey, you are full of $%*#," he said.

"You're just noticing that now?"

"Nope. Known it all along. Just saying it out loud now." We raised our plastic cups and sipped.

Jack never finished the illustration of me in the bra. He e-mailed the magazine, apologizing and explaining that he could no longer make the climb to his studio. He thanked everyone for all the fun over the years. He died four days later.

Jack Unruh was more than a great artist. He was a great soul. I counted him among my best friends. And I'm bold enough to believe—this may be wishful thinking, but I think it's true—that he counted me among his. Bless you, Jack. Thank you. I love you.

Deer, Lies, and Videotape

I was hard at work—losing a stare-down with a blank computer screen in the basement—when the phone rang. It was the call most outdoor writers pray for: a PR guy for a tree-stand company wondering if I'd like to be their guest for a bow-and-black-powder hunt for trophy whitetails in Wisconsin in late November.

I tried to play it cool as I consulted my official 180-day planner. It was as empty as that part of heaven reserved for politicians. The guy asked if I had any objection to being filmed while hunting. A free hunt and the possibility of my mug appearing on the TV screens of hunters all over the country? I mulled it over for a nanosecond before accepting. We hung up, and I lost it, dancing around the basement and whooping like I'd just knocked out Evander Holyfield in the first round. Man, I thought, *this is something.*

Four months later, I was twenty feet up a tree on a cool Wisconsin morning with the cyclops eye of a video camera staring down at me from a second stand four feet above my head. The videographer, Paul, an Arkansas boy who had filmed hunts in seven states so far this fall and hadn't seen his new bride in two months, wanted a shot of me pulling my muzzle-loader up into the stand on the tote rope. I complied.

"Damn," he whispered. "Wrong angle. Could you do it again on the other side of the stand?" No problem.

"Hey," I whispered back. "You gonna get to hunt at all this year?" He patted the camera sadly and shook his head.

We sat and waited. Here I was in high-rent trophy country (the outfitter told us not to shoot any deer scoring less than 150) with a smokepole in my hand, knowing that at any moment a deer better than any I had expected to see on the hoof in my lifetime might saunter by. *This is something,* I told myself. Unfortunately, that something wasn't hunting. I knew because I kept looking at my watch.

Normally, after the first hour or so on stand, I forget the quartz handcuff on my wrist and slip into woods time, measuring the day's progress by the changing light and the passage of clouds, the fingers of the wind on my face, the moods of crows and songbirds and hawks. The workaday chatter of my mind subsides, and I forget to think about how my career is going or the money I'm not making or the bickering of everyday life. My domesticated mind tips over into the hunting mind, the predatory hardwiring that underlies the veneer of modern life. To the hunting mind, an hour means nothing; the innocent rustle of leaves is a matter of life or death; and a change in the wind can bring panic or euphoria. I love when this happens.

But it wasn't happening here. Part of it was because I wasn't alone. Paul was a perfectly nice guy; he knew not to make any unnecessary noise; and he was just trying to do his job. But deer hunting, even in a camp, is essentially a solitary pursuit. You eat, sleep, drink, lie, and joke with your buddies, but when it's time to hunt, you go your own way.

The other distraction was that we were trying to make a deer snuff film. I'm just like any other hunter; I've watched scores of them. Personally, the more I hunt, the less interesting they are to me. Sure, it's exciting to watch some guy nail a trophy. But it's a pale substitute for the real experience, and the guys in the videos always seem to be acting, not hunting. That fist-pump after the shot gets hollower every time you see it. And the longer I sat in a tree with a camera watching, the unhappier I became.

We sat on stand for three days and never saw a shooter deer. I kept up my end of the bargain, vowed never to hunt on camera again, and felt a mixture of frustration and relief when it was all over. Two days later, I was back in the woods, alone and hunting happily. The taking of a wild deer remains for me a personal thing, a momentous thing, maybe even a sacred thing. Fellow hunters, rest easy. You will not be seeing me in your living rooms anytime soon.

Father Knows Less

Some bleak February mornings it's all a guy can do to rise, eat an eighteen-ounce bag of white corn Tostitos, and go back to bed. Then one morning you wake to a sun that makes you feel like lost luggage that got sent to Jamaica. A sun that warms to the bones. A few hours of sun won't stir up any fish. They're too smart for that. But something pulls you anyway, if only the ritual. If only to pay your respects to the river.

Emma wouldn't like it, but she needed a shot of the natural world herself. For too long she had tarried in YouTube's slanted universe of banana-peeling cats and hamster steeplechases. I wanted to remind her of an even better large-format website: the outdoors. I knew it would be a tough sell, especially coming from the Homework Monster, Mr. Eat-Your-Peas. So I offered a choice: clean her room—which I defined as "that state in which a stranger could tell whether the floor was carpeted or not"—or go fishing with her old man.

"That's blackmail!" she cried.

"Blackmail is a form of extortion through intimidation," I explained. "This is more like 'the lesser of two evils.'"

"Oh," she said, surveying a room that made the Middle East look tidy. "Okay. But I am *not* touching worms."

It was balmy when we arrived, nearly 60 degrees, the river running high and cold. I headed for a hole that sometimes yielded an early crappie. I tied on marabou jigs tipped with worm and clipped on bobbers three feet above. Emma pointed to a painted turtle sunning itself just as it plopped back into the water. "Good eye, honey," I said. We cast out. Nothing. We cast again. And again.

I complimented Emma on her casting. But she was reeling in too fast. I tried to show her how to pop the rig with a low rod tip and reel more slowly. Coming from anyone else—a hated teacher, the hairy-handed orthodontist, or Satan—the suggestion might have merited consideration. Instead, she shot me a brief you're-kidding-right? look and kept reeling too fast. I backed off. Her good humor, welcome as the February sun, was just as likely to dive behind a cloud.

I'm not the greatest parent, but I knew some positive reinforcement was in order. "It's fun being out here with you, monkaloo," I said. "I'm really glad you came." She didn't say anything—I'd known she wouldn't—but I wish I had a recording of the assenting noises she made. Brief but wondrous, like birdsong.

After ten minutes, Emma said, "Daddy, is it okay if I don't fish?" I'd seen this coming. "Sure, honey," I said, even though it meant we'd be leaving in five minutes. I began not catching fish more quickly.

After twenty minutes, I went looking. Em was kneeling on a sliver of beach nearby, working on an arrangement of small sticks, stones, and grass. Similar arrangements lay on other rocks. Each was a little stone altar protected by a twig tepee. A sheaf of bright green onion-grass, bound with a single strand of some wheat-colored grass, lay atop each altar. They were astonishing things, a child's unaffected and unself-conscious response to the natural world, springing from a place that I, like all adults, had paved over long ago. Implicit in these small shrines was the understanding that everything here—water, rock, turtles, plants—was alive, powerful, holy.

"Monk," I said, "these are . . . amazing. They're beautiful. What do you call them?" She shrugged, adding a final twig to one of the tepees. "Just things I did," she murmured.

We had switched places. I was suddenly the one who needed to see. I forgot about fishing. I tried to photograph the scene in my mind. I wanted to hold on to it. Emma is changing quickly. By the time you read this, she will be thirteen. She may no longer make temples at the water's edge.

"Okay," she said. She placed a last stone. "Let's go." Emma's intuitive nature extends to knowing when she has power over her father. That night, she insisted on dinner in front of the TV, on which we watched *Hannah Montana*, her touchstone teenage sitcom for the last four years. I hate this show, with its canned laughter and dumb jokes. I watched anyway. It was my own small offering to the mystery of my child.

Some Home Truths

Fall is a busy time in the animal kingdom. Hormone levels rise markedly. Daytime activity increases. Feeding and travel patterns change. The sexes largely segregate themselves. Males who were on friendly terms all summer now avoid contact. When they do meet, the hostility may escalate into fights.

What's amazing is that the same thing happens among deer.

It's true that the average deer brain is only about one-sixth the size of the average human's (although scientists believe that rises to one-third in the case of David E. Petzal). In evolutionary terms, however, whitetails are clearly the more successful and highly evolved species. Our team, *Homo sapiens,* has been around for 200,000 years. Fossils of *Odocoileus virginianus* found in Florida date back 3.5 million years. That ought to tell you something.

True, deer are dumb by our standards. No whitetail has ever posted a cat video to YouTube, gone bankrupt buying a thirty-thousand-dollar bass boat on credit, or forced its offspring to take forty hours of standardized tests each year. But they leave us in the dust in other areas. Their ability to detect danger so exceeds ours that we call it a sixth sense, which is code for "We can't even measure it, let alone explain it." When it comes to skills like concealment and using natural camouflage, forget it. I have seen bucks walk into thickets the size of an airplane bathroom and—counter to everything I know about logic, physics, and literary criticism—disappear. Deer are also quick to recognize and interpret patterns. A big buck, for example, will often bed within yards of a WMA parking lot and watch fools like me walk right by all season. I strongly suggest that you point out these examples of their intelligence at your next back-to-school night, especially if you don't want to serve on any committees.

To me, no fact so eloquently speaks to a deer's mental superiority as its complete avoidance of home repair. We don't know whether this has always been the case or whether they owned and overhauled houses before recognizing it as the fast lane to extinction. Sometimes—while retrieving a stuffed animal or a new ukulele flushed down the toilet by my daughter—I imagine the crucial moment. Maybe it was a lone buck homeowner assessing his house on the 2 million BC real estate market. *Who am I kidding?* he thought. *No paint is going to hide that kind of termite damage.* And he simply walked away.

This is exactly the type of adaptive behavior humans should imitate if we are to survive for another 200,000 years. Yet recently, displaying the self-delusion at which our species excels, I purchased a multistoried roofed dwelling far larger than I could afford. Then, as if to further compound my mistake, I stopped listening as soon as our home inspector said what I wanted to hear—that the place was "up to code and in good shape." So I missed the rest of the sentence: "by Republic of Liberia standards."

I appreciate the fact that whoever hung the gutters thought it would be funny if the water had to run uphill to get to the downspouts. As for the elevated back deck, one foot of sway for every 10 miles per hour of wind seems—at least potentially—hazardous. And a hammer and pry bar should not be necessary to open and shut most of the windows.

I have every intention of fixing these problems. But for now, I intend to advance my own species by intense field study of the most widely distributed ungulate in the Americas. And if this should involve a tiny amount of hunting, that's cool, too.

Like millions of my kind, I dream of bagging a buck with antlers the size of a chandelier in a Las Vegas strip club (not that I've ever been in such a place). At the same time—due to genetics (ours) and hunter density (also ours)—I know that the odds of this are absurdly low. The average hunter's chance of killing a B&C buck is well below

1 in 1,000. To be conscious of two contradictory ideas at once and still be able to eat donuts is a uniquely human skill.

Whitetails aren't great at abstract reasoning, but I suspect that if they were, they'd decide that I'm on a fool's errand. And I'd be the first to agree. At this time of year, however—and I consider what I'm about to say a sort of public service announcement to the girlfriends, wives, and families of deer hunters—that part of the hunter's brain goes on vacation. Leaving the other, more primitive part in charge. Which is totally convinced that the 1,000-to-1 figure applies only to other guys.

The real questions, I suppose, are these: Is such thinking an evolutionary adaptation that will help *Homo sapiens* survive? Or is it a symptom of our inevitable doom?

I honestly don't know and—at the moment—don't particularly care. But I do know this: It's almost November. And I'm feeling pretty good about my chances.

In the Face of Failure

As the old year winds down, a man takes stock of his performance. Even adjusted for inflation and moral turpitude, I'm not a candidate for the gifted-and-talented track. Yet there's a certain bracing satisfaction in facing the truth head-on. Afterward, you take a hard look in the mirror and say, "Dammit, son, you need to come up with better excuses." Here are a couple of mine.

Issue: My fly-fishing skill peaked about twenty years ago. Since then, a graph of my improvement closely resembles that of Abraham Lincoln's pulse. In 2014, I was visited by a feverish desire to do better. As with most fevers, this one should have been allowed to pass. Instead, I booked a lesson with Lefty Kreh, the best fly-fisherman alive. First, he wanted to see me cast. Then he didn't. He thought for a moment, then gave me his analysis: "That was awful." Lefty took my rod away and began throwing perfect loops. Fly casting, he explained, is similar to swinging a bat or golf club. You accelerate smoothly to an abrupt stop. In my hands, a fly line becomes a physical example of Obsessional Defiant Disorder—negative, disobedient, and hostile. In Lefty's, it is bewitched into a living thing that wants only to do his bidding. I was aware I was watching genius. This, I thought, must be what it felt like to see Fred Astaire dance or Ted Williams hit. "It ain't about strength," Lefty said. "I'm eighty-eight years old. I don't have any strength left." Then, to show me what I would never achieve, he dismantled the rod. And threw the same perfect loops with half of it. I didn't know whether to kneel before him or break his arm.

Afterward, I left my spinning gear behind on my next outings, the better to focus on the long rod. I'll spare you the details, but I've had more enjoyable root canals. I actually began to dread fishing. Then I snapped, said to hell with it, and went back to the basics that had first lit my fishing fire—a 5-foot UltraLight Ugly Stik, a spinning reel, 6-pound mono, and a 3-inch white grub on a leadhead. I got so absorbed in catching Potomac smallies that I lost track of time, coming out of my trance as sunlight faded.

Excuse: Some men's lives, like mine, are too brief to attain fly-fishing proficiency. I will continue to admire those who throw pretty loops on our nation's rivers and streams. Me, I'd rather catch fish.

Issue: In 2014 I resolved to up my bowhunting game by descending from a perfectly good tree stand to hunt on the ground. This was pure hubris, Greek for "not a good idea in your case." My reasoning was as follows: When hunting from a climber—or any stand, really—once you've picked your tree, you've placed your bet. After that, you're just waiting for the roulette wheel to stop spinning. If you do get lucky, you still have to make the shot, of course. But you're not going anywhere for a while.

Hunting on the ground would be harder but more rewarding. I'd shoot fewer deer but would increase my woodcraft at all levels—stalking, tracking, reading sign, and imitating various shrubs. There were just a couple of problems. Deer had already nuked the understory in the woods behind my house. There weren't any shrubs to imitate. The best I could do was pretend to be a rather slender tree holding a compound bow. Later, when a friend invited me onto the better land on his lease—mixed hardwoods with mountain laurel and loads of big-buck sign—I gave it another go. I saw nothing for the first two hours. Then, with a slight breeze in my face, I spotted a buck eighty yards off. He looked like a small cow with no neck and half a picket fence on his head. He was moving purposefully, as if late for an appointment. I still don't know how he made me. I didn't move. I didn't have time to start hyperventilating, although that would have come. He didn't even give an alarm snort. He just somehow zeroed in on me, swapped ends, and vanished. It took about five seconds. That was enough to send me back up into the trees.

Excuse: I don't really have one. What I tell people is that at least one big buck out there has binoculars. And knows how to use them.

This was also the year I vowed not only to remember the difference between pitching and flipping but also to finally become proficient in both techniques. I saw a video in which Kevin VanDam said your backyard is a good place to start. Which is why I am forwarding the vet bill for the neighbor's cat to Mr. VanDam. On a more positive note, I can attest that Mustad UltraPoint KVD Grip-Pin hooks are every bit as effective on small game as they are on bass.

The Stalk

Nothing is more intense than getting so close to a mule deer you could reach out and touch him. Except trying to make the shot.

I'm on my hands and knees on an uneven outcropping, holding my bow flat against the rock, moving forward an inch or so at a time. The midday sun, high and slightly behind me, throws my shadow just forward of my head. An erratic wind gusts from 5 to 20 knots and back down again. I've been timing my movements with each surge in the breeze to cover the tiny noises that now sound to me like avalanches: a pea-size pebble rolling a few inches as I shift my foot, the horrendous scrape of my cotton pants cuff against the stalk of some tiny high-plains plant. Fifty yards back—a lifetime ago—I removed my boots, forcing myself to slow down even more, to move even more quietly. Now I'm methodically trashing a brand-new pair of twenty-dollar Filson socks in the prickly pear and gravel up the back side of this giant igneous rock. A pair of socks for a crack at a big muley buck is a deal I'll take any day. He's close. When the wind stills, I can actually hear the drone of flies buzzing around his eyes.

At the moment I have two problems. The little one is that I can't find places to put my hands and feet that will allow me to come to a standing position and take the last two steps forward. (Also complicating the situation is the fact that my body has begun to tremble.) The bigger problem is that all of a sudden I'm drowning. I can't get any oxygen in my lungs even though I'm sucking air as heavily as I dare. It's not the altitude, which is slightly over four thousand feet.

It's certainly not physical exertion; I've barely moved eighteen inches in the last five minutes. No, the cause is that after a forty-five-minute stalk guided by outfitter Chad Schearer, who has been signaling me into position with big orange flags from half a mile away, I've finally just taken a quick peek over the edge of the rocks. And there, six feet below me, bedded down calmly in the shade, lies a wide-racked, deep-forked, 4-by-5 muley.

Most muley hunters get up before dawn, glass the animals as they head into bedding areas, and attempt to stalk within rifle range through trees or other cover. You can also try to connect this way with a bow, though the majority of archers use tree stands or blinds to ambush the deer near water holes or crop fields at dawn or dusk. But if you hunt muleys with Schearer, who runs Central Montana Outfitters, you don't do anything the conventional way. Instead of rising at 4 a.m., you have a leisurely breakfast and start glassing around 9, after the deer have left their nightly feeding areas and are beginning to bed down. Midday (I got on this deer at 11:30) is prime time. Stalking ends around 3 p.m., by which hour the deer are up and slowly transitioning to feeding areas. At dusk, on the twenty-thousand-acre ranch we're hunting, you can set up in a makeshift blind of branches stuck into the dirt as you hunker down in a ditch at the edge of one of the many alfalfa fields. But it may feel anticlimactic by then to let the deer come to you.

You can stalk to within yards of a bedded mule deer at lunchtime because of the unique geology of central Montana. As soon as I drove into this country, what struck me were the "stegosaurus" rocks—perfectly vertical spines of stone busting out of the crests of hills—that looked exactly like the plated armor on the dinosaur's back. The rocks were so uniform as to appear man-made, vestiges of some ancient civilization. The technical name for such formations is *igneous dikes*, and there are few places on earth where they and mule deer coexist.

What Schearer has found is that the muleys—especially the larger bucks—escape the warm sun of summer and early fall by bedding at the foot of these rocks, and that they have been doing this for decades, if not centuries. Some of the beds I check look almost like shallow trenches, hollowed out from many generations of use. The deer nearly disappear into them. This means that even on land that Schearer has been hunting for years, he sometimes finds deer hard to spot, especially in the fall after the muleys have turned the same gray-brown as the rocks. We spend hours each day glassing for them with binoculars and spotting scope from elevated areas on the ranch. It's a little unsettling to survey a huge expanse of country with the best optics available, knowing that there must be half a dozen or so good bucks in it looking back at you, and you can't see them.

I'm still starved for air, still stuck on the rock. As I crouch down, senses overloading my brain like an ocean liner bearing down on a rowboat, I notice in a vaguely disembodied way that one of the vanes on my nocked arrow has come halfway unglued and now hangs raggedly from the shaft. Normally, I'd yank it off, since an arrow with two vanes still flies almost perfectly true, whereas one with a ragged third vane drops like a rock due to the increased drag. But arrow trajectory is not a major consideration on a two-yard shot, and fixing it now would sound like ripping an entire bedsheet in half.

It's not like I've never taken a deer before. I've reached out and touched them at two hundred yards with scoped rifles and watched them drop silently to the ground. I've shot them at fifty yards with muzzle-loaders and slug guns, close enough to see the hair blow up, see the animal stagger under the shock of all those foot-pounds, see its legs churn the air a few times before it lies still. I've killed them with a bow at twenty yards, well inside the animal's bubble of security, close enough to see his coat ruffled from his last bed, close enough to see the shaft go in black and come out red on the other side. It's personal at that distance; an individual deer that you're killing. The elation and the guilt (say what you will, I do feel guilt) are proportionately greater as you get closer.

But at six feet the fletching will barely have cleared the bow when the broadhead enters the deer. My hand may be on his flank when his

77

muscles twitch for the final time. What I'm feeling is the emotion our ancestors must have felt tens of thousands of years ago, the one that surfaces when we truly confront what it means to be alive. It is awe in the original sense of the word: a strange mingling of terror, veneration, and wonder. It has always made men shake, and it is making me shake now.

I risk one more peek over the rocks. He's still there, and apparently still suspects nothing. If anything, he looks slightly drowsy. I am trying to keep from coming completely unglued, but I can't stop shaking. My rational mind is a faint ember, while my autonomic nervous system, the part that usually hums along quietly in the background, has turned into an arsonist. Intellectually, I know that this stalk—successful or not—poses no physical danger to me. Either I'll get the deer or I won't. But intellect is not in charge at the moment. My primitive brain is. And it's saying *code red*.

The geology that makes this kind of hunting possible requires its own kind of tactics. You need a buddy who can see the deer and signal you with the flags because you are almost always approaching via an angle opposite to where you glassed the buck. You'd never find the animal without help. (Using electronic transmissions to guide a hunter to game is illegal in Montana. It wouldn't be effective anyway. Mule deer got their name because of their big ears; they'd hear a radio and bolt long before you knew where any were located.)

The key to effective communication is a few basic signals rather than a bunch of complicated ones. The flagman watches the deer in a spotting scope or binoculars and holds a banner on the side that he wants the hunter to move toward. (When he first started hunting this way, Schearer and his buddies signaled each other using Cheetos bags stuck onto arrow shafts. Now he buys the big blaze-orange banners with wooden handles that truckers use, which he says are perfect.) On this approach, for example, the deer is bedded along a hundred-yard ridge of rock. And because I can't see Schearer and the flags unless I am so close to its crest that the deer can see me as well, it has taken me three painstaking approaches to get on him.

When you're in position at last, right on top of the deer, the flagman holds the banners directly in front of his body and makes a downward stabbing motion. If the animal moves or busts you, he waves the flags overhead repeatedly, and you go back to the truck and look for another deer to stalk.

Another challenge this style of hunting presents is that you have to be disciplined enough to wait until the buck has bedded down for the bulk of the day before you start. A mature buck may change its bed three to five times, chasing the shade over the course of a morning, before he finally settles in. There's obviously no percentage in stalking an animal that may be gone by the time you get there. Not only does the buck have to be bedded in a spot where he's going to stay for a while; the wind must also be right. Schearer says he sometimes glasses an animal for four or five days, waiting for favorable conditions, rather than educate a trophy deer with a failed stalk. The presence of smaller bucks and does bedded nearby that will give you away is another major consideration. Sometimes that negates the stalk before you've even begun. Other times it means adding an extra mile or so to your approach.

Nevertheless, this ranch contains so many different places where deer bed that you can usually find enough animals to work all day long. Schearer has had clients connect on their first stalk, though it takes most hunters six or seven tries before they get it right. He had one who was a champion target archer, who could put four arrows in a tennis ball at sixty yards, but who couldn't hit anything with fur and eyes. That guy methodically blew five stalks a day for five days. He made noise, got seen, got winded, or missed the deer at fifteen feet. In the end, Schearer says, he led the guy up and did everything but aim for him. The fellow finally got his buck.

Frank Roberts—who owns a share in the ranch and has been guiding for Schearer for many years—says, "Heck, usually we do it until the hunter is sick of it." They get many stalking opportunities because this area has nearly constant sunshine, especially in the fall, and averages a scant sixteen inches of rain a year. In fact, this part of Montana is suffering through a five-year drought. But we've had three days of rain and snow, more precipitation than the ranch has seen in ten years. The deer are bedding low in heavy cover instead of up in the rocks. This could be my only chance.

But I'm having trouble closing the deal. That's because a successful stalk requires two very different skill sets, and the ability to switch from one to the other in the blink of an eye. During the approach, caution rules. You cannot move too slowly, quietly, or carefully. Most people, Schearer tells me, blow this part because they rush it.

Then, after what seems like an endless period of doing everything you can to leave the animal unaware of your presence, you must draw your bow, step up to where you and he each have a clear view of the other, and shoot. A shot at an unalerted deer is the exception here rather than the rule; Schearer has told me that on this particular stalk there will be no way to get a shot off without the buck's seeing me. Once I stand, even if he doesn't pick me up immediately with his 270-degree vision, he'll see my shadow and know instantly that a predator is above him. After that, I may have two or three seconds before he's gone. I nodded my head dutifully when this was explained to me. But my adrenaline was already running high then. Schearer could have told me my mother was a bus, and I would have nodded solemnly.

Now I'm flummoxed. I cannot find a way to avoid making noise before I'm in final position to shoot. There's just no way to cover the two steps to get into place without scraping brittle stems and loose scree. (By now, I'm also positive that the buck can hear my heart beating.) I'm still on my hands and knees, unbalanced, agonizing. At some level, I know that time is running out, that accepting that I'm going to make some noise getting up to shoot is better than never taking a shot. It's just that my body has stopped taking orders from my brain.

Indecision is not a luxury you have at this distance. When I finally bite the bullet and begin to rise, the buck is already up and moving away. He's not doing the mule deer pogo; he's not even walking stiff-legged, so I know he hasn't winded me. But heeding that sixth sense that prey animals are born with, he has decided to change beds. And he's out of range by the time I draw my bow. He takes his 9-point rack with him as he lazily meanders out of sight.

I am heartsick, disappointed, and frustrated. Yet an unexpected sense of elation, of being vividly alive, floods me. So does a feeling of addiction. This is hands down the most intense hunting experience I've ever had. I want to do it again, right now. I walk back to the truck quickly, where Schearer is waiting with a look of commiseration on his face. "Bud, you were so close. Believe me, I know exactly how—"

I cut him off with a shake of my head. "We'll do that part later," I tell him. "You think we should go back and have another look at that little canyon?"

Schearer is smiling as he fires up the truck. And you can almost read his thoughts: *Hooked another one.*

II

The Stand

The most ordinary deer stand can somehow turn itself into a spiritually powerful place. I don't pretend to understand how this works. I do know that you can climb into one with a stranger and come down four hours later knowing things about him you probably don't know about your best friend.

I was sitting on a folding chair in a tower stand in central Arkansas on a raw October morning. I had the barrel of a loaner rifle, a 6.5-by-55 Swedish, resting on the rail as Mike Romine and I scanned a big cutover field with pine woods on three sides. He'd warned me that the deer on his club's lease rarely showed themselves for more than a few seconds. Mike is fifty-eight, with hands calloused from a lifetime of working outside. I'd only met him the day before, but there was something about him that I'd liked immediately. He seemed uncommonly aware of the gift of being alive.

Around 9 a.m., Mike rattled and a big 8-pointer came to the edge of the woods three hundred yards away. It was a trophy—the biggest rack seen on club property in years, I learned later—but it was farther away than I felt comfortable shooting. I was almost glad that brush shielded its brisket. The deer melted back into the pines. We just sat for a good while. Then Mike, still watching the field, started talking in the singularly casual voice that some men reserve for the weightiest things. A little more than two years ago, his wife's younger brother had committed suicide in his favorite stand not far from where we sat. Mike had been twenty-one and Barry thirteen when they met. "Basically, he was my little brother. We loved each other. I was the one who got him into deer hunting and the club. He loved hunting and loved this place." Mike was the last to see Barry alive and the first to see him afterward. He'd arrived to find blood spattered on the walls of the stand and his brother-in-law on the floor next to a 20-gauge slug gun. With an EMT on speakerphone, Mike had administered chest compressions and breaths to a dead man until a police car arrived.

I didn't know why Mike was telling me this. The reason didn't matter. What did was that I'd just entered his world. Beneath his calm voice, I felt the emotional annihilation a suicide inflicts on the survivors—devastation, anguish, anger, and bewilderment. When Barry had blown away his own heart, he had taken a great many others' with him. The news had just about done in Barry's parents, his four sisters, a slew of nieces and nephews. I was overcome by this rush of knowledge and by Mike's selflessness. Here was a man in great pain who was nonetheless more concerned with others' suffering than his own. I blinked back tears and pretended to study my side of the field.

Mike had watched the coroner bag up Barry's body. He'd stood there alone and watched as the little caravan of cars appeared and disappeared as the road rose and fell and finally curved away. He'd thought of how our lives were like that road—with highs and lows and places where the way ahead seemed to have washed out altogether. Mike believed that God had given us the promise of ever-lasting life, but that first we had to do due diligence to this one, see it through even the bleakest times. And that we had a responsibility to love each other, help each other along the way.

What a man, I thought. *What a tough, brave, tender son of a gun.*

I remembered reading somewhere that most suicides were cases of mistaken identity. Which I understood to mean that acute depression— a tidal wave of unbearable self-loathing and despair—fooled you into thinking that your suffering and feelings of worthlessness were your identity rather than things you were going through.

I didn't say anything, but I reached out and clamped Mike's shoulder for a moment. We didn't say anything else about it. Mike rattled a couple more times. We saw two does cut the corner of the field as they traveled from one section of woods to another. But we didn't see the big buck again or any others. Two hours later, two men who had been strangers climbed down from the stand having shared something that I still can't quite put a name to. I felt richer for it and hoped Mike did, too. I hoped that the telling of his grief had lessened its weight.

As for me, I felt a mix of things. There are few honors higher than having a stranger trust you enough to share his deepest thoughts. And I did feel deeply honored. But I was also a bit anxious. Now I had to be as good a man as the one Mike had taken me for. While walking away, I glanced back at the stand. It looked like any other. Its power was as mysterious to me as anything else that had just happened. But I knew it was real. I'd felt it.

If Hunters Ruled the World

Tuxedos with hand-warmer pockets, chewing tobacco that smells like a cycling doe, and numerous other signs that the guys in orange and camo are calling the shots

[1] The entire month of November would be a paid religious holiday.

[2] You could go to a fast-food restaurant and order a McBackstrap sandwich with extra garlic and fries.

[3] Men with big butts would be renowned for their "outside spread."

[4] Taxidermy would be a required course in elementary schools.

[5] Golfers would have to leave the links at once if you spotted a good deer on the course and wanted to stalk it.

[6] Failure to do so would result in the golf course's being converted to an eighteen-hole food plot. The sand traps would be turned into mineral licks.

[7] Guys who hunted your stand without permission would do a mandatory seven to ten years.

[8] You would be fined by the police if you were stopped and found *not* to be in possession of a weapon.

[9] After one week, reports of violent crime would cease altogether.

[10] All jackets would come with a built-in safety harness and hand-warmer pockets, even tuxedos.

[11] There wouldn't be any tuxedos.

[12] The government would announce a "race for the cure" and throw billions of dollars into research to eradicate buck fever.

[13] Your wife would complain that you're spending too much time around the house and tell you to "drop that paintbrush and get your sorry ass out to the stand."

[14] At parties, a tending grunt would be considered a sophisticated way of showing interest in a member of the opposite sex.

[15] Gas stations would have attendants that approached from the downwind side to fill your gas tank, then spray and clean your windshield with Scent Killer.

[16] Women placing singles ads would state their times in the one-mile deadweight drag, 150-pound division.

[17] All vehicles would come with bloodproof seat covers standard.

[18] Game wardens could not come within three hundred yards of you unless you signaled that it was okay.

[19] A warden's first words would be "If this isn't a convenient time, sir, I'd be happy to come back later."

[20] Convenience stores would stock shells, broadheads, and black-powder accessories in little bowls by the donut case.

[21] If you showed up at a fancy restaurant in full camo and reeking of doe urine, you'd immediately be shown to the best table in the house.

[22] Bars would have "sparring areas" where you could put on an antler helmet and go head-to-head with other hunters to let off steam.

[23] A chewing tobacco would be developed that, when mixed with human saliva, turns into a powerful deer attractant.

[24] The dollar bill would feature a picture of the Hanson buck.

[25] Landowners would come around to your house and beg you to hunt their property.

[26] If you gave your wife or girlfriend a scoped .30/06 on her birthday, your anniversary, or Valentine's Day, she'd say, "Honey, you're the best!"

[27] The State of the Union address would be given by a deer biologist telling you the best places to hunt.

[28] "I just felt like they were gonna be moving this morning" would be an acceptable excuse for why you were late to work.

[29] Each day's weather report would start with wind direction and velocity, barometric pressure, and times for the beginning and end of legal light.

[30] Reality TV shows would feature six people turned loose during the rut in an extremely rural area with a sharpened stone and a grunt call. First one to bring in a 150-class deer wins $1 million.

The Slam Man

Jeff Budz is the greatest turkey hunter alive. He has the most grand slams ever recorded. No one in the sport is more driven or accomplished. So we gave him the ultimate challenge: Get Bill Heavey a gobbler.

Jeff Budz turned the Expedition's engine off and blew a coyote call out over the South Dakota prairie. When he heard the first distant gobble, he took off wordlessly at a ground-covering jog and glassed a distant field edge. Jogging back toward me, he veered down a pine-studded ravine to the right and motioned to me to follow. When I finally reached him, he was almost to the top of the ravine wall, waiting for me. I clawed my way up. "Look, dude," I whispered. "I'm in decent shape for a guy my age, but I can't keep up with you."

"Nobody can," he whispered, not bragging but merely stating a fact. "Just get to me as fast as possible. I want you as close as my pocket on my right side. Keep your head lower than mine. If I make a fist or squeeze your shoulder, freeze. If I point and show fingers, that's the direction of the bird and how many yards away he is times ten. If I tell you to shoot, come up with your gun shouldered, put the sight halfway up his neck, and kill him."

I nodded.

Budz pulled a turkey fan from his vest and raised it slowly above the lip of the ravine, looking through the feathers. His hand squeezed my shoulder. I froze. Then he pointed, showing two fingers. "Shoot the one on the left," he whispered.

Trembling, I rose, saw the two toms at twenty yards, and aimed at the neck of the left one. The gun roared. The bird began to flap away. I shot again, and it disappeared behind an apron of brush. Budz's head dropped. "I don't see how . . ." I mumbled.

"At least you missed clean," he said. His cheeks bulged slightly with the two calls he carried in his mouth simultaneously—one for sharp yelps and cutts, the other for soft clucks and purrs. He threw a call after the departing birds. And one called back. Budz's eyes got big. "It's not over," he said.

First Impressions

When my editors asked me to join Jeff Budz on this five-day, three-state road trip, with his girlfriend, Jenny Slaton, and a couple of his pals, I was hesitant. Calling Budz a turkey "maniac" is like saying the Kardashians "like" publicity. I'd never met him, but I knew his reputation as the turkey-killingest man alive. A friend who'd hunted with him said that "he makes your definition of *hard core* seem *half-assed*."

When I wrote to him with some concerns, Budz responded, "Don't worry. I'll take it easy on you." This turned out to be a lie.

Hearing the tom gobble again after my two whiffs, Budz rode his heels down the thirty-foot embankment we'd just clambered up. He looked like he was enjoying himself, as if he were skiing. I slid down in a three-point stance—both feet and my butt.

We chased those two toms for hours and miles on the two-million-acre Sioux reservation where we'd started our odyssey. Budz would catch sight of them, gauge their mood and direction of travel, and figure out how we could snake along a ravine or follow a finger of woods or belly-crawl hundreds of yards to get in front of them. Eventually we did. And eventually, he told me to shoot again. I was using a Benelli Super Eagle II with a Carlson choke designed specifically for the Hevi-Shot Magnum Blend shells I was shooting. Budz said it could kill a bird out to seventy yards. Maybe that was the problem. Maybe I was just too damned close. Because the tom was only thirty yards away, standing in the open. And I missed again.

Having been asked to hunt with four strangers, I'd hoped to make a good first impression. The first two misses were setbacks, but I was able to rationalize them as hiccups, momentary losses of poise. This third miss made me feel like I was on a bobsled run of failure, gathering speed. I started to dissociate. It wasn't *me* who was missing. It was some guy who had rented my body for the day and hadn't read the manual.

The turkeys, at this point, decided that we should both see other people and flew across a ravine so deep that we couldn't see the bottom. Budz charged after them. Things that demoralize normal people—a bottomless ravine—energize him. "People always complain that they don't like hills," he later told me. "I love hills. You know that metallic taste in your mouth when you're maxed out physically? I love that taste."

After only hours in the field with him, it was clear that Budz was the most driven hunter I'd ever met. It would be tempting to dismiss him as a whack job, if it weren't for his accomplishments. At forty-nine, he's registered ninety-one grand slams, each of which involves tagging all four subspecies of wild turkey. That's more turkey slams than anybody in history and about forty more than his closest living competitor. When he discovered that there was something called a super slam—killing a turkey in every state but Alaska (where they aren't present)—he was initially crestfallen to learn that three hunters had already done it. A closer examination, however, revealed that each of the three had used guides. That, Budz realized, meant that the distinction of completing a self-guided super slam was up for grabs. So, over the course of about fifteen years—much of it spent living out of his truck, poring over maps, knocking on doors, and eating PowerBars and Fig Newtons—Budz completed the feat in 2014. During one stretch, he killed ten toms in ten states in twelve days. He figures he averaged about three and a half hours of sleep a night.

Reaching the Bottom

We descended into the deep ravine and climbed up the other side. It was getting late. We were walking along a flat, brushy hilltop, looking for birds, when Budz grabbed my arm. The toms, twenty yards ahead of us and just coming into view, had no idea we were there. "Shoot!" Budz said. Then he pleaded, "Please shoot those turkeys!"

I shouldered the gun and realized I had two red heads lined up perfectly in my sights. The world slowed. Even I knew this was a once-in-a-lifetime opportunity. But whoever had commandeered my body decided that it was a good time to practice flinching. My shot hit the ground ten yards in front and ten yards to the left of the birds. Hevi-Shot, incidentally, is devastating on dirt, at least in South Dakota. The turkeys spread their wings languidly and glided down the long hill we'd just scaled, back into the thick woods.

Budz said nothing and walked off a few yards to be by himself. He was facing away from me. His head and torso were bobbing rhythmically, like a man banging his head against an imaginary wall. It reminded me of the TV footage you see of people at the Wailing Wall in Jerusalem. A strange thought coursed through my brain: *Maybe they'll put up a Wailing Wall in South Dakota in my honor.*

The bobsled run was over for the day. I had just medaled in the Loser Olympics. I felt for Budz. He had done nothing for the past fifteen hours but try to spoon-feed me chip shots at wild turkeys. My only part in all this was to aim a stick at the birds and then move my right index finger. That, obviously, had proved too complex a task. I wanted to melt into a little puddle of failure and soak into the ground.

To his credit, Budz handled my meltdown like a pro. He composed himself, told me it was okay, and even managed a smile before we trudged back to the truck.

This was just the first day.

Jeff's World

When you hunt with Budz, you enter Jeff's World, which is a different reality. You get up every day at 3:30 a.m. If you aren't up by 3:45, Budz will shake you awake. If your motel room door is locked, he will pound on it until you wake up or the manager calls the police. You're in the woods before dawn, you don't leave until after dark, and you will spend most of that time jogging, scrambling, and belly-crawling. You will want to sneak rocks into Budz's vest to slow him down.

In Jeff's World, the dominant personality is a teetotaling Christian who is so relentlessly upbeat that, around 2 p.m., when you feel like you've been awake for thirty-six hours, you will want to put a bag over his head so you can leave Jeff's World if only for a few minutes. When you do fill your tags for one state—*if,* in my case—you immediately jump in the car and drive hundreds of miles, mostly at night. In Jeff's World, driving during the day is a kind of sin. That's time that could be spent doing the only thing Budz cares about, which is hunting turkeys.

As strange and oppressive as Jeff's World is, you will find yourself liking Budz himself. He's outgoing and easy to talk to. He is open about the fact that he's a little crazy. "If I were a kid in school today, I'd be on tons of ADHD medication," he says. A germophobe who carries disinfecting wipes everywhere, he prides himself on traveling light but cannot imagine life without Chapstick, hand lotion, and Charmin. He's an obsessive-compulsive who likes things organized his way. When friends want to mess with him on trips, they don't rearrange the whole truck. They move little things. They put the pen one tray over on the console or a seventh shell in a pouch that had six. "That unnerves him much more because he's not sure what's going on," says Bob Brammer, a friend for thirty-five years, who is also on the trip.

Did the world's greatest turkey slayer learn at his father's knee? Of course not. That guy would have had nothing to prove. Budz's parents divorced when he was four. He grew up in Illinois with his mom, a real estate agent who worked hard to feed Budz and his two sisters. He learned to survive, to be on his own. He vowed never to be dependent on anyone else. Once, he heard a woman who'd been rude to someone explain that she was always that way until she'd had her coffee. Not wanting to be that kind of person, he vowed at that moment never to drink the stuff. Boom. Door closed. On to the next thing.

When I ask Brammer to describe how they met, Brammer smiles and Budz winces. "His mom came to me in seventh grade," Brammer says. "She said, 'He talks a lot. He's going to need a little help getting through school. He's my only boy. I'll pay you five dollars a week to look out for him.' I looked him over and said, 'Make it ten dollars.' She said, 'Deal.'"

Budz didn't start hunting until a friend took him out in college. He killed his first turkey in 1989. "I knew I'd found something," he says. He liked everything about turkey hunting. He didn't need anyone else. He could be as aggressive as he wanted, could hunt by his own rules. "I knew I couldn't hunt like everyone else, though—a day here, or a weekend there."

He first heard about grand slams in 1993, and completed one the next year. Again, he'd found something. He called turkey biologists in every state for information as he drove. He scoured maps of public land for remote areas. He knew how to talk to farmers, and there's something about the guy that's just hard to say no to. He finished up his self-guided super slam in Arizona with a bow-killed Merriam's tom. I ask why he used a bow, and he says he knew the photo accompanying any story about his feat would be from that last hunt, and a bow would make the accomplishment that much more impressive.

By 2019, he expects to register his one hundredth grand slam, a number once considered unreachable. But he doesn't just want to lead the pack in grand slams. He wants to make history.

Getting Hosed

On the second day, with everyone else tagged out, Budz announced that he and I weren't leaving South Dakota until I put a turkey on the ground. I accepted this with surprising equanimity, either because of sleep deprivation or because there was nowhere to go but up.

It took a while. We got on some birds at dawn and chased them all over creation but never got close enough for a shot. After lunch, we went from one hilltop to the next, calling. Eventually, a gobbler answered a loud yelp from Budz's box call. We couldn't see the bird, but Budz took off as if he knew exactly where it was. Glassing from behind a cedar, he spotted two toms and a few hens in a draw about five hundred yards off.

We made a wide swing right, entered the mouth of the draw, and crawled our way to a downed tree. Budz pulled out the fan again and clucked. Finally, he clamped my shoulder. "When I tell you, come up and shoot him. He's only twenty yards off."

There was a quaver in his voice. Here was a guy who had killed hundreds of turkeys and put guys like me—okay, not exactly like me—on hundreds more. And he still trembled when the moment came. I rose up with the gun shouldered and saw the tom heading straight at the fan. I couldn't shoot at his neck, because his head was forward, right in his center of mass, as he charged. So that's where I shot—and killed him convincingly.

"That's what I'm talking about!" Budz exulted, punching me in the shoulder. Then he got quiet. "Now let's get after the rest," he whispered, and took off. I almost ran right over my bird. Budz figured the others were just over the next rise, but when he peered out from behind the turkey fan, they were gone.

"That's all right. You did good back there," he said. "He was only a jake, but you nailed him." I was a bit disappointed to have killed a jake, but at least I didn't miss. As we returned and I picked up the bird, I noted that it felt pretty heavy. It also had a 9-inch beard and spurs that looked to be about an inch long.

"You sure this is a—" I started to ask.

"Hosing you, man! That's a big tom! I bet he's three years old." I could see at that moment how much he'd wanted me to succeed. Now that I had, the pressure was off and he could enjoy my success and his. I was so happy that it didn't bother me that I would never hear the end of how badly I'd screwed up that first day.

Unstoppable

The next three days I spent hunting with Budz, Jenny, and his buddies were a blur. I limited out in Kansas before 8:30 on our first day. Then I tagged two more toms in Nebraska for a total of five, which is three more than I've ever taken in a season. But I couldn't tell you which birds I killed where or even the names of some of the towns we stayed in. And it took me about a week to recover.

One of the most telling moments came when there wasn't a turkey in sight. It was midmorning. The road was greasy, so we drove on the grass alongside. We were doing fine until the Expedition came to an abrupt stop. Budz had high-centered the truck on a hump. He, Jenny, and I got out to see the vehicle resting on its belly like a stranded turtle.

Budz tried jacking up all four wheels in turn. Jenny and I gathered stones from the road and carried them in cupped hands; we pulled branches from a dead tree and shoved them beneath the wheels. Nothing helped.

A strange look entered Budz's eyes, as if he and the vehicle were the only things that existed. One of them needed to yield. And it wasn't going to be him. "Have to dig her out," he said flatly. We had nothing with which to dig except the flat end of the tire iron. Didn't matter. Budz intended to dig out an eighteen-foot, three-ton SUV, stranded atop heavy clay soil choked with deep-rooted prairie grass, with the equivalent of a large screwdriver.

He wormed his way beneath the front bumper and disappeared. Then he went about digging in a cold, wordless fury. Handfuls of clay and grass flew from beneath the vehicle. It was like a nature video about a bear or wolverine digging its winter lair, where all you see is the dirt coming out of the hole. It was a little scary. He wasn't digging like somebody who had a stuck car. He was digging like a prisoner who had to tunnel his way out of his cell or be executed in the morning.

I wanted to help, but this had clearly become Budz's fight. He didn't seem to want or need anyone else's help. When he finally emerged, his shirt and pants were plastered to his body. It was the first time I'd seen him sweat or breathe hard. Then he got in the vehicle, started it, drove forward, and called, "Let's go kill some turkeys."

Later, I asked Jenny where his fury had come from. "Don't you get it?" she said. "That car was the only thing between him and the turkeys." I nodded, but it still took me a minute to understand. If I get a car stuck, I size up the situation in terms of what my options and capabilities are. Budz never asks those questions. The car needed to be unstuck so we could hunt turkeys. There was no thought about whether he was capable of getting it unstuck. He doesn't think that way. His capabilities are whatever is needed to remove the obstacle in his way. No money? Sleep in the truck. No refrigerator? Eat food that doesn't require it. The bird is strutting atop a mountain, a cliff, or a flagpole? You climb the mountain, cliff, or flagpole. The fate of anything in between him and turkeys has been decided long before the obstacle even presents itself. Obstacles, by Budz's definition, are just things to be obliterated in order to get where he wants to be.

The Future

Budz was once quoted in this magazine advising anyone who wanted to follow his example to smash his wedding ring with a hammer. This is interesting, considering that he has brought his girlfriend along on the trip. Could it be that Budz, as he closes in on his one hundredth slam, is discovering that there's more to life than turkeys?

On our last night, eating tacos in a brightly lit chain restaurant about to close, I ask Budz what he intends to do once he reaches one hundred slams. "I'm going to slow down a bit," he says, then catches himself. "Wait. I'll never slow down. Let's just say it won't be such a priority."

With his closest living rival in the forties, he says he can't see one hundred slams being surpassed in his lifetime. "They'd have to kill me. And even then, it'd still take, what, another fifteen years?"

There it is. They'd have to kill him. That's the only kind of failure he can imagine. But, I persist, surely someone will overtake him eventually. All records, after all, get broken.

"Not mine," he says. Then his face brightens as he eyes me, Jenny, and Brammer in turn.

"We leave at nine tomorrow morning for the airport. We can sleep for almost four hours and hunt till eight. Who's in?"

He's definitely not dead yet.

Meat Matters

When I first started hunting, I went to the deer woods with visions of wall-hangers dancing in my head. My dream deer, however, was no ordinary trophy. He was Kong, king of the whitetails, the one other bucks saw in their nightmares. Jacked on delusions of fame and fortune, I sat glued to my stand from dark to dark. It was only a question of time before I arrowed a freak, a beast with a cow-catcher on its head, forever to be known as the Heavey buck. Whenever deer hunters gathered, a lively debate would arise as to the most intriguing facet of my success. Some would argue it was the beast itself—a nine-and-a-half-year-old 23-pointer that scored in the low 250s. Others would say it was that I had shot the buck in my underwear while changing in the parking area of heavily pounded public land that hadn't yielded a decent buck in years.

Like so many fantasies about myself, this one bit the dust shortly after I met Paula Smith. Initially I knew her only as a shed fanatic, a woman who hunted for dropped antlers each spring the way other people reported to work. Gordon Leisch, another friend, provided Paula a room in exchange for help with the upkeep of his house. At some point, I learned that Paula and Gordon ate wild meat almost exclusively. Gordon, who is seventy-seven, once came home smiling from his annual physical. "Doc looked over my blood work and said, 'I don't know what you're eating, but whatever it is, keep it up.'"

In the course of a year, they'd go through two or three deer, a few turkeys, and some rabbits and squirrels. A nephew occasionally gave him a goose or a brace of ducks. He and Paula often invited me along on fishing trips to the Chesapeake. We'd launch Gordon's 17-foot skiff and fish for spot, croakers, stripers, and bluefish. The two of them processed everything themselves, double-wrapping and labeling each package for the freezer.

Nobody loves big antlers like Paula Smith. But when it comes to the pot, she's all about does. "Give me a nice fat one-and-a-half-year-old doe, maybe eighty pounds. Cook that tenderloin up with some oyster mushrooms, a little chestnut stuffing? Good as it gets, honey."

I shot the occasional doe myself, usually at the end of another season during which the Heavey buck and I had somehow missed each other. I'd drop my doe at the nearest processor I knew of, a guy whose other sideline was selling undersize cords of green firewood. I'd throw the meat in my freezer and eat it as the mood hit me. It was just meat. I didn't give it a great deal of thought.

That changed the day I casually mentioned to Paula that I was going to pick up a deer from the processor. Unwittingly, I had hit on one of her three hundred pet peeves. But this must have been in the top five, because she became so incensed she couldn't speak for a moment. I was afraid she was going to swallow her cigarette. "Are you serious, Heavey?" she finally sputtered. "You know what kinda guy puts out a DEER PROCESSING sign where any idiot driving by can see it? *The kind who blew up his last house cooking meth, that's who!* You shoulda just told the guy, 'Hey, I'm a dumbass. Whyncha bag me up fifty pounds of whatever crap you got on the floor?' Because I guarantee you that's what he's doing."

Like most of Paula's harangues, this one humbled me. Outsourcing my deer processing—even to a reputable butcher—suddenly felt unconscionably lame. And so, under Paula's watchful eye and abusive tongue, I learned to butcher deer myself. She taught me that if you pay attention, the deer's body practically talks to you, telling you where to sever the joint, where to cut across the grain of the meat, and where to cut along it. Then I learned something else.

I'd long known how to hunt, kill, field dress, cook, and eat. But—and I still don't understand this completely—it was the act of butchering that closed the circle for me. With my hands inside a deer's body, I felt the mysterious and powerful contradictions—the mixture of exhilaration and sadness, of pride and humility—that, for me, have always been at the heart of hunting.

As for the Heavey buck, maybe he's still out there. Maybe he's on somebody else's wall. What I can't figure out is why it took me so long to realize how fantastic venison is. It's as organic, free-range, flavorful, and healthy as meat gets. These days, a young, fat doe wandering into sight gets me pretty excited. Don't get me wrong. I still keep an eye out for giant bucks. But when I leave the woods dragging a doe, I'm on my way to a trophy meal.

Not the Same

I was on an early-season deer hunt in western Kentucky this year when I ran into a guy I hadn't seen in a long time: me.

I was hunting with a couple of "industry" guys who figured they could count the trip as work if they invited me. It was late September, only nobody had told the weather. You'd wake up at 4:30 and it was in the mid 80s. By afternoon, it was 100. We were hunting feeders, usually not my idea of a fair fight. But everybody said it was the only way to see a deer. A months-long drought had scorched the food plots, a late-spring freeze had killed off the mast, and every step you took in the woods cracked like a rifle shot. If there was ever an unlikely place and time for a surprise encounter, this was it.

By the third afternoon, tired of being carpooled to and from my stand, I opted to hunt a spot I'd found by walking the roads, a parched little food plot half a mile from the lodge. The com was long gone, but there were fresh droppings, some of which looked big enough to have been left by a buck. A ladder stand commanded the spot, but another hunter told me it caught full sun and was like sitting in a Dutch oven. I scrounged an old climber and lugged it with me that afternoon. By the time I reached eighteen feet, my shirt was shredded, my forearms were bleeding (short sleeves and hug-the-tree climbers are not a good combination), and I was dribbling a steady stream of sweat onto the ground. I opened my spray bottle of Scent Killer and slowly emptied it onto my head and over the rest of my body.

Two hours later, three does and three fawns came tiptoeing out of the pines. They were taut as guitar strings, coming and bolting four

104

times, spooked by the twigs breaking under their own hooves. Finally they started feeding. One drifted my way, stopping to nose the pine needles at the base of my tree. She caught a whiff of something wrong and started swinging her head around, trying to locate the source. The one place she failed to look was straight up. The encounter got my heart redlining. I shut my eyes, pressed my forehead into the bark, and shrank the world down until it consisted of the pounding in my ears and my new task in life: inhaling for four beats and exhaling for eight. Long minutes later, I picked out the biggest doe and began a slow pivot. When she turned broadside I drew, aimed, and let the arrow go.

All six deer were within touching distance of one another, and at the shot each exploded on an arc unique to itself. It was like a fireworks shell you could see but not hear. I saw my arrow hit low, saw the red blood bloom on her coat as she leaped. I must have nicked her heart because she died in midair. I'd never seen a deer depart life so decisively. She bounded into the air fully animated and came back to earth inert.

We'd been encouraged to shoot does to maintain the land's carrying capacity and the ratio between the sexes. And yet, I felt uneasy as I walked toward the deer. I knelt, stroked her neck, and apologized for having taken her life. Then I made my first cut. As I worked, a feeling of regret kept dogging me. It was as if it had been decades rather than months since I'd last done this. I looked at her muscled heart and the dark liver as if seeing these organs for the first time, heard the sloshing of blood in the now-empty body. It was unnerving. Something, it seemed, had changed in me.

The bungee cords holding me to this particular place and time went slack. I was no longer the guy on the licenses and ID cards in my wallet. Suddenly, I was nothing more or less than a lone man in unfamiliar country in the almost-dark, holding a bloody knife, standing over an animal whose life he'd just taken.

I flashed on the first buck I had killed with a bow. the euphoria of mastery, of besting a wild thing at its own game. I'd dipped a toe into the river that day, been initiated into the mystery and knowledge that all life feeds on other life. It had been both wonderful and terrible, humbling and pride inducing. I remembered being immensely relieved to discover that it hadn't been wrong to kill.

But I was no longer that young hunter, the one with more years in from of him than behind. I'd changed, and so had my experience of hunting. I understood in my bones what I'd only understood in the abstract until now: that just as I had hunted and taken this deer, so was something just outside my awareness stalking me. My arc on this earth would end as irrevocably as the deer's had. And there wasn't a damn thing to be done until that day except to live as fully as possible. Some things hadn't changed. It hadn't been wrong to kill this deer. I still loved hunting. It was hunting, after all, that had helped me make sense of my true circumstances. But I had to admit that, like life, hunting was turning out to be a lot more complicated than I'd thought.

Boys Should Be Boys

Memory really doesn't give a damn what you think. At the yard sale of the mind, memory is the whack job who shows up and ransacks every box—driving off the paying customers—and yelps in triumph at striking its own kind of gold: an old VFW flyswatter bespattered with its kills. Memory has a mind of its own. Here are two odd bits of 2010 that haunt me.

It's a soft June evening and I'm picking serviceberries from a tree along the bike path. Foraging, the very skill that enabled our species to survive, is now highly suspect behavior. Pick berries in a public park and strangers will stare as if you were a sex-offending terrorist. There is just one group that suspends judgment. At some point, I look up and find one of its members watching from ten feet away. "Whatcha doing?" asks the boy. He is six or seven and has wandered off from his father, who is fifty yards away, a cell phone clapped to his head as if it is the only thing keeping him alive.

"Picking berries," I answer.

"You can eat these?" That the fruit trees in storybooks have counterparts in actual dirt has not occurred to him.

"Pick a dark one. They're the sweetest." He picks, tastes, and his face lights up, the primordial hardwiring suddenly activated for its inaugural run.

"This is awesome!" he murmurs, abuzz with ancient knowledge. With the father now approaching, the boy calls, "Dad! C'mere! We have to do this every day!"

"Thomas," the man says, "what's our rule about eating things we find?" His voice is the strange singsong of a judge deaf to all appeal. Joy flees from the boy's body. He slumps. For an instant he looks older than his father. It hurts to watch, and then I'm explaining that serviceberries taste similar to blueberries and that one of their names, saskatoon, comes from the Cree, who were especially fond of the fruit. I hand the father one. The slight nod he gives while chewing makes me hope he will reconsider. But it is only the formality of reviewing the evidence. His mind was made up before he came over. "Not bad for a wild berry," he says. I understand the words individually but have no idea what he means by them. "Well, Thomas, we'd better be going." I wave good-bye as the boy is led back to the safety and sterility of the great indoors.

And now, whenever I ponder the stunting disconnect between modern man and nature, I keep hearing his strange words. They seem an epitaph for a lost way of seeing, a lost way of living: not bad for a wild berry.

It's July. At a campground with a group of primitive-skills enthusiasts, I encounter an attractive single mom with two boys, three and seven, who are dying to try fishing in the pond behind the shower house. They have only a broken Dora the Explorer outfit and its blister pack of hooks and bobbers. Suddenly, my mission is clear. Every boy has the right to a first fish. On this particular planet, no man is granted a greater privilege than to be present and to assist in the realization of this moment.

I set the boys digging for worms in the wet leaves by the outflow. I tell mom to scour the parking lot for a truck with fishing tackle in it, then to find and flirt with the owner until he gives up twenty-five feet of line. From the nearest stand of bamboo, I saw two twelve-foot lengths with my Leatherman. In twenty-five minutes we are just about ready. The line is 40-pound mono, so thick I have to shave the tip to fit it through the hook eye. David, the younger boy, decides to keep digging for worms. But Seth is determination itself. In him I see the boy inside me I had almost forgotten. "What about a bobber?" he asks, pointing to the blister pack. "Seth," I say, "I'm going to tell you a secret. We'll catch more fish without the bobber. It makes the worm float wrong. The fish get suspicious." His eyes widen and he nods.

The rod is long, so I put my arms around his and four-handedly we swing the worm into the watery world. It lands eight feet out and is falling when a bluegill nails it. Seth, bowstring-taut, yanks so hard that the fish sails directly overhead and lands in the grass behind us. We whoop and pump our fists before catching more: two bluegills and a largemouth.

Two weeks later, his mother calls to say that Seth has been telling everyone he meets, "I'm going to tell you a true secret about fishing. If you're trying to catch a fish, do not use a bobber."

"Are you still there?" she asks. I am. It's just that some memory— deep, strange, and overwhelming—has taken hold of my throat.

Hands Off My Stuff

Fifteen months ago, Michelle and I—in the great American tradition of utter financial cluelessness—bought a house twice as large and expensive as we needed or could afford. Now we're putting it on the market and looking for something less . . . insane. The hardest part for me is acknowledging that I own more hunting and fishing gear than anyone who has not already appeared on *Hoarding: Buried Alive*. It's as if some minister told me at an early age, "We enter and exit this world with nothing. In between, a man's spiritual salvation depends on getting as much of the Cabela's catalog into his house as possible."

It hit me when I combined my inventory into what looked like a landfill's worth of perfectly serviceable gear. *Wow,* I thought, *maybe I am a true, clinical hoarder.* So I did some research. It turns out that serious hoarders often are emotional, creative people who are also indecisive. That is totally not me. If you disagree, I will burst into tears and then perform "Ecstasy of the Heat Pumps," an original interpretive dance depicting last winter's utilities bills. Then again, maybe I won't.

Update: Okay, having spent some time on the Hoarding website, I'm officially pitching myself as a candidate. They got me at "we will offer assistance with finding licensed therapists as well as professional organizers." On second thought, never mind. For one thing, the show got canceled. But I don't really need therapy anyway. What I need is dynamite. A few examples of stuff I can't part with:

I don't own a single waterfowl decoy, but I do have a huge Primos decoy bag, a perfect place to store my thirty pounds of old tree-stand harnesses. Most are from the torso-only days, before we knew that hanging from your armpits kills you just a bit more slowly than hanging from your neck. The point is that there's sixty yards of good nylon webbing and seat belt buckles in there. What if I suddenly need to make, say, a really secure canoe seat for a keg of beer? A man wants to be prepared for things like that.

There's a set of commercial fisherman's foul-weather gear—Guy Cotten parka and bibs—that I got for a brown bear hunt in Alaska, where it's not unheard of to get two weeks of steady rain. It's made of Nylpeche, a polyester fabric coated on both sides with PVC, which was perfected for professional watermen. Thing is, you put that stuff on and you look competent. I was wearing it home after a bowhunt in a sleet storm when I joined two other guys trying to push a woman's car off the muddy shoulder of a road. One dude looked at me and said, "You look like you know what you're doing. Whaddya think?" I can count on one hand the times I've been mistaken for the most skilled guy in a group. I looked around and noticed a pile of gravel left by a road crew forty yards off. It had a shovel stuck in it. I suggested we try some of that. It worked. It was one of my proudest moments ever. You think I'm throwing that suit out? No way.

Then there's my collection of about four hundred hand warmers, some of which date to the last century. Almost all are past their expiration dates. But those dates are only there for legal reasons, like the ones on instant mac and cheese, which has the shelf life of quartz. Just the other night, we lost power. The kids were terrified that Taco the bearded dragon lizard would freeze. Taco never stirs from atop his little electric warming pad. For all I know, he might have died two years ago. To quiet the kids, I splurged, uncorking three 2006 toe warmers that I'd been cellaring in the garage. Two out of three warmed up right away. That's a pretty good ratio. Throwing those away would be crazy. Suppose a rogue glacier busts loose and comes barreling down the East Coast? A guy with four hundred hand warmers would be a kingmaker.

I have an extra-stout 5½-foot St. Croix spinning rod and Shimano reel the size of my head that I got to fish for large tarpon from small boats in Costa Rica. The surf was so strong we couldn't launch, so I fished the mouth of the river from shore with a lighter outfit. Which was how I put a 4/0 hook all the way through my thumb. My lure had snagged on some vegetation, which I failed to notice was floating. When I yanked, there was nothing between my hands and a 2-ounce jighead but tropical air. I nearly fainted from the pain. An American doctor guest removed the hook and arranged for a tetanus shot to be flown in the next day. He later told me he'd been afraid I might go into shock.

Long story short, I have yet to use that outfit. My sense of how the world works, however, is that the moment I do get rid of it, I'll again be invited to go fishing for tarpon. I have mixed feelings about this. Either I'm hanging on to that outfit to be prepared for that invitation or to ensure that it never comes. All I know for sure is that the rod stays.

Cross-Country Skiing Among the Cree

When the Polar Bear Express finally clanks into the town of Moosonee at the southern tip of James Bay in northern Ontario, we climb down from the train and turn our backs into the arctic wind like a troupe of synchronized penguins. Our group of nine American and Canadian cross-country skiers, led by outfitter Tuckamor Trips, specializing in Canadian wilderness travel, has journeyed to the tribal lands of the Mushkegowuk (or "Swampy") Cree for five days of skiing and cross-cultural interaction in the company of three Cree guides. I've come out of a twofold curiosity. I want to see how Indians fully versed in modern technology (snowmobiles, computers, and Kid Rock) manage to hold on to their tribal identity. And, having never skied anyplace farther north or less crowded than resorts in Vermont, I want to see what it's like to ski and camp in winter on their turf. Waiting for us on the platform is Phil Sutherland, a friendly bear of a man and our head guide, dressed in jeans, jogging shoes, and a thin warm-up jacket. My hand, momentarily pulled from a mountaineering mitt, is cold when I greet him. Phil's, bare, is somehow warm.

You don't get to a place like this by accident. The nearly 200,000 square miles of forested bog—known as muskeg—that make up the lowlands of the James and Hudson bays is one of the largest wetlands left on earth: home to four kinds of geese, golden eagles, moose, beavers, muskrat, wolves, fox, and lynx. The waterlogged ground keeps roads at bay, and the only significant settlements cling to the edges of the bays. To reach the twin towns of Moosonee (mostly nonnative) and Moose Factory (an island in the Moose River where the Cree have a reservation) you cover the 186 miles north from Cochrane aboard the decidedly subsonic Polar Bear Express, which teeters along at thirty-five miles an hour through endless forests of spruce, fir, aspen, and poplar.

As we form a line from the baggage car to Phil, standing in the bed of his pickup and begin passing gear, he bestows nicknames that have a fearful sticking power. Charles, a Princeton-educated lawyer-turned-nonprofit-housing-developer on his third Tuckamor trip, is dubbed "Chuckie." (Though two days later, when he protests, the moniker is immediately dropped.) Fernando, a Colombian-born systems analyst from Ottawa, becomes "Colombia." On a whim he declines to explain, Phil christens me "Bwana." At one point, he looks at me and deadpans, "You bring'um Indian trinkets, Bwana?" Then his eyes crinkle and he gives his big, hearty laugh. Secretly, I am thrilled. These people don't give a damn for white-man etiquette.

We soon discover that this disarming teasing and an almost physical need to laugh loud and often are ingrained parts of Cree culture. So is the welcoming of strangers. Phil leads a caravan of three vehicles over a plowed strip of the frozen Moose River into the Cree village of Moose Factory. (Despite the name, no moose were ever assembled here. In 1673, the Hudson Bay Company set up a fur trading post on the site. The post's head was known as a "factor," and his home was a "factory.") At Phil's own modest wooden house with satellite TV broadcasting a curling championship in the background, our group—six men, three women, ranging in age from early thirties to early seventies—digs into huge platters of roast Canada goose, blue goose stew, homemade bread, vegetables, potatoes, and coffee. We meet his wife and children, hold his new baby grandson. We take showers in his bathroom. We lay our pads and sleeping bags shoulder to shoulder on the floor of his living room. Tomorrow we'll ski twelve miles up the Moose River to Phil's hunting camp to pitch a teepee, learn about Cree customs, and eat the insane amounts of calories your body requires to ski and camp in winter.

The Cree have been living in this part of northern Ontario for about three thousand years. For most of that time they were a nomadic people who traveled by foot, snowshoe, and canoe, their movements echoing those of the game they lived on. Elaborate rituals for placating the spirits of the game that sustained them were passed down. When a bear was killed, the hunter cracked its knuckles to free its spirit from the body. At the ensuing feast, an offering of food was placed in the fire and the men greased their hair with the bear's fat for good luck. Even the bones were honored, placed in the forest on a platform above the reach of dogs so that the bear might continue to give of himself.

This way of life was nearly snuffed out after the fur traders arrived, bringing with them the traditional white man's gifts: firearms, alcohol, and tuberculosis. The Hudson Bay Company fur press still stands here today. A Cree trapper laid his beaver pelts in it and watched while the screws were turned. A musket could be acquired for its height in compressed beaver pelts. As many as 90 percent of the Cree may have died within the first two generations after contact. Many of those who survived did so by keeping their distance and holding on to the old ways. As late as the 1950s, it was common to find groups of families living together in the bush, coming into town once or twice a year to sell furs and buy supplies.

Our itinerary calls for a reasonably early start each morning, about ten to twelve miles of skiing carrying daypacks containing lunch and the extra clothing we'll need anytime we stop moving. Arriving before the afternoon temperature drop, we'll help the guides with camp chores and sleep either in a canvas tepee or Cree hunting shacks, both heated by woodstoves. Phil's two Cree cousins, Clarence Trapper and Jim Chum, will carry our gear in snowmobiles ahead of us, packing a trail through the two-foot-thick snow as they go. Bill Pollock, who runs Tuckamor Trips, has learned the hard way that it's necessary to have backup routes ready to adjust to varying weather conditions in this part of the world. This year, for example, a rare thaw upriver has left the snow too slushy to ski there. We'll ski along the river as planned to Phil Sutherland's hunting camp, do a day trip of the surrounding area, then ski west over a woodland trail to another hunting camp the next day, then spend two days retracing our path to Moose Factory.

It's an overcast, windy day as we set out on the river. As the town recedes behind us, we ski into a white desert. Snowfields stretch for half a mile over the ice to either side before hitting woods of scraggly spruce and balsam fir. Here and there are tracks left by snowshoe rabbits and the foxes that hunt them. After the first ten minutes I shed my parka, as David and Uli, a couple from New York in their late fifties, politely zip past me. While this is beginner-level skiing, there's a fair amount of it and the pace is brisk. Most of these folks, though older than I, are extremely fit. While skiing, I'm comfortably warm. The moment I pause for a drink the cold finds my bones. I don't dare stop for the sandwiches in my pack until I'm standing with my backside toward the fire waiting for us at Phil's camp on Makachanau Island.

The first order of business after lunch is to put up the canvas teepee. The guides don big homemade snowshoes with moose-hide webbing, then wade into the woods to cut long spruce poles to support the teepee and green boughs to insulate the floor. Phil sprinkles a handful of tobacco—a plant sacred to virtually every native tribe in North America—on the tamped-down snow and walks to the four compass points of the site, intoning a brief Cree blessing. Then he directs us in tying four poles together at their tips—two groups of two lying parallel in the snow—and in walking them up and spreading them to form the freestanding skeleton of the teepee. We lay on more poles to round out a circular footprint for the tent. Lastly, we place poles in small pockets sewn into the upper corners of the white canvas teepee itself and hoist the fabric up to drape it over the poles. The raising requires the entire group: five or six people to do the actual work and at least that many to yell "It's gonna fall!" whenever one of us loses control of an eighteen-foot pole. After the tent is up, there is a small gap at the top where the canvas sides didn't meet. Clarence doesn't like it. Any hole means heat loss. He steps out of his coveralls and boots, grabs two tent poles, and shimmies up the inside of the canvas like a human fly to close the flap. Awestruck, we stare at him as if he has just sprouted wings. "Old Indian trick," he jokes shyly. At last the thing is up and we begin laying the boughs, which will provide insulation from the snow. The smell inside is heavenly, sort of like Pine-Sol without the disinfectant. Clarence assembles a woodstove inside and soon the place is warm.

After a dinner cooked and eaten around the woodstove in one of the three small shacks that make up Phil's camp, we all pile into the teepee for Cree 101, our nightly informal talk by the guides. Clarence, thirty-two, is unusual among his generation, having spent much of his youth learning the old skills with his parents, who built a cabin in the woods and lived most of the year there subsisting on what they could hunt, fish, and trap. "We'd get a moose most years and that would be enough meat for months," he says. He tells us about "Indian time," a more elastic version of the continuum than the one you measure with a wrist bracelet. He says he learned the hard way that a phrase like "in a little while"—which can mean a full day among the Cree—means no more than an hour or two for the people he guides.

He says he's noticed that Cree and whites have almost opposite views of two social conventions: small talk and visual contact. "We're pretty comfortable with silence," he says. "In fact, a person who's just talking to talk—just chattering—seems like somebody who's uncomfortable or anxious to us." Similarly, he says, in Cree society, staring or looking someone directly in the face indicates either hostility or a declaration of love. "It took me a while to get used to white people staring," he says. "Now it doesn't bother me." He rolls over until his face is about a foot away from David, a tall forest ranger from New York, and stares him straight in the eye. "So," he says at last, "how's it going so far?" Everyone cracks up.

The night starts off warm in the teepee, and we fall asleep quickly after a long day. At 4 a.m. the fire in the woodstove goes out. It's dark as the inside of a cow, but you can tell by the changes in our breathing that every one of us is awake. It's a Canadian standoff, each of us hoping another will fold, get up, and brave the cold for the two minutes it will take to restoke the fire. No one moves. I squirm deeper into my bag, pull the drawstrings so tight that only the tip of my nose is exposed, and drift in and out of slumber. When I finally crawl out of my bag at seven, my water bottle is frozen solid.

The next day, we ski an out-and-back course about seven miles each way through the woods on a trail to the French River. It's a gorgeous route, passing along a creek bottom overhung with alder, then past virgin white spruce seventy feet tall that may be 250 years old. I glide over a frozen lake and into a frozen jungle of tamaracks on a windless, sunny day. I'm feeling more confident today, sucking in the cold, clean air and sliding along at my own pace. Only Chuckie—I mean Charles—who purposely uses ancient wooden skis and bamboo poles precisely because he wants to force himself to slow down, is behind me. But it doesn't matter. My skiing settles into dance, a moving meditation of legs and lungs and arms. I pause in a clearing where the tracks of rabbits and foxes mingle and realize I hear nothing—no voices, skis, airplanes, not even the wind. Suddenly, I'm completely at ease. I realize I can do this, that I'm fine. I have a good sleeping bag and enough clothes. A dry place to sleep and a fire to keep me warm. Out here, these are the things that matter. A half-mile up ahead, smoke rises from where the guides have made a fire. I press on to hot vegetable soup and big cold-cut sandwiches. I eat knowing I will have burned it all up by the time I make it back to camp.

That evening, I take my turn as Phil's helper in the kitchen: fetching wood and water, kneading the dough for the bannock bread we fry up to go with the stew. An hour before sundown, while most of the others are napping, Clarence, Phil, and I knock off for a tea break in the cook shack. I'm sitting hunched forward on a crate, trying to stretch the muscles in my back. "You okay?" Phil asks. "Just a little sore," I tell him. He clears a space on the bed, motions for me to lie down, and gives me a five-minute back rub. I can think of handful of people on earth I would feel comfortable doing this for, most of them immediate family. But Phil is no more self-conscious about this than if he were helping me put on my coat. When he's done, he lights a cigarette and goes back to his tea. "You hear about the 1956 Indian hide-and-seek champion, Bwana?" he asks. "They just found his body last week." It's a joke so old I'd forgotten it. His eyes crinkle. He laughs his big, hearty laugh.

Car Talk

I didn't want to clean out my car. My mama made me. "You are not driving Aunt Joyce to the airport in that rat's nest," she said. "Get it washed. And see if they can do anything about the smell." With these words my mother witched me from an adult back to a twelve-year-old with acne. Mothers have had this power since time immemorial. Attila the Hun's mom? I bet you a Calais 4-by-8 DC reel (the $649.99 one that electronically adjusts brake force every one-thousandth of a second and also predicts winning lottery numbers) that when he came home after conquering much of the known world, she was standing on the porch, shaking her head. "Running around wild with your hoodlum friends. If you'd stayed home like your brother Bleda you could have had a real job with medical and dental by now."

To comply with orders, I first had to empty my car, an action that runs counter to every fiber of my being. A clean car is a sterile car, and so is the man who owns it. Women, who have the luxury of carrying purses—mysterious pouches containing breath mints, spare stockings, and Taser guns—do not get this. They do not understand that a man's vehicle is his four-speed multi-tool, his wheeled tackle box, his hunter's Quik Mart, the campus of his continuing education. And that it smells fine to us the way it is.

You need a 100-grain mechanical broadhead? Take your pick: There's a Rocket AeroHead Sidewinder in the ashtray or an NAP Spitfire in the glove box. At least that's where they used to be. You want to see if anybody's home in that pond we just passed? Yeah, it did look kind of fishy. If I remember correctly, there ought to be some watermelon black Senkos and Zoom Salty Super Flukes in baby bass right under your floor mat. Used to be some 4/0 Gamakatsu G-Lock hooks in a Lipton tea bag envelope in that door map pocket. There are probably a few snagged in the carpet under the seats as well. You'll find a six-piece takedown tucked right next to the jack. Careful, though. It's been through two summers there, so that 8-pound test is probably more like 2-pound now. Catch a hog on it and you're looking at a new IGFA light-tackle record.

Ever grabbed a three-meat sub on the way to where the pavement ends and forget the condiments that transform mere calories into food? That little hatch between the seats is a veritable spice rack, with little packets of ketchup, mustard, sweet pickle relish, pepper, salt, horse radish, soy sauce, and nondairy creamer. (I wouldn't put that stuff in my coffee on a bet, but it makes a heck of a fire starter.) Napkins are with the eating tools and a bottle of VizWiz lens cleaner tucked up on the visor. I find it cleans hands as well as glasses. And I promise you this: Your fingers will never, ever fog up again.

One of the most important benefits of a properly neglected rig is that you can always find something to do when you're cooling your heels. Just last week I was stuck in my internist's waiting room. All the good magazines had been stolen, leaving me the Hobson's choice of *Cosmopolitan* or *Redbook*. It was either "Sex Tips of a Hollywood Hooker" or "Give Your Meatloaf That South-of-the-Border Zing!" Both promised to drive the man in your life wild. I bopped out to the parking lot and rooted around for an unread copy of *Quality Whitetails*. Did you know that deer are immune to poison ivy? They actually eat it year-round, often preferring it to other foods because of its high protein content. Gospel truth. Or that you may reduce coyote predation on deer fawns with a diverse food-plot mix that provides plenty of food for grasshoppers, a staple of the coyote diet? (Or that I'm having a colonoscopy in October? I just got the news!)

My point here is that you can't rescue a busted hunting or fishing trip, learn about food plots, or improve sandwich quality in a vehicle ruined by excessive cleaning. But a son disobeys his mama at his peril.

I kept excavating and found a Frisbee I'd taken on a smallmouth trip some years ago, cherished for its dual use as toy and food plate. A Looney Tunes ball cap I'd gotten at a NASCAR race in Richmond in 2002, with Bugs Bunny on one side and the Tasmanian Devil on the other, turned up; a cementlike layer of dried baby vomit on the bill had damaged its value as a collectible.

Last, I took my emasculated vehicle to the Mr. Wash. They washed, buffed, vacuumed, and finished the desecration with the same hideously sweet disinfectant that the New Jersey Turnpike Authority uses in its restrooms. When I finally picked up Aunt Joyce, she got in and winced. "What is that awful smell?" I explained that it was the odor of maternal pressure and asked if she'd mind if I lit a cigar to freshen the air. "Please do," she said. We had a nice ride to the airport.

I'm trying to reverse the damage, but a well-equipped car is like a good stinkbait. The right ingredients are just the beginning: Time alone allows them to settle into their optimum relation to one another.

Going to Pieces

Hunting and fishing have gotten me through some of life's rougher patches. When some defeat of the heart or career left me paralyzed and clueless, when what I believed suddenly no longer obtained, I still knew what to do in a deer stand, on a smallmouth river, or on a bass pond. But what once came with ease in these places now hurts sometimes. Chronological time is the steady progress of calendar days. You can push back against this. Although I am fifty-eight, for example, I'm often told that I have the tact and emotional intelligence of a fourteen-year-old. Then there is body time, the toll the years take on your bones. Body time is unsteady. It's a series of long plateaus punctuated by sharp declines. If you graphed it, it would look like stair steps.

I think I'm falling down the stairs.

Last year, for the first time in my life, I got tennis elbow. Twice. Once in each arm. The first came last December, when, frustrated at having to cancel an afternoon hunt, I shot arrows in the backyard for the better part of an hour. I felt fine the next day. The day after, I woke with my left arm on fire. I could still lift it fine, I just needed to scream at the same time. The doctor said the tiny tears in my tendons could take up to a year to heal. I suddenly felt ancient, smaller. I sat there and listened as he explained how tendons are different from muscles. They're fibrous and inelastic, receiving little direct blood flow. The only good news was that I might halve the recovery time if I carefully followed his rehabilitation protocol of stretches and exercises.

In six months, I was shooting again—very carefully, after warming up, and only a few arrows at a time. My trusty left arm was renegotiating its terms. *I'll still dance with you,* it seemed to say. *But you can't take me for granted anymore. I want some consideration. Try my patience and I'll ruin your season. Are we clear?*

I was still processing this when my right arm—not to be outdone—decided it wanted some attention, too. I'd been practicing my fly casting, mostly so that I wouldn't humiliate myself when Jack Unruh and I went smallmouth fishing at Harpers Ferry. Once more, I awoke with an inflamed arm, this one even worse than the first. I got a cortisone shot without even checking to see whether it was covered by my insurance. It did wonders. I'm happy to report that the trip went fine and that I didn't totally embarrass myself on the river. When Jack said, "Those guides must've liked you," a sort of pride welled up in me. Unfortunately, he hadn't finished. "Because I've never seen people trying so hard not to laugh."

On top of that, I've got back issues. Many men ignore this, hoping the condition will resolve itself. You've seen these guys. They're the ones who only hunt from ladder stands they didn't put up, who can't go out on the water unless the boat has a motor. They're in the club I'm fighting like hell not to join. After wasting three and a half years seeking help from medical doctors, I found a physical therapist who works on athletes and dancers, people who have to show up. Terry Sneed is a strong, no-nonsense woman who has me lie on a table while she digs into the pockets of evil in my back and buttocks with her fingers, knuckles, and elbows. I let her put me in traction and strap electrodes to my muscles. I let her plunge actual needles into the knotted muscles of my back and butt. She once slapped a toilet plunger (new, I'm pretty sure) onto my back, then pumped it. The suction draws blood to places that are starved for it. "And, honey, you've got a lot of places," she said. "You're as locked up as anybody I've ever seen."

When I ask how long I'll need to see her, Terry sighs and says, "Took you a long time to get this crooked. Be a while before you get straightened out." My state, she notes, suggests a lot of asymmetrical exercise. I pantomime shooting a bow. "So that's it," she says. "You ever think of stopping?" I look at her. "Got it," she says.

I'd be happy to tell you about my other physical "challenges" if I didn't recall how tedious I found such talk back when I was young and immortal. I don't know how many good years I've got left. I do know that the prospect of losing the ability to fish and hunt more or less on my own terms motivates me to work out regularly and hard, to pay Terry to search and destroy the kinks in my twisted body, and to pay closer attention to my aging forearms. I won't win this battle against time. No man does. The best you can do is draw it out as long as possible. And when my turn comes, I intend to go down swinging.

The Rope Report

If a form requires me to specify a religious denomination, I sometimes declare myself a tithing member of the Church of Cabela's-Bass-Pro-Shops, since at least 10 percent of my annual income goes to these two institutions. When I'm not dipping into Emma's college fund for the latest gizmo, I'm reading their websites' unedited customer reviews. The comments of your fellow sportsmen can help you make a more informed purchase. They also provide insight on the mindset of the modern American outdoorsman. And damned if some of us don't sound like we fell out of the Stupid Tree and hit every branch on the way down.

Take something as straightforward as a pull-up rope for your tree stand. There was a time when a guy would find some rope, measure off the desired length, and cut. Afield, he would tie one end to his belt, the other to his gear, and climb. Simple, right?

Maybe once upon a time. The twenty-first century is a specialized age and we want specialized, hunting-specific tree-stand ropes, designed by tree-stand-rope experts and manufactured in China. You want a camo rope, of course. (No telling how many monsters owe their lives to foolish hunters using single-color ropes.) You want little plastic clips on each end. (Otherwise you'd have to tie—and untie—actual knots.) And you want the rope premeasured to thirty feet. (Few tape measures are this long, and face it, America has pretty much outsourced all advanced math problems.)

At Cabela's and Bass Pro Shops you can find a three-eighths-inch braided nylon rope that satisfies the above criteria for $5.99. Last I checked, 38 reviewers on cabelas.com had given it an average rating of 4.1 stars out of 5, while 12 reviewers over at basspro.com had awarded it an average of 4.5 stars. (What's up? Are Bass Pro Shops guys less demanding or are Cabela's devotees just really particular?)

One five-star review at Cabela's actually pronounces it "one of the best designed ropes I have used." Another, after calling the product "a necessity," zeroes right in on its crucial weakness: "The downside is that it could knot somewhat." Bingo. Over at Bass Pro Shops, one reviewer sounded as if he'd spent the last decade wandering in the Tree-Stand-Rope Wilderness: "Finally, a pull-up rope made for those of us who hunt higher than 20 feet!"

I read reviews like those and—remember, we're talking about a piece of string—wonder whatever happened to self-reliance. Don't get me wrong. I'm as lame as they come. My pull-up rope was designed for people who hurt themselves opening their own refrigerator. It's the Strapper, thirty feet of tangleproof black nylon tape that you wind into its own plastic housing with a little folding crank. I love the damn thing. I paid $16.99 for it. And I still sometimes find myself halfway up a tree with a deer coming in and my Strapper lying unclipped on the ground.

What bothers me is what Ötzi would think. Ötzi, you'll recall, was the mountain man who lived some 5,300 years ago, whose body was discovered in the ice at 10,500 feet in the Alps in 1991. He is both the oldest fully preserved human and the first prehistoric man found with his everyday belongings.

The clothing and gear of this Copper Age man are remarkably sophisticated in their way and well suited to their tasks. Ötzi's coat, hat, and leggings were each made of pieces of tanned leather carefully cross-stitched together with sinew. His beautiful bearskin hat looks like something you'd want to wear on a December morning on stand. His leggings tied to his belt so they wouldn't fall down and to his shoes so they wouldn't ride up. The shoes themselves incorporated a woven net to hold insulating grasses around the foot, tanned deerskin uppers, and soles of thick bearskin to which additional strips of leather had been sewn on the diagonal to increase traction.

Ötzi carried a yew-handled ax with a blade of pure copper and a handy flint dagger that rode on his belt in a reinforced sheath. A U-shaped length of hazel wood is thought to have been part of an external-frame backpack. He was found with a quiver and arrows. The preferred fletching fifty-three centuries ago? Same as ours: three-part radial, only attached using birch tar and nettle thread instead of epoxy.

Ötzi's tools say that he knew how to fix things. In his leather pouch were a flint scraper and drill. He also carried a bone awl and a tool that incorporated fire-hardened stag antler to work flint. He might have carried live coals in a birch-bark vessel found to contain charcoal and green maple leaves as fire-resistant insulation. If that went out, he could make fire with the tinder fungus and flints he also had. His kit contained what might have been prehistoric Band-Aids: lumps of polypore fungus, known for its antibiotic and styptic properties, strung on leather thongs, the better to hold the fungus where it was needed.

He sounds like a pretty self-sufficient guy. And here's the kicker: Researchers say that if Ötzi himself didn't make all the gear he carried, he almost certainly knew how to.

Ötzi probably died knowing secrets of hunting and field craft that we'll never know. But I'll venture this much: I bet you a bearskin hat the guy would have made his own pull-up rope.

Inward Bound

This just in: Carrying a cell phone in your pants can lead to fewer and slower-swimming sperm, according to a recent South African study. In men, that is. Researchers think the radiation emitted by the phone is to blame. All men should take note, but I am particularly concerned. While I swim with all the speed and grace of a beer bottle, I have always believed—deeply, with the absolute certainty of a man whose beliefs have no basis in reality—that my personal reproductive cells could outswim bluefin tuna. In fact, they would dominate Olympic competition. Don't laugh. If the Olympics has room for Ping-Pong and trampoline, it has room for sperm races. I'm thinking 2016 should have both an individual 25-centimeter sperm freestyle and a 1-meter four-sperm relay.

Anyway, to limit the damage, I vowed to carry my smartphone near a less critical part of my body: my brain. I found an elegant solution online in the Aryca Headlamp Style Head Strap Mount. The site shows pictures of four satisfied users, all of whom—I'm not making this up—are fishing. During my headband research, I was surprised to note that there are still folks who contend that smartphones and the hyperconnectivity they afford us are not unmixed blessings. These killjoys point to "studies" in which heavy Facebook and Twitter users were found to be lonelier and to have fewer "real" friends than other people. Further, these prophets of doom claim that the instant gratification of the Web inhibits empathy for others and that people significantly underestimate the time they spend online.

This is ridiculous. These are the same people who say that Bigfoot doesn't exist, despite the fact that there are new TV shows about him every week. As for the Web destroying empathy, that's just a crock of—hang on, Jim just sent me, wow, a Vine video of a crocodile chowing down on this dude who fell off his Jet Ski! OMG! His girlfriend seems really upset. This is hilarious! I'm totally retweeting this.

Where was I?

Oh, right, the naysayers.

My personal outdoor recreational experience has been, like, awesomely better since I came into possession of an iPhone. True, I don't actually spend as much time outdoors as I used to, but—whoa, check this out! Marcos just sent me a video of a leopard cuddling a baby baboon! That is so cute. Almost as good as the one of that elk jumping on a trampoline. It makes you wonder how people lived before we had access to this kind of knowledge.

So anyway . . . um . . . oh, I remember now. The reason I don't need to go outdoors as much anymore is that my smartphone brings the outdoors to me. If I can have real-time trail-cam photos telling me what size bucks are around and when, why should I drag myself out of bed at zero dark thirty just to go sit in a tree? And my new FlyCaster app, highly recommended on the website of a magazine called *Field & Stream,* is like having a trout stream in your pocket. (Or strapped to your head.) For one thing, it's got way better water than any of my local streams. And there's a new fish biting every fifteen seconds. It makes me realize what a chump I was back when I'd put the canoe on the car roof, drive someplace, and then go hours, or even the whole day, without a bite. And FlyCaster has this metronome thing that times your cast and sounds a chime when you get it right. Okay, I've never actually heard the chime. The point is, the thing's so true to life that it makes you want to throw the phone on the ground and stomp on it. (Tip: The $99 "comprehensive" AppleCare policy does not consider fly-fishing-stompage to be accidental damage.)

As for the claim that we spend more time on the Web than we think, that's—hang on, it's the kids at my office door. They want to shoot their bows and need my help. I'll be there in a sec. Oops, another text. You have to see this. This guy made himself actual steel claws like

Wolverine, got on water skis, and is slashing at leaping Asian carp! Great helmet-cam footage. Oh, he just hit a tree! LOL!

I'm thinking a helmet cam would be awesome for capturing my outdoor experiences. There's one online that mounts a little camera alongside your ear. But this chest mount might be cool, too. Like if I was playing a huge marlin. No, I'm going to go with the ear cam.

Okay, time to shoot with the kids. Wow, it's almost dark. C'mon, you guys, let's go. What do you mean you don't want to now? You'd rather play Roblox and Infamous 2? Wow, they look totally glazed over. They're addicted to these damn video games. Sometimes—I hate to say this, but there are times when a man has to stand up and speak the truth—I think computers are ruining our kids.

The Bear Essentials

I recently returned from the annual SHOT (Shooting, Hunting and Outdoor Trade) Show in Las Vegas. It's a four-day orgy of stuff you don't need. Yet. But if the marketing guys push the right buttons, you'll change your mind. Weird as it is, SHOT is a core sample of the American outdoorsman's psyche. And what we secretly long to be is one of two things: an elite sniper, or the first member of a three-man SWAT team through the door. The identity of the enemy is unclear, but it doesn't matter. What does is that we are up to the mission. We are professionals, immune to either fear or pity. We are competent, lethal, not to be messed with. And all that stands between us and our heroic best selves is the proper hardware: ARs in exotic calibers—the 6.5 Grendel, the .300 Blackout—that bristle with night scopes, lasers, computerized ballistics calculators, and silencers the size of salamis.

By the time I got home, I felt strangely tainted. I'd been exposed to too much technology, too much of the invisible desire machine that makes us want it. So I did what I've done every few years for about four decades. I dipped back into the flat-out best hunting story ever written, William Faulkner's "The Bear."

I warn you. Faulkner is everything that SHOT is not. He doesn't give a damn about being user-friendly. If anything, he goes out of his way to be difficult. His stream-of-consciousness style veers from reality to myth and back again. He'll uncork a page-long sentence without warning. He often dispenses with fact entirely in pursuit of truths larger than mere facts. If you're confused, you've got company. Scholars still debate whether the thing is a long short story or a short novel. It often reads as if Faulkner wrote "The Bear" for an audience of one—himself.

But it's worth the whistle. Whatever his faults, Faulkner has hunting in his marrow. Read this description of wilderness and hunters who go there "with the will and hardihood to endure and the humility and skill to survive, and the dogs and the bear and deer juxtaposed and reliefed against it, ordered and compelled by and within the wilderness in the ancient and unremitting contest according to the ancient and immitigable rules which voided all regrets and brooked no quarter."

Told you.

The story unfolds through the eyes of Ike—first as a boy of ten, then as an accomplished woodsman of sixteen. He is the youngest in a group of hunters who journey each fall to the Big Bottom to run dogs on deer and other game. To Ike, hunting isn't a pastime. The woods are his school, his path to manhood, his only possible salvation. He is ravenous for the skill, humility, and pride by which a man may prove worthy of being called a hunter. For as long as Ike has been alive, the main event of the annual trip has been the hunt for Old Ben, who is not just a bear, but *the* bear. He's a mythic creature, the spirit of the wilderness made flesh—ancient, indomitable, destructive, elusive, light-years beyond such man-made concepts as good or evil. He has absorbed countless charges of ball, shot, and bullets, all "with no more effect than so many peas blown through a tube by a child." The hunters no longer expect to kill Old Ben. The chase is more ceremony than hunt, an offering to the ancient primacy and unfathomable power of the natural world. And these same men—and, by extension, all men—have already doomed the wilderness. They—we—don't hesitate to exploit and destroy it for their own gain.

I won't ruin the story by telling you how it ends. It will lift your soul even as it breaks your heart, the way hunting exalts your skill as it sears you with knowledge that the world won't miss a beat at your exit.

It's tough to explain why you love a given book, especially one as convoluted and difficult as this one. I reread "The Bear" because it affirms things I believe. Because it articulates them better and more deeply than I can. Because underlying every word I feel Faulkner's knowledge that hunting is how certain men fill a need felt by all of us—to connect an individual consciousness to the universal one, the one that has always been and will be, the one whose powers, rhythms, and mysteries move all things.

Even when Ike is sent back to the city to replenish the hunters' store of whiskey, the mere fact of clearing weather and the prospect of hunting make his world more vivid. "He felt the old lift of the heart, as pristine as ever, as on the first day; he would never lose it, no matter how old in hunting and pursuit: the best, the best of all breathing, the humility and the pride."

There is no Faulkner booth at the SHOT Show. Maybe there ought to be.

True Grit

In case you ever get thrown in jail—and I'm not suggesting that you do—you probably already know which of your friends you'd burn your one phone call on. If you're lucky, he's not just a guy who would post your bail but one who would also pick you up at 4 a.m., make sure you're okay, and even tell the cops that you couldn't have robbed that orphanage because the two of you were getting drunk in a strip club at the time.

I know who I'd call. Jim, my friend of more than thirty years. We've each seen the other through a divorce, periods of high drama and low money, and various births and deaths. Twenty-five years ago, I held his eldest son the day he came home from the hospital. Sixteen years ago, when my baby daughter stopped breathing at four months, I can't remember who I called first, but it was probably Jim.

I do remember his fortieth birthday party, billed—accurately—by his then wife as "world's oldest man turns forty." And I remember my fiftieth, a surprise party at which I arrived three hours late. My wife at the time was displeased that I'd kept a houseful of guests waiting. "People mostly sat around being polite. Then the curtains caught fire and everyone sat there like they were paralyzed. Jim pulled them down, ran outside, and stomped the flames out." At the time I remember thinking, *That sounds about right. Jim would be the guy to do that.*

And now the jerk is dying. At first he thought the pain was a strained stomach muscle from kayaking the Potomac's whitewater. When he finally went to the doctor, the diagnosis was pseudocysts, benign and mostly fluid, on his pancreas. Then they were true cysts, but still no cause for alarm. Then cancerous. Then inoperable, wrapped around major arteries. Jim told me all this in a matter-of-fact phone call. He made it sound like he might be getting the flu. I stopped researching the ailment after five minutes. It was just too grim. Pancreatic is the black mamba of cancers—aggressive, lethal, and pitiless. Seventy-three percent of those diagnosed are dead within a year, the lowest survival rate among all twenty-one common cancers. As I sat at my computer, the bottom fell out of the world. I felt the huge, bored yawn of the abyss. It's strange. Until then, I had no idea how much I loved the guy.

He's taking Elvis-level pain meds, which allow him to sleep at night. He's halfway through six weeks on chemo, after which they'll scan again. Then, if he can take it, a short rest and more chemo. There's a snowball's chance that radiation might buy some time. But the doctors no longer talk timelines, much less any chance of a cure. Jim—wisely, in my view—hasn't asked. Now it's all about controlling his pain until there is no more pain.

Jim is an Oklahoma boy. By which I mean that while we've been texting and talking more often than in the past, we rarely mention his cancer. He's still working, trying to leave something behind for his wife and two twenty-something sons whose children he'll never hold.

We shot sporting clays the other day. He was gaunt, twenty pounds lighter, skin stretched tight over his skull. It was probably a miracle that he could shoot at all. He was short of shells, so I offered some of mine, Winchester Xtra-Lite Target loads, which have an ounce of shot. He declined, saying the shop sold ones with seven-eighths of an ounce. This from a guy I'd once seen lift a washing machine off the floor so it wouldn't scratch the linoleum. As we walked to the first station, I looked down. "Bud, what happened to your ass?" I asked. His buttocks were flat planes, as if sliced away. He shrugged, told me he now requires a pad to sit on a wooden chair, that his clothes hang off him like a scarecrow. "Don't know how much sense it makes to be investing in new ones. Or even what size to get."

And then he shot my lights out. He missed a few of the high crossers that have always troubled him, but on most stands he broke four, five, sometimes six out of six birds. "Damn," I said. "They might have to put chemo on the list of performance-enhancing drugs." When I dropped him off, we just shook hands and said, "Later."

A few days after, he e-mailed that he hadn't realized getting ready to die involved so much paperwork. He was still keeping the news from anyone he didn't have to tell. There wasn't a whiff of self-pity in any of it.

I wrote back that it was pretty damn selfish of him to get cancer, that it showed little regard for his friends and family, and that he'd been brought up better. Who, I asked, was I supposed to call from jail now? I said that in light of his weakened state, I could probably kick his ass and just might the next time I saw him.

His reply, in its entirety, was "Well you could try."

It was the most courageous response imaginable. I lost it, hard, knew better than to even try to stop the tears. I let them come. And tried once more to come to terms with the unbelievable fact that this is actually happening.

III

Task Master

Faced with a task that can no longer be ignored—two months' worth of laundry, a refrigerator reeking of the bloodworms you put in six weeks ago and then forgot—every man should have this coping strategy to turn to: First, take a deep, centering breath. Next, shut your eyes and relax your mind. In the mental space just created there will arise a miracle—a pre-task task at once more urgent and less odious. Once you've seen to this pre-task, you will totally get down to the other one. I mean it.

What sorts of pre-tasks arise in this suspended moment? The sudden need to replace all your fishing line is a good example, especially if you use braided and must first lay down fifty yards of mono backing. Then, of course, you need to join the mono and braid, for which I use either the blood knot or double uni. That is, I start with one of these. But since neither quite works up the way it looks in the diagram, I usually switch to the other halfway through. Then, to further ensure the knot's integrity, I incorporate aspects of the surgeon's loop, the water knot, and other flourishes unique to me. By the time I've done fourteen reels I can no longer remember the original dreaded task.

Sometimes, the more imperative duty is a practice round of arrows. Archery is a highly perishable skill, and once you're engaged in the original chore, it could be days before you practice again. I prop open the storm door to my study with a cinder block, prop open the main door with a phone book (the only use I've found for a phone book in the digital age), and stand at the rear of my office. This gets me a

141

forty-yard shot, provided I miss the overhead light. Forty yards is a longer shot than I would take in the field unless conditions were perfect or a whitetail deer were somehow involved, and tends to reveal errors in form. As I draw and settle for the shot, I repeat the mantra of master coach Terry Wunderle: "Steady forward pressure with the bow arm. Steady rearward pressure with the release arm. And see if just once you can keep from punching the trigger, numbnuts." Having shot your five arrows, you walk out into your unmown lawn and discover the bicycle your child reported stolen. The dandelions, waist-high and nodding agreeably, would be prize winners in some cultures. (You wish you lived in one.) And so you go in search of the mower. By now you've forgotten there was even a task to avoid.

Can't find the kitchen table under a stack of bills? This is just the moment to make sure that every blade in the house has been honed to an arm-hair-shaving edge. Different blades respond to different sharpening systems, so it's wise to have a variety. The Benchmade Mini-Griptilian riding in my pocket now, for example, touches up nicely in a Lansky Crock Stick sharpener. On the other hand, my Fallkniven F1—the deceptively vanilla fixed blade issued to pilots in the Swedish Air Force, which minces pimentos and guts elk with equal ease—prefers a diamond stone. I have fillet knives that rival surgical scalpels, but only if honed on the fine rods of a Spyderco Tri-Angle sharpener. This device also has a 12.5-degree setting that sharpens the very scissors I can barely refrain from testing on the utility bills.

You can extend this coping strategy to more than just distasteful chores. Once, on the very day of a colonoscopy, I realized I had never inventoried my flashlights. Clearly, this had to be done prior to anyone's installing five feet of cable up my butt. Like any outdoorsman, I own lights for purposes general and specific. The fifth tackle box that I looked in yielded the tiny Petzl headlamp reserved for tying knots when night fishing. From my ScenTote locker, I retrieved a pencil-size Streamlight Stylus, a sort of anti-flashlight, output equal to three horny lightning bugs, which is just what you want for stealth in the deer woods. Camping, on the other hand, requires a range of lights, like my go-to outhouse light, a SureFire G2 Nitrolon. It's way more powerful than the task would seem to require. But the middle of a moonless night is precisely when I have the least faith in scientists' assurances that Bigfoot does not exist. Remember, these same guys took seventy-six years to downgrade Pluto to a "dwarf planet." Here's my take: If Pluto can get smaller, Bigfoot can get bigger. I want the ability to blind the big ape for a three-second head start, and the G2 gives me that.

Having finally accounted for all my lights, I was at last ready to get down to the real task: battery testing. I was thus engaged when the doctor's office called to ask if I were sick, as I'd missed the scheduled procedure. I explained that an unforeseen situation requiring my immediate attention had come up. Which was the absolute truth.

Dr. Jekyll & Mr. Eye

Call, commands Ray in the half-light of a late April dawn.

Putting striker to glass, I scratch out some soft yelps and listen. Silence. Lots of it. A whole truckload of silence. A bunch of turkeys gobbled in the distance when Ray owl-hooted with his voice fifteen minutes ago. It was an amazing hoot, born deep in his chest, a place normal humans have no vocal organs. (I will not learn until after returning home that he was a hoot owl national champion even before he held that title in turkey calling.) Since then it's been a funeral of a morning.

"Again," whispers Ray. "Not like you're the ugliest girl at the dance. Call like you're horny. Go on."

We're set up in a blind at the head of a brushy ditch leading up to a cornfield. This is prime turkey country, near the town of Kirksville in northern Missouri. Ray Eye is not exactly irritated, but we both know there would probably be a bird on the ground by now if we were doing things his way. The standard deal is that he summons the gobbler and the dumbass outdoor writer pulls the trigger. Then the writer poses for a hero picture and lies about the hunt. I had to go screw up a good system, trying to learn something by doing the turkey calling myself and having Ray critique. That was bad enough, and it didn't get any better when he heard me call. "My God," he'd said with a wince last night in the motel. "Look, I can put you onto turkeys. But I can't make 'em commit suicide."

Reversing the Curse

Right now it looks as if my ten-year turkey curse (don't ask) may continue. I try again, a longer series, the way Ray instructed last night: each yelp a little longer, louder, and higher than the previous one. This time a chorus of gobbles answers. The sound runs straight up my spine.

"That's more like it," Ray mutters. He does something behind me with the video camera. "Call again." I do, the same rising, urgent cadence. The turkeys gobble louder, closer. "Coming in. Get your gun up." And then, magically, improbably, four red wattled heads come jerkily into view. The birds take vicious pokes at our jake decoy and strut for the foam hen twenty-two yards from the blind. All four are jakes themselves, short-bearded suitors with bumps for spurs. They're legal birds, everything a turkey-cursed wretch like me could ask for.

More than forty years of turkey encounters should have made this routine for Ray. Instead, he's audibly stoked, his breath coming in short, quick gasps as he films. I'm suddenly dying for oxygen, too. I have to scootch my folding stool forward and slightly uphill to get the barrel out through the blind's shooting port. The jakes are oblivious, alternately strutting and sparring with one another for the hen's favors. An eternity passes before Ray whispers, "The dominant bird is on the far right. I'd take him." I exhale, center the bead halfway down the neck, and wait until Bachelor No. 4 comes out of his strut. The gun roars and slams into me. For a frozen moment I am in midair, flying slowly backward, looking up into the blackness and smiling. I land hard on my back against the tripod, still smiling. Ray's eye never leaves the camera, but he gives me a congratulatory slap on the back and offers an arm to lean on as I regain my seat.

It's 7 a.m. Should the world end today, pulverized by a killer asteroid, I will die a happy, successful turkey hunter at last.

An Ozark Original

I have come to Missouri to learn from Ray Eye, called "America's premier turkey hunter" by that bible of turkey hunters everywhere, the *Wall Street Journal*. He has his own TV show, *Eye on the Outdoors*, plus video series and sponsorship deals, and is a sought-after speaker at seminars and sports shows nationwide. He sold Ozark Mountain Calls, the company he founded, to Hunter's Specialties in the mid-1980s and helped that firm develop its H. S. Strut line of calls. Anybody who is anybody in the world of turkey hunting knows Ray Eye. But I get the opportunity to be around a lot of "name" hunters, and too many of them want to be celebrities even more than they want to hunt. They morph from die-hard hunters into egomaniac-idiot-jerks. This has not happened to Ray. One reason may be that he has an agreeably twisted sense of humor, which he attributes to poisoning from his early attempts at making diaphragm calls with plumber's lead and expired condoms that he got free from a pharmacist. He likes to wake up hunting clients at 3:30 a.m. by sticking a flash camera ten inches from their faces and yelling, "Wake-up time!"

His practical jokes are legendary among his friends, and he travels with a full-face, professional-quality rubber clown mask. One time, there was a know-it-all teenage boy in the group of hunters Ray was accompanying. The kid's attitude got on Ray's nerves, so he announced that he had to leave that evening to check on another camp and would return the next day. Instead, Ray slept in his truck that night, rose well before dawn, and ensconced himself in the blind where the boy would be hunting that morning. "When that kid backed into the blind with his little penlight, I was half lying down, my face about the level of his thigh," Ray remembers. "In fact, I find people are more afraid of small clowns than big ones. Anyway, he bumped into my leg, turned, and when he lit me up, I said"—and here he slips into an eerily convincing imitation of a psychopathic carnival clown—"'Heh, heh, heh, I'm so happy to see you. I've been waiting for you.'" The kid screamed, dropped his gun, and took off running. Which, according to Ray, was pretty much the idea. The only problem was that the boy was still inside the blind. "He must have moved that thing twenty yards before he finally stopped screaming. I mean just ass-over-teakettle, full-out running. He wrecked the blind, a brand-new Double Bull, big sturdy thing. Just went ape. For a minute I was worried I'd traumatized him for life or something. But he was fine. And it seemed to work. He's been real polite to me ever since." Ray is laughing so hard that he has to wipe his eyes.

As you might expect, Ray gives and receives dozens of abusive phone and e-mail messages each day.

At heart, Ray Eye is a dinosaur. Like pre-1964 Model 70s, he is something they stopped producing long ago: a boy from a family farm in the hardscrabble hills and hollers of the Ozarks of southern Missouri, a place where the Eyes lived for five generations. The plumbing was a limestone spring bubbling up through a rock near the front door, the bathroom was a detached structure with natural wood paneling, the plowing was done behind a horse, and it took a pretty good hike and a pretty good reason to make a telephone call. A boy growing up in that time and place didn't take up hunting and fishing any more than a beagle takes up chasing rabbits. It took him up. Some of Ray's earliest memories are of being carried down the mountain on his father's back in the dark to go duck hunting on some nearby lakes and ponds. He was hunting squirrels and rabbits about as soon as he could walk and was sitting in deer stands alone by the age of seven. He fished, gigged frogs, looked for morels in the spring, and ran traplines for foxes, muskrats, bobcats, coyotes, and raccoons. He was just eaten up with all of it.

The Turkey Mystique

"There was always something mystical about turkeys," Ray says. "You'd hear a gobble way up on the mountain now and then, but you'd almost never see the bird itself." Even the hill people rarely saw them. When he was in fifth grade, Ray got up during show-and-tell and talked about seeing some birds fly over the road at the sound of the family truck. He was promptly sent to the principal's office for lying: Everybody knew wild turkeys were extinct. He recalls a sudden thunderstorm one spring day. With black clouds rolling in and the first peals of thunder rumbling in the distance, the hills suddenly came alive with gobbles resounding from every ridge. "I just stood there with my mouth open," Ray says. "Stupefied." He learned to call with his mouth, since he could make more turkeylike sounds that way than he could with the calls available at the store. He also practiced on the one his grandfather had made: slate salvaged from a schoolhouse blackboard and a striker cut from an old cedar fence post, set in a corncob handle. Mountain folks are secretive people, and the local hunters were especially closemouthed about turkey lore. But even the rumor of someone bagging a gobbler was enough to set the boy begging for a ride to hear the tale and possibly learn a new trick.

Like all young men in the mountains, Ray had to leave to make a living. For a while he worked as a welder and delivered rechromed auto bumpers to shops in East St. Louis. But he hated punching clocks, answering to bosses, and being in a place where all the angles were 90 degrees. Eventually he went home, ran his traps, skinned deer at meat houses, pushed snow with a blade on his Jeep, and guided turkey and deer hunters whenever he got the chance. Often, after a hike of six or eight miles back into the forest to roost a bird at sunset, it made more sense to Ray to burrow into the leaves and sleep there instead of walking out and trying to come back in before first light. The next morning, he'd either kill the bird or not, then head straight to whatever work he had lined up.

Ray had been entering turkey-calling contests since high school, and it was his ability to work his mouth on turkeys and audiences that would eventually bring him fame, if not fortune. "In the seventies, I was still calling with my voice but also making calls," he says. "Guys would ask to buy them at contests. Then stores started carrying them and asking me to come down and demonstrate." One day, during a demo at the local Walmart, a fellow offered Ray three hundred dollars to fill in for a no-show speaker at a turkey seminar being held at the community college. "I walked into an auditorium with three hundred guys in it," Ray remembers. "Talk about a pucker factor." After a few minutes, he discovered that if he just talked the way he did to his hunting buddies, people listened and laughed. So he told them about the time when Uncle Lee guided a new hunter carrying a quail gun who wanted to take a crack at a gobbler that was hung up sixty yards out. Uncle Lee already had the stranger's money, so he agreed, then watched the man drop the gobbler cold. Deer slugs, the man proudly explained, unaware that the ammo was completely illegal during turkey season.

A Skeptical Eye

Ray's lack of pretension hides a dark secret, one that only begins to seep out after you've spent a few days with him: He thinks that most of us weekend turkey hunters are—not to put too fine a point on it—fools. Why, you ask? Because we accept conventional turkey wisdom as truth without testing it for ourselves. Like the idea that birds become call-shy, or that turkeys won't come downhill, or cross water, or go over fences. Or that you shouldn't use turkey calls when you're roosting birds in the evening. Or that turkeys only gobble in the spring. Ray lives in the turkey woods, spring and fall. Spring birds alone consume three months of the year, from the beginning of March until the end of May, from Florida to Hawaii to Texas to the Midwest to New England. If he's not hunting, he's out in the woods gathering video footage of birds. (He has footage of them gobbling in July, crossing three-strand barbed-wire fences, flying across rivers, and running downhill to a caller.) All this time afield has led him to some definite conclusions about what works, what doesn't, and how the weekend hunter approaches things.

"Look, I call up turkeys for numbnuts writers like you for a living," he says, grinning, as if to imply he's just stating what we both already know. "I have to produce."

The lightbulb illuminating what passes for turkey expertise came on early for Ray, when as a boy he read a magazine article that maintained the only way to call in a gobbler was to yelp three times, wait ten minutes, then do it again. He hiked up the mountain, located a tom gobbling on the roost, and proceeded as instructed. After his first yelps got a response, he sat down with his watch to wait. Meanwhile, a real hen started yelping and cutting nearby, the tom answered, and the two of them immediately started calling hot and heavy, found each other, and wandered off. "I was stuck there looking at my damn watch with nine minutes left before I was supposed to call again," says Ray. "That's when I realized the experts didn't know squat."

Subsequent experience has only reinforced that belief. Everywhere he goes, he encounters skeptics, guys who say, "Well, maybe that'll work where you hunt, but it won't work around here." He ignores such talk as much as possible when he's giving a seminar, but every once in a while he's forced to confront the local hotshot. "There was this guy in Alabama one time, and he just wouldn't give up," Ray says. "The seminar became like a gunfight, so I finally agreed to go hunting with him. We're out in the woods in the dark, and he says, 'Go ahead and hoot. But if you don't do it just right, they won't answer.' So I did a pig squeal just to jerk his chain, and a turkey hammered right back." Ray killed that bird. "That guy and I ended up being good friends."

Man Overboard

Once, having capsized a raft while steelhead fishing, I found myself upside down while getting worked over by the rapids. That first stunned moment underwater was like waking to a different world. I didn't know where I was, how I'd gotten there, or that I was in danger. I remember bubbles going in one direction and familiar-looking gear going the other. Bubbles and gear, I thought. I had a vague impulse to follow but couldn't decide which group I belonged in, bubbles or gear. The river itself finally shook me awake just as I was about to fill my lungs with water. I chose bubbles and wriggled to the surface like a tadpole seeking its first breath.

I mention this because I had an encounter a year or so ago that was not dissimilar. I capsized in love. I'd been bopping along in my life— maybe not winning any races but keeping my head above water—and suddenly I was upside down with bubbles going one way and every- thing I knew about myself going the other. I was stunned at the pull I felt for this woman, stunned that a bruised middle-aged skeptic was capable of such feeling. I'd known her for several years but she was married and lived in another city, and our paths seldom crossed. When next they did, we were both separated. I still don't know exactly what it was about her that spoke to me. I do know that I was soon desper- ately in love, and also transformed, energized, and elevated by that love. The only thing I feared more than making a fool of myself was what might happen if I didn't. In short, I had fallen out of the canoe.

I told her. I said that I could feel her presence in my bones. That she seemed to have awakened some unnameable thing that I'd given up for dead. It was full-blown, stage IV love. She was flattered, not without feelings for me, but confused. She asked what I loved about her, why, why now, and how I could be sure. I told her it didn't work that way. Some love doesn't obey traffic signs or bother calling ahead to ask if now is a good time. The fact of it is its reason, its explanation, like a river, it's there. It has always been there. You just never noticed.

In those heady months I remember feeling wonderfully vivid, both more and less like myself than ever before—a bald eighth grader, a boy with a retirement account. She told me that her grown daughter, seeing the two of us together briefly, had pegged me at first glance for a goner. It was true. I began letting other cars merge in front of me. I flattened the barbs on my hooks. I tipped waiters 20 percent.

The relationship was not without friction, unavoidable between strong-willed people but something I thought we could work out. She became tentative, then distant. And one day she showed me the door.

In a just world, the ground would have opened and swallowed me. This world definitely has some work to do in that department. The same love that had buoyed me up now sucked me under. I lost weight and sleep. I replayed certain conversations incessantly in my head. Her absence was palpable, a stone in my stomach. Whereas I had become a shadow. I could walk through a motion-detector alarm and not set it off. Somewhere far above, I knew, the river of the world ran on. I just couldn't muster the will to follow the bubbles up.

Five months in, still sick with grief but increasingly sick of it as well, I did the only thing I could think of. I went fishing. I strapped the canoe to the roof, threw two rods in back, and drove to the river. It was late spring by the calendar and sunny, but the river wasn't buying. It ran high, fast, and cold. The run of migratory white perch was over but there still might be a few herring around. I had a new smoker gathering dust in the basement. Herring, I'd been told, were good candidates.

I anchored at the edge of the main channel, and on the bucktail's second bounce the line quickened with life. The fish shivered and ran for the channel. From twenty feet down, I pulled a herring up into this alien world and admired its coat of bright chain mail. I caught another, then another. When next I looked up, the light had slanted and the fish scales on my pants were winking some lost code. The dead world had come to life again. For the first time in months, I'd inhabited my own body. Beguiled by the river, I'd briefly wriggled up to the surface again. I wasn't all right. I wasn't even close to all right. But I now felt that I might be, in time. Because all the evidence indicated that I was still alive.

The Sky's the Limit

The modern outdoorsman never quite shakes a feeling of being historically misplaced: born too late, domesticated too early. Standing on my front porch, I ponder my neighbors' living AstroTurf. These inedible monocultures, the product of great care and regular doses of poison, are the merit badges of suburban existence. They baffle me. I see them as the upholstery of empty lives. But the true outdoorsman, no matter his neighbors' preoccupations, masters his own fate. Let the clogged gutters and accumulated dryer lint of modern life drive lesser men to desperate measures—male enhancement creams, madness, even golf. Should circumstances keep me from heading to the wilds, I'll make the wilderness come to me, taking adventure where I find it.

Exploit #1. I take Emma to visit my mom, and they decide to bake oatmeal chocolate chip cookies, as I had hoped. Now I will have time to hunt and track the scraggly woods nearby. Although actual hunting is unlawful inside the Capital Beltway, the hunting instinct knows no law and needs no weapon.

A thin belt of woods rims both the inner and outer loops of the Beltway. It's little more than a fig leaf that developers offer homeowners, the pretense that they live somewhere other than a stone's throw from an eight-lane racetrack open twenty-four hours a day. In more than a decade of "hunting" these woods, a Yosemite never more than sixty yards deep, I've yet to encounter another human. Already this year, I've found a lone cedar tree girdled by a rub glowing bright as a yellow lantern in the understory gloom. The tree sits two hundred yards away from the house where I grew up. In short, a bedded trophy deer is likely listening to your radio as you sit snarled in rush-hour traffic.

These woods, inside I-495 and nearest my mom's house, contain lots of deer. I see their trails and tracks, droppings and scrapes. Recently I realized that the woods bearding the outer loop may be even better. Less accessible and thicker, they have steep south-facing slopes that are magnetic to wintering deer. They back up to a private golf club, through which you may not cross to reach this forgotten stretch of public land.

One day it dawned on me that a sewer pipe I'd been driving over for decades was a direct conduit there. The first time through, I was nearly paralyzed by claustrophobia and the roar of eighteen-wheelers overhead. Now the pipe, nearly five feet in diameter, has become my personal wilderness portal. I enter, straddling the two-foot-wide stream running along the bottom. With one hand tracing the top to keep me from bumping my head, I start the eighty-yard duck walk toward a tiny circle of daylight hanging in the distance. Arriving, I slow my pace. At the pipe's mouth, I'm in full-stalk mode. From four feet inside, I watch three does grazing fifteen yards distant, oblivious. They move off after five minutes.

As I take the decisive step into the open and give an involuntary grunt at the pleasure of standing upright, something explodes in the brush ten yards away. It's a buck, flag flying, gone an instant later. He reappears, crossing an opening on the hill, four tines of the right main beam visible, each distinct and tall.

When I return home, Emma, dusted with flour, mouth smeared with chocolate, takes one look at me and says, "Daddy! You're tracking mud into Grandma's kitchen!"

Exploit #2. A weekday afternoon's freak winds—the radio says 28 miles per hour, gusts to 50—have the trees in my neighborhood dancing like Merrill Lynch executives at bonus time. When I suggest to Emma that we go fly a kite, she jumps on the idea. Twenty minutes later, I am stringing up a cheapo Dora the Explorer kite in the local dog park. The fifty yards of string it came with seem limiting, so I've brought a two-piece spinning outfit spooled with 8-pound Stren Super Braid. I hold the kite until the string running between me and the handle in my daughter's hand is taut. When she calls "Now!" I let go.

Soon all fifty yards are out. It's fun enough. But Dora, if she is to be true to her name, needs a longer leash. I attach the fishing line to the handle with a uni knot and open the bail. The kite shoots up like a missile. "Whoa!" Emma shouts, running in little victory circles. In twenty seconds, the kite is six hundred feet up and threatening to spool me. Line zips off so fast it's all I can do to force the bail shut. I hand the rod to Emma. "Dad! It's like the biggest fish ever!" she squeals. She plays the sky fish to one side, then the other, then tows it back a few steps and lets it pull her forward. Eventually, she tires of the marvel, ditching her dad to play with the dogs that have arrived. It takes me long minutes to land Dora. She seems energized by the ride, reluctant for it to end, and bucks hard the whole way. I've never tangled with tarpon on light tackle, but I imagine this might be how it feels. They generally aren't found in the skies above Virginia at this time of year. Unless you know where to look.

Turkeys: Life on the Square

Moving slowly through the forest on an uncharacteristically warm November day, my companion gestures at the disturbed oak leaves and pine needles all around us. "This wasn't here two days ago. They came through and just rototilled this place," he whispers. This is our second stop of the day. We passed the morning in a stand of white oak above a just-cut cornfield. "They're all over the place. I counted forty-six of 'em in a field the other morning."

Gerry Austin drops to one knee and delicately brushes away leaves and needles to reveal a gobbler's J-shaped dropping. He rubs it between his fingers and shows me the little granules that remain.

"Weed seed," he whispers, shaking his head and smiling. The rain this year has transformed the Taghkanic Hills, rolling mixed forest and farmland just east of the Hudson River valley, into a supermarket of mast, berries, and crops. In the midst of this abundance the turkeys have, naturally, opted for weed seed.

Last summer was so dry that by fall the woods were barren. Patterning birds was—comparatively—a breeze. If you saw birds feeding in a field one morning, there was a good chance you'd find them there the next. Gerry got his limit easily and cut two more notches in the handle of his turkey knife. This year's different. Oh, he got the first one easy enough. He ran ("although it ain't exactly runnin' when you're sixty-four years old") out into a flock and busted the birds with a round from his worn Mossberg pump, then set up and called them back. An hour later, a nice hen raised her head once too often as she came cautiously through the tall grass toward his yelp. But that was nearly two weeks ago. Since then, he has hunted more days than not and patterning turkeys has been like trying to predict when Cher's next plastic surgery will take place.

The truth is, Gerry has only been seriously obsessed with wild turkeys since he retired nine years ago. (On the other hand, once he gets interested in something, he doesn't fool around. He's got more than twenty notches on his knife.) Before that he spent twenty-three years with the New York Conservation Department hunting featherless turkeys. He specialized in slob hunters, the kind of guy who decides that whatever walks in front of his gun has just come into season.

"I always figured you take the money, you do the job. And it musta been the right job for me, because, hey, I loved it," he says. He bombed around the back roads of Columbia County in his state car, a pink station wagon. It was dangerous work and the spotlight that came with the car wasn't strong enough, so Gerry replaced the bulb with one from the landing light of a small plane.

"People generally couldn't stop fast enough with that beam bouncing off their rearview," he says fondly. "Only I couldn't keep it on more than a minute before it'd short out."

During deer season he worked around the clock and his wife, Barbara, stocked up on groceries so she could stay by the phone and relay tips to the dispatcher, who'd radio them to Gerry in his car. Once he made ten one-hundred-dollar busts in a single day. Guys up from New York City accustomed to buying their way out of trouble got a rude awakening when they opened their wallets in front of Gerry. Some of the locals didn't much appreciate his zeal, either. He'd give first-time juvenile offenders a second chance, and he knew there were families in his jurisdiction that wouldn't have meat at all unless they took a deer once in a while, but he wasn't big on wiggle room. When it got so he couldn't take his family out to a restaurant without finding his tires slashed, he figured he must be doing something right. "Hey, I always thought you ate better at home anyway."

Gerry silently leads the way past a number of well-built deer stands (one of them his) to a hillock in the middle of the woods from which we can see a hundred yards in every direction. This is old country, settled in the 1700s. What was once pasture is now forest, threaded by stone walls almost decomposing into the leaves like ancient bones. Stuffed in Gerry's pockets are calls of his own making: a three-piece wingbone from a young hen, which he likes in the fall because it gives the high-pitched yelp of a young bird, and two box calls, one sassafras (similarly squeaky) and one chestnut (old reliable).

We set up with our backs against trees and do nothing but listen for ten minutes. Once the squirrels have accepted us and gone back to work, he issues a five-note yelp on the wingbone. We wait. With each puff of wind, a few more of the year's last leaves let go. They fall slowly, like rust flakes in water. A sparrow lands three feet away and bathes in the dust, trying to work out a crick in its neck. Every twenty minutes or so, Gerry calls again.

There comes a moment several hours in when it seems pretty clear we won't be bagging any birds today. It's too warm, the woods too quiet. Still, there are three good reasons for keeping at it: First, wild turkeys never do what they're supposed to. Second, every moment hunting brings you that much closer to your preordained next encounter. Third, nobody has come up with a better way to pass a fall afternoon than sitting quietly in the woods with a shotgun in your lap and hope beating in your heart.

Finally, Gerry stands and stretches, peeling back his head net. I've got to head home, but first he wants me to stop by the house. He shows me some fox, beaver, and muskrat skins in his shed. He likes to recount the stories of how people with weekend houses up here are horrified at the idea of his trapping animals until a beaver girdles the trees in their front yard or a coon hisses them out of their attic. Sitting at the kitchen table he feeds me the black walnut cake Barbara makes from the nuts he gathers each year; the piece is slathered with honey from his hives. We eat slowly and watch goldfinches at the feeder outside his window. A flag flies in the yard.

Gerry's father took off when he was four. His mother died when he was ten. By fourteen, he was earning his own way in the world, and he bounced around quite a bit before settling into the Conservation Department: working on a dairy farm, in a sawmill, pulling a hitch in the air force, and working as a guard in a maximum security prison. Along the way he learned a lot of practical skills, including to never quit a job until he had a better one and to never waste anything: wood, meat, or breath. Although he grew up poor, he was never particularly impressed by money. He figures he's happier than most rich people. On the wall in the living room is a piece of needlepoint given to him by a former secretary. The conservation officer's creed is knitted into it. It reads in part, "... grant that I may earn my meal ticket on the square ... deafen me to the jangle of tainted money and to the rustle of unholy skirts."

The basement is crammed with sacks of hickory nuts and butternuts, split wood for the stove down there that heats the whole house, and uncountable planks of cherry, cedar, walnut, and apple wood he turns into box calls. He doesn't sell them, but he'll give you one if he likes you. Before I leave, he fills my thermos with coffee, loads me up with two jars of honey, a hard maple box call so pretty I don't know whether to use it or put it in a glass case, a three-piece wingbone call, and a bag of deer jerky.

"Too bad we didn't get on any birds," he says as he walks me to my car. I thank him and tell him I had a great time. "Hell, you don't know what a great time is, bub. Come back in May and we'll get you a turkey." I tell him it's a deal.

Grand Guns

My grandfather, who gave my father his name and me mine, died when I was sixteen and still too young to be curious about old men. I do remember that as early as age nine, going to visit my grandparents after church was the best part of Sunday. After ushering in the rest of the family, Granddad would take me aside, lower his voice conspiratorially, and say, "My little .22's waiting in the closet for you." And off I would scamper to get the single-shot, bolt-action rifle, which I dry-fired endlessly, mostly prone on the big Oriental rug in the living room.

It was a Ranger M34, a gun likely made by Marlin for Sears, Roebuck & Company. I studied that rifle. Its lines. They bespoke intention, restraint, and consequence. There was nothing nonessential to that gun. It was unlike anything in my nine years of experience.

I loved shooting that gun—the solid lock of the bolt, how the bead settled into the notch like the moon setting between two hills, the crisp click of the trigger. It was a bond I had with my grandfather. He had originally gotten it for my father and Uncle John back when they were boys and the family lived in the Panama Canal Zone. Granddad set up a rifle range in the basement of their quarters. A large steel plate deflected the bullets into a sandbox. Dad gathered the spent bullets and melted down the lead to make toy soldiers. He had shot a fer-de-lance that he'd found in his tree house with that rifle.

My father? The stern man who shined my shoes before church so ferociously that I often wondered what that particular cow had ever done to him? It was a thunderbolt to realize he'd been a boy who killed extremely poisonous snakes, shot a gun inside the house, and

161

liquefied metal over open flames. It was this object of metal and wood that made me see that.

When the .22 passed to me, I kept it at a friend's farm. It was the cheapest and plainest of the four rifles there. It was also the most accurate.

I never knew Granddad had had any other guns until Uncle John died. I was at his house, near Annapolis, Maryland, while his wife was going through his papers. Lying on the piano stool were a Winchester Model 94 .30/30 and a Colt .380 hammerless stamped U.S. PROPERTY. When I asked Aunt Joan her intentions for the guns, she said, "I'm going to throw them in the Severn River. I don't like guns."

I didn't say anything, but my mind was doing wind sprints. The Severn River, I knew, was largely indifferent to the fate of these firearms. Whereas I suddenly wanted them desperately. I needed them. I let a couple of minutes pass. "Tell you what," I said casually. "I'm headed back that way. I'll throw them in the river for you."

The .30/30 was a shooter. It pointed nicely and had the potential to shoot one-inch groups at a hundred yards. I knew that millions of deer had fallen to such lever-action guns and tried hunting with it. But the top ejection meant it wouldn't take a scope, and the iron sights went dark half an hour before the end of legal light. After watching a few deer disappear into darkness when I shouldered the rifle and tried to aim, I went back to a scoped .270. The smart move would have been to sell it. I didn't make the smart move.

At first I'd thought the Colt was Uncle John's sidearm from the air force. But some digging revealed that such pistols were issued only to brigadiers and above during World War II. That meant just one thing: It was Granddad's gun. All I'd known about his soldiering was that it was a tough act to follow. My father chose the U.S. Naval Academy instead. Granddad had headed the Army Corps of Engineers' 2nd Engineer Special Brigade, a force of 7,000 men and 400 officers engaged in the evolving science of amphibious warfare in the Pacific. The 2nd ESB made eighty-two combat landings and engaged in the longest stretch of continuous combat operations of any military unit during the war. I came across a photo of Granddad from the time. He was all intention and purpose, even standing at attention in some sandy wasteland. Like the .22 itself. The caption read: "Leyte, Philippines. 12 March 1945. Gen. Heavey with Aide, Lt. Williams, at ceremony to present Presidential Citation to Co. A, 542 EBSR. Cocoanut trees in background cut by artillery fire on day of landing."

Collectors pay thousands for these wartime Colts. Granddad's is staying in my gun safe. I check on it every so often. I heft it and somehow feel connected to my co-conspirator at Sunday brunch so long ago, the old man who would lower his voice and tell me that his little .22 was waiting for me in the closet.

Gee Whiz

Pheasant hunting is, by any rational standard, crazy. You spend a bunch of time and money getting to someplace like South Dakota, where they have tons of birds and the government actually enables people to chase them. In most of the country, if the truck ahead of you pulls over and four guys with shotguns hustle out, a logical reaction is to put your vehicle in reverse and floor it. In South Dakota—where it is legal to hunt the ditches along public roads—you just smile and wave.

Once you get to South Dakota, what you want to find is a motel made of cinder blocks—preferably inside and out. Cinder-block construction, generally, signifies a joint that will put up with dirty dogs, dirty shotguns, dirty boots, and the cleaning of colorful nonnative gamebirds in the parking lot. This is a messy job. If I happen to be involved, no one driving by dares stop, including people who already have rooms there.

Three friends and I recently stayed at just such a palace near Pierre. There was Jack Unruh, responsible for the flattering illustrations of me you see on this page each month. I once overheard him saying that he tries to show me as "someone who aspires to be a sex offender but doesn't have the nerve." There was another old friend, Richard Stucky, a farmer from Kansas. He has done more hunting and fishing than anyone I know. He does his best to disguise that he can't begin to fathom how I—a guy who nearly fell over backward in fear the first time he flushed a pheasant at close range—am allowed to write for a national outdoor magazine. And there was a friend of Richard's, Brett Soileau, a Cajun whose machine shop makes custom tools for oil companies. Brett should be made to hunt with a .410 loaded with Ping-Pong balls. He dropped everything he shot at and usually limited out in the first hour. This made me wish that he were less likable and that I could understand his accent. These guys had four dogs they had trailered from as far away as Dallas. One of them wandered over to me, tail wagging, and casually peed on my feet. "No big deal," Jack said. "It's a dominance thing."

You can't hunt pheasants in South Dakota until the civil hour of 10 a.m. We nevertheless rose at 6 sharp, mostly because Richard and Brett are country boys who can't sleep any later. We'd mess about with the dogs, speculate about the weather and the birds, and then go to a diner. The deal here was to drink several gallons of coffee each and discuss the merits of hash browns, home fries, and "breakfast potatoes," which are just french fries that have been run through a garbage disposal. Then we would compare ham, bacon, and sausage.

The actual hunting involved fighting your way through fields of thick, head-high vegetation. This included millet, milo, cane, and other crops that Richard would patiently reidentify for me each day in the hope that some of it would take. We'd set up a blocker at the far end of each field and advance with the dogs leading. I felt privileged to witness the nearly telepathic connection between men and the dogs they have trained to disobey them. As soon as the dogs were released, they bolted so fast I could have sworn I heard the whoosh of outgoing e-mail. "Back, Daisy!" the dog's subordinate would yell. "Dammit, you boneheaded mutt, I said back!" You didn't see the dogs. You followed their progress by the rippling stalks, rather like the scarier scenes in *Lost*. Meanwhile, approximately all of the pheasants in the field would pitch out of it well beyond gun range, set their wings, and kite downwind. They do have a lovely glide.

Smarter, saner men would learn from this experience. Us, we kept at it. Eventually, after loading and unloading the same two shells a dozen times, you'd be fighting your way through another field of head-high Velcro when you'd get lucky. A feathered Bouncing Betty would detonate six feet away, making more noise than anything with feathers ought to be capable of. And then the big bird would helicopter itself up and fly straight into the sun, making it impossible to determine whether it was a rooster ("Shoot, dimwit!") or a hen ("Don't shoot, dimwit!").

Occasionally, a bird would actually offer a shot. In past outings, I'd been complimented on my efforts at conservation of pheasants by shotgun. For this reason, I'd been shooting trap regularly. It paid off. There were at least three times—possibly four—over the three days of hunting when I was personally responsible for the death of a pheasant, including one that caused Richard to bob his head in a gesture of respect. "Heckuva shot, Bill. Way above your potential."

On the last afternoon, on the last push, the sun lit up the fields with amber light against dark clouds. The low hills undulated to the horizon, looking—I guessed—much as they had for thousands of years. I was crunching my way along, hopeful of flushing a bird. I was pleasantly tired. I was hanging out with guys who liked and understood one another. It struck me that I was happy.

Back at the motel, the four of us crowded into one room and helped ourselves to Jack's bourbon in plastic cups. I asked Jack what the hunt dates were for next year. I told him I was in. And that while I still thought pheasant hunting was crazy, I'd realized it was the kind of crazy that worked for me.

Dyeing to Connect

Emma is fifteen, the age at which she wonders why it took so long to see that you, her father, are an idiot. It's not just that you are clueless about who she really is. You also embarrass her, mostly by existing. You talk to people you don't know, which is totally uncool. You ignore her request to walk behind her at the mall so that no one will suspect you're related. You choose inopportune moments to channel the Jamaican man who lives inside you.

A child's developmental task at this age is to separate from her parents. And since I only see Emma on alternate weekends, she has to pack a lot of rebellion into that time. She does this by wearing earbuds all the time, including in the shower. She dresses in clothes that would be appropriate at a tomato fight with zombies. Knowing that her father hunts, she declares herself a vegetarian. She mostly eats pizza, as long as it doesn't have any vegetables on it. Overwhelmed, I look to parenting books. These are all written by experts with grown children, some of whom benefited greatly from drug treatment programs. The books assure me that my daughter still needs me. She needs my love and attention. She needs me to set limits so she knows what to rebel against. And she needs me to drive her to buy the purple dye she is applying to her hair at this moment.

Every fifteen minutes, I am summoned to the bathroom to paint bleach or dye on another strand of hair, which she then wraps in tinfoil. The Splat Oxide label says the bottle may explode if left unused for more than two minutes. A drop on the toilet seat burns right through the paint. The color Emma chose is Lusty Lavender. I wish that I were making this up.

It wasn't long ago that my daughter would fish and shoot her bow. Now, the fact that I approve of these activities is reason enough to reject them. I even tried forbidding them. This was met by the kind of eye-roll that only a fifteen-year-old girl can do, the kind that would strain the ocular muscles of a normal person. She said, "That's, like, Child Psychology 101. I'm not an idiot, you know."

"I never said you were an idiot." I knew as I spoke that this was a textbook example of the wrong thing to say. But I'd already said it.

"Yes you do! All the time!"

"Like when?" Again, huge mistake. (Why was I taking the bait? What was wrong with me?)

"Like right now! Like whenever you're awake!"

I said nothing.

These days, getting her outside for longer than it takes to walk to the car is a victory. Recalling that Emma had once voiced an interest in shooting, I decided to get her a sporting clays lesson. The chief qualification for the coach was that he not be me. I called Rhys Arthur, a noted Level III instructor. Unfortunately, the lesson fell on the day after I'd briefly confiscated her phone for refusing to surrender it by 9:30 p.m. When it comes to taking revenge, the Mafia has nothing on teenage girls. Emma waited until we arrived to announce that she had no intention of shooting. I remembered a therapist's words. "When your kid is pushing your buttons, don't react. You have to be like Lucite." I breathed deeply. I tried to picture myself encased in polymerized methyl methacrylate. I couldn't. What I saw was more like a dry cleaner's bag. "Okay," I said brightly. "No problem." I took the lesson while Emma sulked, earbuds firmly in place beneath her earmuffs. At a certain point I missed four birds in a row, prompting a rare smile. Rhys saw the opening and got her to try his .410. "Forget about the gun," he said. "Just focus on the bird." Em missed her first two shots but dusted the third. She smiled again—twice in one day!—then caught herself. Remembering her mission, she sat down and rededicated herself to sulking.

It was a forty-five-minute drive to her mother's. I was desperate for one moment of connection before the weekend was over. I invited her to plug her phone into the car stereo and play me a song she liked. It was "I'm There" by Hey Violet. It wasn't bad. I told her I liked it. Part of the chorus went:

'Cause no one wants to be alone . . .
You just have to say the word and I'm there

Something happened during that ride. Somehow we both softened a bit. Being the target of her resentment and anger hadn't been fun. But maybe I'd misread them. Maybe they were symptoms of things deeper and harder to express—the fear and confusion of being a teenager. Maybe what she needed wasn't fatherly wisdom and advice. Maybe what she needed was something more fundamental, simpler—the knowledge that her father loved her beyond all reckoning. That he would always love her, no matter what. That was one thing that I did know how to do.

When I dropped her at Jane's I had to sort of corral her into a hug. She resisted at first. After a moment she gave in and hugged me back. "I love you, monk," I said. "Always will." I squeezed. "Love you, too, Daddy," she murmured. And then my purple-haired daughter skipped up the steps to her mother's door.

Buddy Trip

The author and artist—colleagues and longtime pals—set out on a trout fishing adventure in the Wyoming wilderness. But an episode of true and honest fear changes everything.

Knee-deep in a riffle on a pristine trout stream high in the Wind River Range, I'm getting ready to cast into the next pool. I'm three days into a five-day, pack-in-on-horseback fishing trip, and I'm feeling a little anxious. I'm not used to having this many things go right at the same time. There seem to be trout in every pool. I'm catching some of them. On a fly rod. But the real kicker? For the first time ever, I'm hooking more trout than trees. It's great but also a little spooky.

I lay out a false cast, release the next, and the Royal Wulff drops right where I was aiming. Then comes a splash and a glimpse of a square tail. I'm still not over the shock and awe of consistently hooking more things with gills than growth rings. I stand there transfixed, with no more sense than a man at the yard sale taking place in his own navel who has just discovered the tool bin. The singing reel jolts me back. The fish darts around the pool like someone caught in a fire and frantically trying a series of locked doors. I bring it to hand. It's a fat 12-inch brookie, nobody's monster, but more than good enough for me.

Damn I'm glad Michelle and I decided to do this. And we wouldn't have except that Jack Unruh, who'd already booked the trip for himself and his wife, Judy, invited us along. I first encountered Jack around 2002, courtesy of the aggressively insulting caricatures of me that he drew each month on the back page of this magazine. (Jack is a celebrated illustrator, revered by his peers, who has won every major illustrator's award possible. In 2006, he was even installed in the Illustrators Hall of Fame. Next to the dryer in the men's room, I believe.) For such an accomplished artist, he didn't seem to have much range when it came to drawing me. I was always one of two things: clueless moron or depraved psycho. That's not fair. He sometimes created hybrids of these, the depraved moron or clueless psycho. No matter which version of me showed up, I could count on several constants: yellow, bloodshot eyeballs, an oversize red nose, and way more blue mascara than I normally wear.

In 2003 or so, having had enough, I went to Dallas with the intent of telling Unruh exactly what I thought of him. I was disappointed that he wasn't the jerk I'd hoped for. He was about twenty years older, a far nicer guy than I am, but also a whack job with a twisted sense of humor. We both loved to hunt and fish. We were both sons of military pilots. Anyway, I never did get around to telling him off. Instead, we went dove hunting on the lease of some wealthy friend of Jack's. I remember that there weren't many birds and that I lost my favorite Filson jacket. And somehow Jack and I became friends.

Ever since, once or twice a year, we've come to count on persuading the editors of this magazine to send us on some boondoggle of a hunting or fishing trip. It's on these pursuits of birds and fish that our friendship has grown. Like most male friendships of consequence, ours remains studiously unacknowledged. As Jack's friend, it's my duty to help him overcome his inability to draw me accurately. On this trip, as on others, I'm doing that the only way I know, which is by helping myself to his fly box each day and to his flask of what tastes like really expensive bourbon each evening.

I look the Royal Wulff over. I know its name only because Jack called it that as he handed it to me this morning. It was new then and looked like a confused little bird in a red vest and fuzzy black shorts, wearing white tails. Jack described it as "a hairwing fly" and "a good prospector." Having no idea what any of this meant, I nodded sagely and put it in my box. Now, repeatedly savaged by trout, the Royal

Wulff is a shapeless lump of feather and fur. The only part that still looks okay is the hook. I remind myself to get more flies from Jack tonight.

Trout Camp

The trip started when we flew to Lander, where we met up with George Hunker, a former National Outdoor Leadership School instructor and an unconscionably fit guy for a man my age. George runs the Orvis-endorsed Sweetwater Fishing Expeditions and has been guiding since 1977. His son, Hank, is assisting on the trip. They weighed our gear, editing it down to fifty pounds each to spare the horses on the five-and-a-half-hour ride. Jack's wife, Judy, had to stay home after breaking her foot two weeks before the departure. The remaining slots were taken by a couple from Indiana, Mike and Carole Edwards.

I'd heard about the Winds all my life without ever knowing much about them. They're a remote one-hundred-mile range, stretching through Wyoming along the crest of the Continental Divide. The Winds have eight summits over 13,500 feet and get so much snow that the backcountry is usually only accessible from mid-July to mid-September. Our camp at about 9,500 feet sits near a stream that George has forbidden me from naming. He will permit me to say it's on the eastern side of the range.

The stream is so overpopulated—brookies, rainbows, cutthroats, and hybrids—that you catch them even when you aren't trying. Yesterday, one hit my fly trailing behind me as I waded through water I'd just fished. They aren't monster trout. Most are 9 or 10 inches, and my biggest so far is probably no more than 13 inches. Catching fish consistently on a fly rod is so novel that size doesn't matter. I'm just crazy for more, hoping to get some muscle memory of success.

At dinner that evening, as I sip Jack's bourbon from a steel cup, George tells of bigger trout in the lakes above. It's two hours' walk and a thousand-foot gain in elevation to the nearest one. Mike is eager to get at bigger fish. So is Jack, which surprises me. I still haven't completely adjusted to the altitude and find myself battling a frequent mild headache and lack of zip. Jack's legs have been cramping up at night to the point that when he needs to pee, it's easier for him to crawl a few feet out of his tent and do it than to try to stand. Last night, he peed a perfect *P* in the dirt, which he proudly shows to anyone who cares to see it. I help myself to another drink. "Take it easy, dammit," Jack says. "I didn't bring that much."

"You can share mine when we run outta yours," I tell him.

"You brought whiskey?" he asks. "Why aren't you drinking yours?"

"I'm trying to broaden my tastes."

"What'd you bring?"

"Rum," I say.

"Never liked it."

"You could learn. Hell, it's not hard."

The Climb

We head out the next morning for the lake and bigger fish. It's steep walking. After an hour, at 10,000 feet with another five hundred to go, we stop for water. "Especially important to stay hydrated at altitude," George tells us. "You get behind, it's pretty hard to drink enough to catch up." He and Hank scamper around like mountain goats, scouting the path ahead and waiting for us to catch up. My head hurts and I'm sucking air as if I get paid by the lungful. And then we top out and find ourselves looking over a huge bowl of a meadow with a picture-book lake set into the far end, at the base of a thousand-foot rock wall. There are open spaces and belts of trees backing up to the wall and boulders the size of houses in the clear blue lake. It's another twenty-minute walk—flat ground, thankfully—to the fishy part of the lake, where we break out our rods.

As gorgeous as this place is, I don't feel like doing much of anything. Jack looks a little weak as well. Nonetheless, he gamely puts his rod together and starts stalking the shore. I'm impressed at how well he's holding up and wonder whether I'll have the stamina for hikes at

10,000 feet in twenty years. I put my hat over my eyes and lie back in some brush to stay dry while I nap. I'm past pretending I feel good when I don't. But I can't sleep, so I get up, put my rod together, and start fishing. No doubt there are some big trout in this lake, but I don't see any cruising, and the water's so transparent that it feels like one false cast would spook anything within a quarter mile.

When I see Jack again, he's a hundred yards away, casting from atop one of the boulders. I can't tell if he's catching anything. Around 2 p.m., George says it's time to start back. Jack and Hank have already left, hoping to pick up any fish cruising the shoreline before the rest of us spook them. We catch up with them at the lake's outflow, where Jack happily reports catching four fish, all 16 or 17 inches. He's smiling, but also looks tired.

The Descent

It's rougher going down than coming up. George admits he has lost the faint trail but says we should hit it soon. We're slogging through a fair amount of downed timber and brush. At a certain moment, I hear an "Ooof!" behind me and turn to see Jack sprawled in the brush. Michelle, Hank, and I rush up to him. "Goddammit!" he says, more embarrassed than hurt. "There was a limb down there and for some reason I thought it would give way," he says. "I don't know why." He huffs again. "But it didn't." We rest for a few minutes. Jack needs help getting up. "I never had my damn legs go out like this before," he says. He sounds irritated. I offer to take his pack—we're each carrying ten pounds of extra layers and rain gear, and Jack has his big sketchbook—but he's not buying it. "I'm fine."

A half hour later, it's clear that Jack is not fine. He hasn't fallen, but his face is pale, his gait slower and less steady. Wordlessly, by exchanging glances, Michelle, Hank, and I arrive at an understanding: They'll walk just far enough ahead to seem unconcerned and I'll stick with Jack. Where the terrain allows, I walk beside him. If not, close behind. For ten years, we've been tramping around together more or less as equals. But something has shifted. Suddenly I'm worried for Jack in a way I have never been before. My own weakness just stops mattering. I need to watch out for Jack now. "Hell, bud, lemme take that pack."

"Nope," he says. A little later, he stops to take off his Stetson and wipe his brow with a pink bandanna. Jack is the only fisherman I know who could combine a pink bandanna and a Stetson and not look silly. He's drenched in sweat now and sucking wind. His skin is grayer. I'm past worried; I'm scared. He's out of reserves, running on pure stubbornness. If he falls again, he might not be so lucky. And it's a long ride out if anything goes wrong. "Whew," he says, and his voice has gotten smaller. "I'm outta gas, bud." I know he's in bad shape, just not how bad, and whether it will lead to something worse.

"I'm getting pretty low myself," I tell him. "But it can't be much farther." Meanwhile, without my permission, the fear that something might happen to this man cracks me open like an egg. My fear floods and overwhelms me. And what I slowly realize is that the fear stems from something I didn't even know I was hiding from myself, which is how much I love this man, how much his friendship means to me. I don't like these thoughts. I want to shrug them off, push them away. They leave me exposed and vulnerable, and that's not a place I want to be.

I try to outthink my fear. *You're overreacting*, I tell myself. Jack, while exhausted, is in no immediate danger. The problem is that a threshold has been crossed. His momentary frailty forces me to confront a different kind of frailty, one not of the moment. Which is that at some point—whether now or in a year or in twenty-five years—Jack will die. No surprise there. I have days when my own immortality seems doubtful. The surprise is that I'm suddenly aware of how large a hole his passing will leave in my life.

Shape up, dumbass. You've got a job here. The next thing I know, I hear myself ordering Jack to hold up a moment. I walk up to him and wordlessly unsling his pack from his back and put it atop my own. I find a suitable stick, break it to staff length against a rock, and put it into Jack's right hand, cupping his fingers around it. I don't look at him as I do these things. I don't know how he's taking them. It doesn't matter how he's taking them. "That stick's a good idea," he says, forcing the tiniest note of cheer into his voice. I'm not sure whether he has actually rallied a bit or is faking it for my benefit. I almost don't want to know. I'm still flooded, staggered by my new knowledge. I can barely contain the guerrilla feelings—love, fear, and astonishment at being so split open—that have breached my perimeter. This, I tell myself, is exactly the kind of crap that happens when what you know in your head migrates south into your heart. I'm not the type who makes friends fast or easily. The truth, I realize, is I don't really know how Jack and I became friends. I don't know why he is so important to me. I know that I'm lucky to have him as a friend. At the same time, it hurts. Because I won't always have him.

"Can't be much farther, bud," I tell him. "What idiot thought this was a good idea anyway?"

"Us," Jack says. We keep walking.

At last, I see Michelle and Hank ahead of us. They say nothing, but both are waving and smiling. They're at the stream. We're back. All we have to do is cross the water. Michelle gets on one side of Jack and I get on the other. The three of us lock arms and wade across. The water, although fast, doesn't even reach our knees. No one says a word about what has happened. George announces that dinner will be ready in a couple of hours. Jack sloughs off his boots and crawls into his tent. I sit down on a log with Michelle and hold her hand for several minutes.

Two hours later, Jack emerges. He's tired—we all are—but his color is better and he's in good spirits. He lifts his flask at me: "You earned a drink today, bud."

"You're running low there," I tell him. "I'm drinking rum tonight."

Jack squints. "You're drinking your own stuff?" he asks. He shakes his head gravely. "Heavey, you sure you're feeling okay?" Everybody laughs, including me. Jack's back. Everything's okay.

Crash Course

I had turned the wheel hard left twenty seconds ago, but the houseboat wasn't cooperating. It was still headed for the shoreline like it couldn't wait to butt heads with some very solid-looking cypress trees. They were thirty yards off and closing fast. Michelle, the kids, and I were ten minutes into a relaxing three days of houseboating on Florida's Suwannee River. We'd been wrong about the relaxing part. Might have to rethink the three days, too.

Time crawls when bad things happen, allowing you a final—but not particularly useful—flashback. Now I'm six years old, sitting atop a ten-cent Speedy the Race Car ride outside the supermarket. As it lumbers from side to side, I spin its ornamental steering wheel, pretending I'm taking a curve. This ride was like that, only bigger and with a different ending.

I was about to yell a warning when the steering kicked in. We took out some branches but missed the trunks and came away with beards of Spanish moss decorating the front rail. Then the boat decided to try the same thing on the opposite shore.

A houseboat sounded so serene. I imagined learning a new river and resuming my quest to interest the kids in fishing. The Suwannee— a federally designated wild river and the only unspoiled waterway in the Southeast—seemed ideal. Stephen Foster, who never saw it, immortalized it in song. Editor-at-large T. Edward Nickens, who did, pronounced it "panfish heaven."

Having never piloted anything larger than a canoe, I wondered about the competency angle. Turns out the sole requirement to rent a houseboat is a valid credit card. Bill Miller, the guy who runs Miller's Marina (suwanneehouseboats.com) in Suwannee, Florida, gave us charts, a manual, and verbal instruction. We were not to run the boat at night, not to leave the river, and not to even think about docking. The two canoes we had in tow were for going ashore, exploring, and fishing side creeks. Bill's son gave us a brief tutorial on the water. He asked if I'd ever seen *Tokyo Drift*. "Just the trailer," I said. "Where they say, 'If you ain't outta control, you ain't in control.'"

"That's it!" he said. "It's like that, sort of a controlled skid." I tried to look like I understood. He had me turn the boat left, right, then in a circle. He said I seemed to have the hang of it and motored off in a skiff. The barge was 44 feet long and 14 feet wide. I felt like I'd just been placed in charge of an aircraft carrier.

Pretty much everything turned out to be different from what we'd expected. The head had been designed for hobbits, not humans. The powerful current meant that it took hours to cover even a few miles. A local bass tournament had been postponed for two months due to high water. The fish were so deep in the cypress swamps that you could lose your way getting to them. Maybe it *was* panfish heaven—because heaven isn't the easiest place to get into.

Unbeknownst to us, however, the river's alchemy had already kicked in. We ate when hungry, went to bed when it got dark, and rose when daylight came. The kids forgot that we didn't have the Internet. They made forts out of pillows and bedsheets on the roof. They chased each other all over the boat. They'd pop up as I drove, goofy faces smushed into the glass in front of me. They grumbled about not getting to swim until we spotted a 12-foot gator. "Okay," Emma said. "Change in plans."

Eventually you get the hang of steering. You don't command something this size. You coax it. It wasn't hard. It just required your undivided attention. You had to be in the moment, which also encompassed twenty seconds hence, the interval before the boat responded. At first, I was frustrated that driving left me unable to supervise the kids' fishing. But this was more river alchemy. It turned out to be a godsend.

Left to themselves, the kids picked up rods when they felt like it. They cast where and how they wanted. I nearly blurted out that there wouldn't be fish in the fast water, but for once I had the sense to shut up. Catching fish seemed beside the point. They were having fun. They kept at it a good while, far longer than they ever had with me. What they'd needed all along was for me to get out of the way. Like so many truths, this one stung a bit. But it was undeniable.

Looking back, that realization—so obvious, so hard to see—was my highlight of the trip. The art of vacations, like all journeys, lies in letting go of what you'd hoped to find so you can discover what's really there. I'd been shown just how much of my ego had been masquerading behind my desire to "teach" the love of fishing. Because you can't teach it. Each person has to learn it for himself. What the kids needed to learn it were the tools and the space.

Besides, I can't wait to teach them how to drive a houseboat.

Bass Land

I've just busted into my boss's office like the Energizer Bunny, had him sign off on a few things to pump his ego, asked his advice on several matters I've already settled, and hurried out as if my one sorrow in life is that there aren't more hours in the day to do his bidding. Now I'm back in my office, computer burning like one of those convenience store fire logs, papers scattered strategically across my desk so that you have to look hard to see what I'm really doing. An innocent man serving nine-to-five in the workforce until his conviction is overturned needs an occasional break. Me, I'm going catalog fishing.

I open up the glossy 420-page four-color wish-book and it's like someone's squirting Hawg Scent directly into my imagination. It's part Publishers Clearing House and part Disneyland, a place where big fish happen to little people and our favorite myths are real. Look, here's a little woman in her fifties from Weedsport, New York, holding up a tiger muskie with a head the size of a coal shovel. How'd she get that sucker into the boat? Over here are a couple of guys who look like they've just been hit with a stun gun, holding up bass so fat they would have exploded if somebody hadn't caught them that very day. And here comes a retired policeman who dredged up a Castaic Lake lunker just a couple of pounds shy of that 22-pound, 4-ounce record. It doesn't look like a bass with its mouth open; it looks like the hole in your clothes dryer with gill plates and fins attached. Hey, it coulda been you or me. I got the very same manufacturer's jig and garlic-scented sparkle frog trailer in my box right now.

I like it in here. It's cozy. All my favorite bassin' pals are right between these shellacked covers. Like Ole Uncle Buddy holding up a stringer of stone-dead crappies, with two beautiful children from the talent agency who would file a lawsuit if forced to touch an actual fish. And those two dudes, with chins like Superman's and headlight teeth, wearing teal and persimmon "fishing shirts," sitting in heavy hydrilla aboard a boat cleaner than a surgical hospital, with Mayan-inspired hieroglyphs on the side, who have managed simultaneous hookups of fish the size of Andre the Giant. They both look kinda pleased, as well they should.

I love these pictures. I want them to be true. I want one of those once-in-five-years hookups, and that gruff uncle with the gold-plated heart to keep the kids away from me while I'm fishing. Hey, I don't just want these things; I deserve them. That two-hundred-dollar spinning reel with seven stainless-steel ball bearings already endorsed by NASA in case there are bass in deep space. I'm entitled to that, along with the commemorative baitcaster and those new lures endorsed by bass pros as "the fish-gettin'est piece (titanium, Naugahyde, or high-molecular-weight thermo-setting polymer) I've ever tied on a line!" I must have the banana-scented grubs and lures that fly away from me and do-nothing lures with cooked-in pork fat and goop that simulates the "real molting fluid" of crayfish so that my sportsmanlike artificial lure is twice as enticing as live bait. I covet the tandem Willowleaf/Colorado spinnerbaits hand-hammered by mad Swiss elves until they gleam in the dark and Teflon-coated hooks so sharp you can splice genes with 'em. My head is swimming under the strain of all the things I long to own.

And then, for just a second, there is a moment of calm, like when the roller coaster runs out of momentum just as you crest the Big Rock Candy Mountain, or that twinkling when you suddenly notice that the wind you've been casting into all day has blown itself out. I take a deep breath, remembering who and what I am. I ask myself, *Do I really need all this stuff?* I mean in my heart of hearts. There is a nanosecond of deep reflection before the answer comes back fast and straight as truth's arrow: Damn right I do! All of it! I need hook bonnets! I need that graphite rod with the Portuguese cork handle so sensitive it'll pull you overboard if a dragonfly lands on the tip, and the camouflage lock-back knife with Parkerized blade I'll lose the first time I set it down on the ground between my feet. Never mind that some of the new soft jerk baits look like what happens if you step on a tube of toothpaste by mistake. Never mind that I don't need a lure retriever shaped like a hound dog or glasses with an FM radio built in or a Nostalgia Tin of last year's lures. I want these things. I want them almost bad enough to pay real money for them.

My phone rings. It's my boss. He wants to know if I meant to give him a coupon for five bucks off a self-cleaning fish scaler that plugs into his car lighter. Suddenly I'm back from Bass Fantasy Land, back with my computer and my nine-to-five. But now I'm ready for a real break in the routine.

Three weeks later it's the second day of a two-day solo canoe float down the upper part of the Rappahannock. Last night I lay on the sand before pitching my tent and wiggled around to hollow out places for my shoulders, hips, and spine. I breaststroked in place while the current's fingers stroked the kinks out of my body, and with the help of dry pine needles got a fire going with my first match. I rubbed garlic cloves over a small steak and cooked it rare, washed it down with two cans of beer, and had three peaches for dessert. Then the summer night sounds came up behind the river's singing, and I watched the embers fade until they looked like the lights of an orange city far below me.

This morning, poking around in thigh-deep water downstream, I found a ledge below which three identical 14-inch smallmouths fell for a smoke-white grub on a one-sixteenth-inch jighead. Two shook their heads at me in anger as they sputtered over the surface like drops of oil in a hot pan. The third fish dove deep, then rocketed north to execute a series of nearly splashless backflips, as if the key to throwing the hook lay in altitude alone. It had taken me a day to leave the world of timesheets and deodorant behind, but this morning it felt like the line to each fish ran through the rod, up my arms, and tightened around something in my chest. Now I look up as a pair of kingfishers flies dose patrol, keeping the shallows honest, and up high a red-shouldered hawk is circling, waiting for any snake, frog, or crayfish to make a mistake. I decide to rest the spot and try it with a different lure after breaking camp.

Now I'm sitting on my island with my feet in the river, sun beating down on me. I like this place, the river splitting around it as if to seal it off from the outside world. And I know that as soon as I get in the canoe the trip's half-over. I fuss with my tackle-sharpening hooks and cleaning yesterday's spiderwebs and crud out of rod guides. As I pull a new floater/diver crankbait from its plastic lamination, the flier inside helicopters down. It tell me where to send my check for a polyester hat, a sportsman's terry-cloth towel, and a patch to sew on my shirt. What seemed so seductive under fluorescent light is absurd out here, a slice of chemically processed tree with ink stains on it. I crumple it up and put it on last night's ashes, cover it with twigs, and strike a match to start water for a final cup of coffee. The plastic flares like a matchhead, the flier wrinkles and blackens, and I'm glad the packaging hasn't gone to waste. I tie the lure on, flattening the barbs with the forceps I keep around my neck. It's time to get back on the water and see who's interested in this thing.

Point Well Taken

For many people, Cape Hatteras is the quintessential Outer Banks experience. Walking the windswept beach along the "graveyard of the Atlantic," whose treacherous shoals have claimed ships for four centuries, they experience the same stark beauty and wild solitude that you feel when you show up at Potomac Mills and realize your wallet did not make the trip with you. Personally, I like Cape Hatteras because the fish do.

Almost every day of the year, you will find people standing in the surf at the tip of the cape holding oversize rods in their hands, waiting to get lucky. Often they do. There are big bluefish, striped bass, and flounder in the spring; smaller "tailor" blues, Florida pompano, spot, and croaker in the summer; and speckled trout, more big blues, and striped bass in the fall.

Around Thanksgiving, while the rest of the country is sitting down to turkey dinners, surf fishermen up and down the East Coast take leave of their senses and their families to journey to Cape Hatteras in search of red drum. When you want to bang a big drum, the largest fish you can reliably catch while standing on the beach, this is the place to do it.

The current world record, a 94-pound, 2-ounce monster so big it looks like a Styrofoam stage prop, was taken here in 1984 by Dave Deuel, a scientist with the National Marine Fisheries Service. In the photo, man and fish look about the same size and look equally stunned. Eleven years earlier to the day, the old record, a 90-pounder, was hooked from the same place. Any serious fisherman would trade his wife's car for a shot at a fish like that.

What's special about this section of the 175-mile-long Outer Banks, the ever-shifting barrier islands between the ocean and the sounds of the North Carolina coast, is the same thing that's special about Rolling Rock beer: the water. Oceanographers consider Hatteras to be the dividing line between the two great basins of the East Coast, the Mid-Atlantic Bight (Cape Cod to Cape Hatteras) and the South Atlantic Bight (Cape Lookout to Cape Canaveral). Here the two currents collide and stir up a kind of aquatic Miracle-Gro for fish. As the single best sentence in *Coastal Fishing in the Carolinas* puts it: "This is a violent feeding ground for the strongest predators, a trap for the weak, a graveyard for the unlucky." Sounds a little like the Beltway, no?

November is the height of the season, when adult red drum congregate in the ocean water cuts between barrier islands to spawn before heading out to winter in the open ocean. Red drum—also called channel bass and redfish—are beautiful copper-colored fish with a distinctive black spot on the tail; they may live to be fifty. Sadly, their numbers have been declining in recent years.

Bob Eakes, the owner of the Red Drum Tackle Shop in Hatteras, doesn't even try to explain the reasons for the mysterious power *Sciaenops ocellatus* has over grown men. He just gives me the facts. No. 1, it's not about putting food on the table. Only "puppy" drum, the ones under ten pounds, are good to eat. The big guys, which regularly reach weights of forty to sixty pounds, are nearly always released alive. No. 2, they're wary critters. While, say, a bluefish will rip into anything that doesn't bite it first and flounder are so gullible they've been caught on bottom-fished hankies, red drum only take the freshest, juiciest baits. Many anglers spend the day playing musical mullet, roving from bait shop to bait shop in search of the freshest offerings. No. 3, they don't like light. Although you can fish for them any time of day, nighttime is the right time.

Eakes is a blond, blustery man who has been up for two days straight coping with the Thanksgiving rush of anglers. But he's not too tired to pass up prime fishing. After I rent a surf rod and reel from him and buy a pair of Red Ball chest waders, I'm still hanging around pestering him with questions. "Tell you what," he finally says across the counter. "You come back 'round dark and I'll take you out fishing at the Point. But don't come late or all you'll see is my taillights."

By eight o'clock we are passing beneath the 208-foot brick lighthouse at the Cape Hatteras National Seashore and Eakes is shifting his truck into four-wheel drive for the sand. All ruts lead straight toward the Point, the place where Cape Hatteras disappears beneath the waves and continues as Diamond Shoals, nine miles of ever-shifting sandbars that have been claiming ships for four hundred years.

The Point narrows to a few yards wide, with Jeeps and trucks parked tightly together. Just feet away is a surf roiling like nothing I've ever seen. It's not big, just restless and afflicted, like something that desperately wants to rest but can't.

It's drizzling slightly as we suit up in chest waders and trudge toward the water. There must be sixty men crammed shoulder-to-shoulder on this spit armed with heavy surf rods, casting six-ounce pyramid sinkers and heavily baited hooks out into the night wind. Each wears a little flashlight around his neck and shines it up against his line periodically to check the tension and see if his sinker has drifted or held tight. Nobody needs to tell me this is no place for beginners.

Eakes finds an open spot and says, "You might want to let me cast your first one out. These fellas can get a little touchy . . ." I hand him my rod before he can even finish his sentence. He slogs out into the surf and slings my bait up into the dark.

I hold the rod and take my place with the others. We stand. After each wave you shift your feet so the undertow doesn't dig you into a hole. We stand some more. No one talks. The water tugs at our legs and lets go, tugs again and lets go again as if it can't decide what it wants from us. Then we stand some more.

Then something strange happens. Time flattens out, leaping off my digital watch and into the landscape. We're waiting, but suddenly it's no longer a matter of seconds, minutes, and hours. It's about tides and currents and wind. It's the moon and migration and mating, the forces that pull at the blood of the fish and tell them when to go. We know they're out here. Several big ones were landed last night. When they're ready, they'll move.

Suddenly I understand the fever. Peel off the externals of high-tech reels and monofilament line and what you have is an aboriginal tribe of men standing stiff-legged in the surf on the edge of the world, waiting in the night to catch a fish that has so preyed upon their hunters' brains that they return year after year whether they are successful or not. The great thing is to take your place, to be there when the big ones are running.

Through the wet air comes a muffled cry: "Fish on!" A man moves forward into the surf, his rod bent and struggling as he lets the fish take line on its first powerful run, the reel hissing its surprise. Two more runs and five minutes later, he has brought the copper-colored animal onto the sand. Flashlight in mouth, he kneels in a circle of light, one hand gently pressing the fish's belly to keep it from injuring itself. Sea creatures out of water are fragile things, their organs suddenly vulnerable to gravity. Another man helps remove the hook and measures the fish with a tape. The first one lifts it carefully in his arms, carries it out to deeper water, and sets it free. There is something about the ritual that brings a lump to my throat.

By now Eakes has left me to go try at another spot. My bait has certainly juiced out and I know if I cross these guys' lines, I'm likely to see a different side of them. But I'm not ready to leave yet so I stand there anyway, feeling the surf slap at my legs and suck at my feet. Several more guys catch fish and move forward to fight them under the lines of the others.

We've agreed that I'll get back to my motel on my own, and at last I reel in, clean my hooks, and prepare for the long walk back. An engine coughs to life as I pass the four-wheel drives. It's a Nissan truck with two guys in the cab. "You guys mind giving me a lift back?" I ask. "Hell, no," the driver says cheerfully, a beer between his legs. "You'll be good for traction. Have to ride in the back, though."

I roll over the side and wedge myself in tight, lying spread-eagle on my back. The air soaks up all sounds but the engine as we pound across the sand. I think of a dark, parallel universe in which fish follow trails and hold councils known only to them. A fine mist is falling on my face from the black sky. I am exhausted and happy. I was there. I saw it.

Turf War

I've always thought that the most significant contribution I could make to the greater good would be to refrain from becoming involved. But when I see a force at work that is fundamentally opposed to the rights of hunters and anglers, I must act. I refer to the American lawn, which in terms of sheer stupidity ranks right up there with our willingness to pay extra for preinstalled holes in blue jeans. I say: Let every lawn be destroyed. I've already begun neglecting mine in earnest. I've also joined No Mo' Mowin' (NMM)—a movement currently consisting of me. It's an uphill fight. But just as a thousand acres of crabgrass starts with one seed, so may NMM grow and thrive until the roar of lawn mowers in suburbia is replaced by the ring of hammers all across this great country as men beat their mowers into fishhooks and casting spoons, lure retrievers and egg sinkers.

How, you may wonder, did we get here? Lawns first arose in medieval times, initially as enclosed communal spaces where livestock grazed. (I'd like to see us get back to this. Imagine Home Depot carrying a line of lawn goats. "Yessir, we do have some with adjustable grazing height. Sorry, they're all rear-discharge only.") As usual, rich people screwed everything up. As they amassed wealth, they built private enclosures. Then the really rich, desperate for a way to show off their wealth before the invention of plastic surgery and designer tunics, removed the animals. They had their servants cut the grass. The transformation of once-useful land into a green flag was a way of saying: "Hear ye, suckers! My wealth is such that I may employ my land and servants in labor that produces nothing of value. Beat that!"

Today, in most of America, the status game continues. And participation is mandatory in many places. There are many communities in which a man who fails to maintain a monoculture of nonnative grass around his dwelling is subject to the wrath of the local homeowners association, which can have him dragged to death behind a team of oxen while a band plays patriotic songs and the kids eat ice cream.

Here are some other fun facts about lawns:

- There may be a reason why *lawn care* rhymes with *warfare*. No one would suggest that cutting the grass is as hazardous as combat. On the other hand, the gasoline-powered lawn mower is not the most forgiving of power tools. When you mow, your toes are 6 inches from a 22-inch-long blade spinning at 3,400 rpm that can eject stones at 200 mph. About 25,000 people a year show up at emergency rooms with mower-related injuries. Many of them leave digits behind. And about seventy-five who really screw up go to that big green farm in the sky.
- According to Scotts Miracle-Gro Company, there are 40 million acres of "turf" in the United States. That's almost a Wisconsin of lawn. The average American annually spends forty hours—one workweek—cutting his share. NMM's revolutionary idea is that American sportsmen should put that time back where it belongs—working a soft jerkbait down a weedline, taking a step upriver every other cast to drift your fly over new water, or sitting with a hopeful heart in a tree stand in the sideways light of an autumn afternoon.
- Americans spend $40 billion a year on yards. NMM believes that expenditure is—what's the word I'm looking for?—insane. It's like saying, "I don't want a bass boat, an ATV, or a deer lease. No sir, I just really want a time-sucking, poison-runoff-producing green carpet surrounding my house." Do you know how many fishing lures my share of that $40 billion would buy? Neither do I—too many zeros—but I'm betting it's at least a dozen, and quite possibly more.

No Mo' Mowin' is a new kind of organization. There are no fees, no ugly coffee mugs, no bad T-shirts. A series of Bill Heavey demotivational

DVDs is in development, but I'm having a hard time getting excited about it. Besides, all you really need to do is just stop mowing. Millions might join us. If everybody stops, there wouldn't be enough oxen around to punish us all.

If going cold turkey is too much, start by planting some fruit trees and native berry bushes. Put in a pond and grow bass instead of grass. Every square foot saved is a blow against the Green Tyrant.

I know that the lawn-free Promised Land is a long way off. It took us a long time to screw things up this bad, and it'll probably take a while before we unscrew ourselves. But I believe that the day is coming when a neglected lawn will signify a man of discernment and prestige. I dream of neighbors who say, "Man, have you seen Heavey's yard? The guy's never home, but those weeds and briers are ten feet tall if they're an inch. I hear he's raising miniature bison in there. How's anybody supposed to compete with that?"

Wild Ride

No matter how many times it happens, returning to the "normal" world after even a few days in the wild still hits me like a sucker punch. Two hours ago, I was in a drift boat sliding past sculpted green hills, their flanks forested with moss-laden oaks. I was slinging plugs for steelhead into water a color my guide dubbed "almost-ready green" on a river I am forbidden to name.

An hour ago, Mikey dropped me at the airport, so eager to get back to the fish that I'm not sure his truck came to a complete stop. Forty-five minutes ago, I realized that I smelled very much like myself. I ducked into the men's room, applied soap and water to a wad of paper towels, and stripped down in a locked stall for the Bum's Rush Airport Spa Treatment. On the way out I glimpsed a guy in the mirror. He had a charcoal smudge on one cheek, the kind of five-day stubble that is anything but a fashion statement, and a wild look in his eye.

A few days away changes your perspective. You forget that "All men are created equal" doesn't include airports. Boarding the aircraft, for example, is a ritual that confirms minute distinctions of socioeconomic class, with status denoted by the periodic table (platinum, gold, silver) or gemstones (emerald, sapphire, ruby). And nobody objects. Ever. Me, I'm in Group 4. And I'm the only passenger trying to cram insulated hip waders into the overhead.

We'd have more space if they packed us horizontally, in coffins. Wedged into a middle seat, I realize my shirt reeks of wood smoke. The travelers to my left and right are studiously pretending that my seat is unoccupied, and I'm not entirely sure they're wrong. My body's here, but my spirit is AWOL, whereabouts unknown. I pick up a magazine, anything to distract myself from the stale air. The first words I see are "Volcanic Ash Cat Is Fat and Happy." I reread them for verification. "Volcanic Ash Cat Is Fat and Happy." I repeat the words mentally until they become a mantra. Their impenetrable nature fits the situation, a smooth stone for the mind's worried hands.

Beneath the words is a picture of what appears to be a cement cat, round as a melon and smiling blissfully. For $29.95 plus shipping, this lump of stone will bring "a sense of well-being to your yard or garden." It's made by "artisans" in the Philippines from "volcanic ash, pumice, and natural stone from one of Mount Pinatubo's biggest eruptions." I examine the magazine as I would an animal track or a seam in the current, trying to decode its message. Eventually, I do. It's telling me that Volcanic Ash Cat is made of cement, in China, on an assembly line.

I insert my earplugs. I always wear them in the air, a trick I noticed that pilots flying as passengers invariably use. Noise is stressful. Unfortunately, the earplugs do nothing to quiet the swarm of things I haven't thought about in a week. I have yet to finalize my divorce and taxes. The stack of bills left behind will have continued its robust growth, and my car needs a new clutch. I pick up *SkyMall,* not recommended reading when you're trying to make sense of anything. But something about the Most Useless Crap on Earth sucks you in. Hucksterism this shameless and exuberant is rare.

In the woods, a square foot of Ensolite foam is my throne, great when glassing or sitting around the fire. Maybe I should upgrade to the $1,250 King Tut's Egyptian Throne, "exquisitely painted in the rich palette of Egypt and finished with gold leaf." Sure, eighty-four pounds is heavy for a camp chair. But kings don't have to do chores.

Perusing the description of the Bottoms Up Boxer Brief, I realize just how little thought I give to how my ass looks, especially in the woods. But maybe I should. The Bottoms Up "naturally adjusts your glutes for an enhanced look." Confidence is everything in fishing, and I don't think thirty-seven dollars is too much to pay for it. Imagine a 20-pound steelie, fresh from the sea, looking up and seeing my enhanced ass. Suddenly, its only thought would be *I'm totally jumping into that dude's boat.*

Pretty soon, the folly of my own species overwhelms me and I can't stop giggling. I want to be the guy who delivers the Beer Pager to someone who will never again fear being separated from his beverage. I want to help a happy couple uncrate the $2,250 life-size statue of Bigfoot, the Garden Yeti. I want to see the relief on the face of some bald guy when he opens his iGrow Hair Rejuvenation Laser, a sort of hockey helmet with 21 lasers and 30 LEDs that, for $695, bombards your follicles until they cry uncle.

By the time we land, I'm fine. I've made the transition back to the world of smartphones and pet cemeteries, dry cleaning and flush toilets. Nothing in this world seems the least bit strange to me now. And I owe it all to you, *SkyMall.*

Home Water

I thought I'd left the Potomac behind when I moved away a couple of years ago. It turns out that the river does not practice catch-and-release. It's barbed water.

In my new digs, I had something in my own backyard that most guys would trade their wife's 401(k) for—a nationally known trout stream. Gunpowder Falls supports trout year-round, thanks to the constant release of cold water from reservoirs upstream. One January day right after we moved in, the whole family was checking out the ice along the river's edge. I spotted an 8-inch brown calmly finning away in four inches of water just feet from Michelle. My wife and the fish saw each other at the same time. Michelle gasped. The fish vanished. That was the closest I ever came to catching a Gunpowder trout. This is likely because the famous stream gets pounded by skilled long-rodders. Dumb fish—the kind I require to succeed—don't last long.

I don't mean to imply that Gunpowder fly anglers are snobs. I'll say that plainly. Go out with a spinning rod and the guys wading past look at you as if trying to decide which fugitive on last week's *America's Most Wanted* you most resemble. Eventually, I did take my 4-weight to the riffle nearest the house. (Why? Maybe I feel off-balance when things are going well in my life and know that fly fishing will immediately fix this.) Anyway, I lost three flies, broke some small trees retrieving others, and restored the quiet desperation I don't particularly like but am used to. The Gunpowder and I went our separate ways.

Next I tried the Susquehanna, a 464-mile-long rivulet known for producing big smallmouths, my favorite fish. I tried near the mouth of a creek, a spot recommended by a bait shop on Route 1. In three outings, I caught five hickory shad and four bluegills. Then I went prospecting in my canoe, sure that I'd eventually find smallies among the river's endless and fishy-looking rock ledges. Everything I saw was too shallow. The fish just weren't there. I'd never seen such a uniform river bottom. And there was a lot of it. The river was nearly a mile across. If 80 percent of the fish live in 20 percent of the water, I figured I could be pushing eighty myself before I found that 20 percent in the Susquehanna.

Not having home water—a place I belonged, a river I knew well enough to fish, even while accepting that I'd never know all of it—was a big hole in my life. But, like new underwear, breath mints, or a circle of social contacts, it's one of those things that you can need desperately without actually being aware of them. One Friday, mistakenly believing Emma had early release from school, I found myself with time to kill and stopped by Fletcher's Boathouse on the Potomac. The road there descends to a single-lane tunnel, built around 1828, beneath the C&O Canal. It's midnight-dark and cool as a tomb on the hottest summer days. Water weeps along the cheeks of the stones in the rough walls. Something happens during that brief passage. When you emerge, there's a granddaddy sycamore—ageless, implacable, survivor of countless floods—standing sentry. And you've entered a different world. Everything built by man down here is conditional, temporary. Down here, the river always gets the last word.

A bunch of the regulars were there, standing around the picnic tables in front of the concession house, people I hadn't seen in a year or longer but who spoke to me as if I'd just stepped out for coffee. It was late spring, perch season. But the wind had been blowing for days and was keeping everyone off the river. "Even if your anchor held, you'd be swinging around like a #@*$-ing kite," Paula Smith groused. We sat there, staring out at the water sliding by. We were all suffering, but at least we were suffering together.

Memories washed over me. This was where I'd rediscovered my boyhood fishing mania when some friends gave me a spinning outfit for my twenty-first birthday, which led to my smallmouth addiction. I remembered once clamping my rod between my jaws to climb a vertical face to get to a tiny, one-cast eddy. I reached for a handhold on the ledge above my head and heard the hiss of what I hoped was a brown water snake. I didn't climb down. I just moved a few feet to the side and tried another ledge. I remembered hooking the biggest smallmouth of my life, a 4-pounder, in two feet of slack water as I headed toward someplace better. My cast had been perfunctory, the kind a fisherman makes without expectation and only in obedience to the idea that you never pass up the chance to have your lure in the water. There was more. The time I'd swamped and lost all my gear sixty miles upriver at White Horse Rapid, a Class III I hadn't noticed until it was too late. Fishing for perch with Dickie Tehaan, Fletcher's savant, and trying to understand how he did it. I had the same lure and had studied his cadence, right down to how high he lifted the rod and snapped his wrist. And he still boated better than two fish for each one I did.

Sitting there, I saw how vain it had been to think that I could just walk away from this river and take up with another one. I might just as well wish I were taller and a better person. There was no point in arguing. This was my river.

Paula said she was going to look for lost lures, which often turn up in certain eddies in the spring. "Listen, me and Gordon are going out Wednesday. First day this wind's supposed to lie down. You can come if you want." I told her I'd be there.

IV

Fishing on the Edge

When you only get to see your daughter every other weekend, there aren't many good excuses for being late. And "I lost track of the time" definitely doesn't cut it. So it was with mixed emotions—none of them good—that I left the house thirty minutes late one Friday to pick Emma up from school. When I rolled through a stop sign and the cop hit his lights, I was pretty sure it wasn't to give me a good-conduct medal. He scanned my car—worm weights and Hula Grubs on the dash, my lunch bag of Doritos in my lap—and asked, "How you doing today, sir?"

"Stupid, sir," I answered. "Today I'm just really stupid." Cops sniff out lies for a living. The truth usually saves you a lot of grief. I told him my story, felt him sifting it. He sighed. "Any chance you've got your registration in there?" I handed it over and wondered what Emma would say about my detention. He came back and said, "I'm not going to cite you today, Mr. Heavey. But you really need to relax, okay?" I couldn't believe this mercy. My arm sort of shot out on its own to shake the man's hand. Except it happened too fast because he stepped back, one hand hovering above his holster. Then he relaxed, shook his head. "See, *that,*" he said, smiling ruefully, "is exactly what I'm talking about."

Emma looked lonely and glum sitting on the school steps. But—to her credit—it only took an ice cream cone and the story about the cop to bring her around. I was the one having trouble bouncing back. I'm not always an ideal companion, and I'd been seeing way too much of myself lately. When my mental plywood starts to delaminate, what I need—contrary to logic—is time with my crazier friends. I needed to go fishing with Steve Burnett.

Steve dropped out of whatever scam he was running in the city about ten years ago to homeschool himself as a farmer in an isolated part of New York. He also sells watercolors that look like postcards from a country no one else is allowed into. He sounds happier and closer to bankruptcy every time we talk. He's also a whack job who sees right through me. I called, invited myself up, and said I'd be there in thirty-six hours and expected to fish.

Steve knew that some local old-timers routinely caught huge trout from the pristine streams around him. We met one, Joe Dibble, at a diner for breakfast. Joe, a sunburned guy of about seventy, had fished, hunted, and trapped the area since boyhood. He was old school: a baitfisherman who threw weightless worms on 10-pound mono with a push-button reel. "Just hook the worm once, through the collar. Browns like big bait, but it has to look natural."

Upon hearing we intended to fish that afternoon, he asked, "You see the river?" Steve, lying, answered yes, and Joe's eyebrows flexed involuntarily. But he did say that big trout could be found where three old railroad trestles crossed the stream.

The water was shin-deep and as clear as our folly. I had a spinning rod and worms. Steve, ever the contrarian, had a 3-weight with a sparkly streamer. "You know this is nuts, right?" I said. "That's why Joe's eyebrows were doing push-ups." Steve has a way of ignoring what he doesn't want to hear. "I see a trestle," he announced, and disappeared into the shoulder-high brush. At last we arrived at the tiny pool. Any trout that hadn't heard us approach now had a good visual. "You're the damn guest," Steve said. "You take it." The rocky abutment was so steep that I carried my rod in my mouth. I lobbed my worm out. Nothing. To make sure that particular horse was completely dead, I cast twice more.

We walked the track to the next trestle. As we went, we compared our aging backs, the morning stiffness, the stretching they now demanded. We noted with pride that we were first-class hypocrites, exactly the irritable old men we'd once forsworn becoming.

The second descent was steeper. Steve climbed down the cut stone gingerly. Then he cast low and drifted the streamer through. He kept at it, as if the trout might have gone stupid.

The third descent was the steepest yet. "All yours," Steve said. But by now something had shifted. It wasn't about the fish anymore. It was about the fishing. About honoring the ritual, seeing it through. I bit my rod again. I was teetering on a rock when Steve—perfectly imitating the fake enthusiasm of a personal trainer—called, "Don't forget to engage your core!" I started laughing, couldn't stop, nearly fell. Here we were, two old farts mincing our way where once we'd have bounded like goats, all for fish we'd never catch. Steve's wisecrack both encompassed and pierced all this. And made me remember what I'd forgotten during too much time alone—namely, that I was alive, straddling the edge between the sublime and the ridiculous, and that this was exactly where I belonged.

I stayed for two more days. We caught bass in his farm pond, cooked them over a fire, and washed them down with whiskey. Looking back, however, it was that moment atop the rock that had put me right again. That moment of rippling laughter at the absurdity and wonder of my life as it sped me along like a stream.

Gear Good!

Since this is an all-gear issue and nobody asked, here's my opinion: Absolutely nothing is more important than having the latest gear. The pleasures of shiny new things are self-evident. The larger consideration is the unspoken promise each new hunk of gear makes. Whether it's the latest gun, fishing rod, or this year's must-have porta-potty—the Thetford 465 Electric, which offers the "next level of efficiency and convenience with a powerful battery-operated flush"—new gear solemnly swears to change your life.

I know what you're thinking: *My current crapper works fine. Would one capable of handling a cinder block really change my life?*

Of course it would. If nothing else, new gear can boost you into the rarified air of a level of poverty that few Americans ever get to see firsthand.

Man's obsession with gear dates back at least 500,000 years, when the first spear was invented. Doug—archaeologists believe this was his name—really just wanted a longer stick to avoid getting smoke in his eyes while roasting his share of the kill. It worked, and meanwhile, the fire hardened the tip of the long stick.

One night, the scent of roasting ibex drew a group of cave weasels. Quickly exhausting his battery of throwing rocks, with a huge weasel bearing down on him, Doug hurled his stick at the beast in a final gesture of defiance. Hominid and weasel were both stunned to see the stick protruding from the animal's bloody breast. The hominids cheered. "Doug! You totally nailed that weasel!" said the chief. That night Doug was awarded the choicest part of the ibex, the eyeballs.

A few days later, Skip showed up with a spear. "The SkipSpear features a critical addition," he said. "A charcoal-rubbed shaft that results in a non-reflective black finish." This, he explained, made it a "tactical" spear. Silence greeted this announcement, for no hominid knew what the hell he was talking about. And yet none said so, lest his peers think him clueless. Instead, each hefted the spear in turn, grunting as if impressed by the weapon's manifest superiority. That night, Skip got the eyeballs.

The great gear race, which continues to this day, had begun. For a while you scarcely dared call yourself a biped unless you were carrying a camo spear. Next it was all-weather spears. One day Rusty, a hominid from the next drainage over, showed up carrying a spear "guaranteed to produce a five-throw group inside a circle the size of a kangaroo heart." That night, the tribe ate Rusty. Then they held a belching tournament to determine who got the eyeballs.

I'm not even going to try to describe the mania surrounding the first atlatl.

My point in all this is . . . I forget. (Incidentally, anybody seen those new high-modulus atlatls with the Circassian walnut nocking point and sharkskin leather handle wrapping? Those look awesome!)

What I mean is that modern hominids have made significant advances since the days of Doug. Judging by our behavior, what we value is money. We value it above time spent outdoors or with our families. I say this because many of us spend our lives at soul-deadening work and then volunteer for overtime, as if money might cure death itself. You would think all this time indoors would slow the gear race. *Au contraire,* my bipedal buddy. Instead, we buy more gear to soothe the misery we experience in our endless quest for money. The beauty of the Digital Age is that you can cop a nice hit of gear while engaged in the very activity that guarantees it will never leave the box.

And I'm just like everybody else. Right now, I'm at my desk working on this column. But I'm also on the Bass Pro Shops website, jonesing for the bass outfit that would release a major jolt of painkilling polypeptides from my brain. The rod is just the ticket for horsing hogs out of the slop, a two-piece, 8-foot, fast-action Daiwa Steez Trigger ($664.99). The reel is a Shimano Calais 4X8 DC baitcaster with 32 settings and a Dartainium drag ($649.99). With shipping, that's $1,333.93. And, no, I don't know what Dartainium is. But I want it.

Oh, I see a few killjoys out there shaking their heads. You say nobody needs a $1,334 bass outfit. You say a rod and reel costing a tenth of that would do just fine. You say that what really counts is something money can't buy: the experience, the joy, and the fact of the fishing itself.

Please. I think everybody knows what's really going on here. Soon I'll have a new reel with a Dartainium drag. And you won't. And that's something you just can't handle.

Bow Crazy

I never expected to find myself here. I'm standing in line at my local Dick's buying a youth-model bow for my daughter. The woman behind me, noting my purchase, asked, "*The Hunger Games?*" Yep, I said and told her that I'd finally caved to Emma's pleas and taken her to see the movie. And that immediately after, Emma had picked up the bow that had sat unused for two years and shot for ninety minutes. It was my twelve-year-old's longest sustained period of concentration since trick-or-treating back in October. And she kept at it. Within two months she had shot out the string. The woman's two boys had also seen the movie. "They're not all that into archery, but they've got snares all over the yard. I almost sprained my ankle in one."

Is this a great country or what?

In case you're not a parent, a tweenager, or really immature, you may not know that archery is having its Cultural Moment. Girls, especially, are taking up archery in record numbers. And suddenly it's cool to hunt and eat wild game, learn about edible plants, and set snares for your mom. The juggernaut behind all of this is *The Hunger Games,* a bestselling book (the first of three) and now a blockbuster movie.

The story unfolds in a postapocalyptic future—apparently the only kind imaginable these days. North America is now Panem, a nation of twelve districts strictly ruled by a corrupt elite in the Capitol. To remind the populace who's boss, the Capitol requires each district to select two children as "tributes" to compete in the annual Hunger Games, a fight-to-the-death competition on live national TV. Tributes kill one another with knives, spears, arrows, stones, their hands, poison berries, and genetically altered killer wasps. Think *Winnie the Pooh* meets *Dawn of the Dead*.

A story like this needs a different kind of heroine. It finds it in sixteen-year-old Katniss Everdeen, a tough, woods-savvy girl who hunts small game to feed her mother and sister. Leaving your district is a potential death sentence, but Katniss knows that the same people who could punish her are also her best customers, buying her squirrels and rabbits on the down-low. Katniss is known for delivering undamaged meat. She aims for the eye and rarely misses. When her younger sister is chosen as a tribute, Katniss volunteers to take her place. She survives the first day by climbing trees too slender to hold the big boys. And when she finally gets her hands on a bow, Katniss kicks butt. Even in the games, however, she only kills when there's no other option. Along the way, we discover how a brave, compassionate girl with a moral compass can survive and—just maybe—prevail in a world where might makes right.

I have some minor issues with the author, Suzanne Collins. First, I totally resent her success. The book and movie are runaway hits. And Collins doesn't know jack about the outdoors. We see Katniss gathering ripe blackberries and strawberries on the same day—which is fine except that strawberries ripen in May, blackberries in July. At one point, Katniss coats her lips with "grease" from a rabbit she killed, an animal whose meat has about as much grease as a carrot. While running flat out from a female tribute who is adept at throwing knives, Katniss narrates, "I keep moving, positioning the next arrow automatically, as only someone who has hunted for years can do." Actually, I can't remember when I last nocked an arrow while running.

Thing is, none of this matters because Collins's story grabs you and won't let go. Katniss is a different kind of hero. Her gender, for example, seems beside the point. She's flawed, an outsider and loner who often can't decipher her own emotions. But she's scrappy, resourceful, and above all, cool. And I, for one, want my kid reading sentences like this: "The meat and plants from the woods combined with the exertion it took to get them have given me a healthier body than most of those I see around me."

Last night, as I helped Emma lug the target back to the shed, she asked, "Daddy, I want to kill and eat a squirrel. How long till I'm ready?" This from a girl who three weeks ago informed me that she was now a vegetarian because "eating animals is cruel." I put a hand on her shoulder and thought of how much she still has to learn, starting with the impossible task of sitting still for long periods. Then there's hunter safety, the need to pull a heavier bow—it's quite a list. I say none of this. I think of what Katniss would tell her.

"Well, it depends on you, monk," I say. "How hard you're willing to work at learning to hunt." Emma's face falls a little. It's not what she wanted to hear. I'm disappointed, too. It's not what I would have liked to say. As so often happens in life, the truth and immediate gratification don't overlap. But I want Emma to learn that telling and facing the truth are the best ways to meet the challenges that await her. Which means that I have to model that behavior even if it stings. All in all, I think Katniss would approve.

Feet First

If you love the outdoors but have finite funds, non-outdoors expenditures are painful things. In my case, no pain compares to that of opening my wallet to acquire so-called dress clothing, which serves no purpose other than to make you look "nice." And the more such an item costs, the sooner it dies. Inadvertently but irreparably, I will either rip it, burn it, stain it, or catch it in a reciprocating saw. There are fruit flies that have lived longer than some of my ties. My personal record is forty-five minutes. That tie never made it out of the box. In brief, I drove to a shopping mall (first mistake), bought a tie (second mistake), and then sought to dull the pain of shopping with Chinese takeout (third mistake). Both the tie and the food appeared to be carefully sealed. There is no such thing as a carefully sealed carton of Chinese food. (Incidentally, should you ever need a dress shirt on short notice and find yourself unable or unwilling to iron one, head for the nearest Goodwill. There, a crisp dress shirt goes for $5.98. A shirt like that, inexplicably, not only lasts forever but will also shatter the blade of any reciprocating saw.)

It is, of course, never painful to purchase outdoor gear, especially if you actually need it. This is doubly true for a vitally important but oft-overlooked type of equipment. I speak of outdoor boots and shoes. I have had feet all my life and what it has taught me is this: An outdoorsman cannot be happy unless his feet are happy. What your feet want at any given moment is comfortable footwear adequate to the task. For me, that works out to about twenty-four pairs of boots and shoes. More or less. Okay, I know that sounds like a lot. But it includes a fair number of outliers, boots for applications so specific they may never be needed again.

There was, for example, a trip to Alaska in January that included travel on unheated aircraft. For that I got a pair of Mountain Pack boots by Northern Outfitters, makers of clothing favored by polar research scientists. The boots cost $185, weighed thirteen pounds, and made me look like I was wearing inflatable apartment buildings on my feet. The open-cell insulation responsible for their appearance works in part by venting moisture as water vapor. What this meant was that on a 30-below morning, I could look down at little wisps of white smoke coming out of the apartment buildings. I cannot convey how satisfying it was to watch this with warm, dry feet. The boots would probably fail in environments where H_2O exists in a liquid state, but at that time and place they were worth every penny.

Once, for a gobbler hunt in southern Mississippi, I read up on the area's snakes too diligently. Eastern diamondbacks, our biggest and most dangerous, are found there. According to Wikipedia, this rattler has "a very high venom yield: an average of 400–450 mg, with a maximum of 858–1,000 mg." A bit further on, I learned that "the estimated human lethal dose is 100–150 mg." In other words, a good bite could kill you eight times. It causes internal bleeding and makes your red blood cells pop like balloons. Hallucinations, bleeding from the mouth, nausea, and vomiting are not uncommon. Also, you don't feel very chipper. Rationally, I knew that 99.9 percent of venomous-snakebite victims in the United States survive. But my upper brain was no longer calling the shots. I got the tallest snake boots available, a pair of eighteen-inch Chippewas. On the three-day hunt, I saw neither turkey nor serpent. I did, however, discover why eighteen-inch boots are rare: You can't bend your knees in them. You walk out of the swamp like Frankenstein with a box call.

The Backcountry Cure

Go on a weeklong paddle trip deep into Quetico, a huge and stunningly beautiful smallmouth and walleye wilderness, and your earthly problems soon come into perspective. Especially on the portages.

As the four of us bustle into the remote border crossing station of Prairie Portage, we find ourselves facing an attractive blond ranger. We're about to head out for a week's paddling and fishing in Quetico Provincial Park, the wilder and less trafficked Canadian version of Minnesota's Boundary Waters Canoe Area. But first we need to get our Remote Area Border Crossing Permits stamped, pay the daily use fee, and buy fishing licenses.

The ranger says she wants us to enjoy our stay in her country. She then lists all the things we are forbidden to do, with a relish that suggests this is her favorite part of the job. We can't, for example, use wheeled carts of any kind on the area's many portages, which have a reputation for being longer and rougher than those in the BWCA. We can't bring in glass containers or electronic devices. We can't use soaps or cleaners within sixty yards of the water. And, yes, this includes the biodegradable ones designed for low-impact camping.

I give a sidelong what's-the-deal? look to my partners, wondering how many more prohibitions there could be. As it turns out, quite a few. Barbed hooks are forbidden. Organic bait is forbidden. This is to discourage the spread of invasive species, like the earthworm, which has destroyed much of the forest duff layer. "The Europeans brought them here," she sniffs, as if—despite her appearance—she herself were not of European descent.

We've just taken a twenty-minute boat ride with our outfitter, who dropped us at the clearing that marks the portage trail. We humped our gear down here to the ranger station by the next lake. We're eager to be on our way. But next we get a detailed tutorial on crapping in the wilderness. All solid human waste is to be disposed of in single-use, six-inch-deep cat holes, which are to be refilled so that no evidence of human disturbance remains. Further—here she looks up to make sure we're all paying attention—"all used toilet paper is to be collected, carried from the site, and burned rather than left in the hole." The four of us nod, as if collecting and burning our used toilet paper is something we always do, even in our own homes.

"This is some of the most pristine water left on the planet," she says by way of a good-bye. "We'd like to keep it that way." Her tone suggests that if we really cared about the wilderness we would have stayed home.

We walk outside, blinking in the bright sun. It's Steve Burnett who breaks the silence. "Hey, I got an idea. Let's all go take a crap on her back porch." It's an intriguing notion, but after much discussion, we decide against it.

It's only now—at a remove of a thousand miles from my daily life, about to head into the wilderness—that I realize how badly I've needed to get away. Initially, I'd balked when Steve invited me to join him, his brother Doug, and Doug's son Matt on a trip to the Boundary Waters, which is a semiannual rite among the Burnett clan. I didn't have the time or the money. It took a push from Michelle to change my mind. "You need to go," she'd said. "You've been acting more and more . . . aggrieved by the world."

Her words stung as only the truth from someone who sees right through you and somehow loves you anyway can. I'd been spiraling downward for months and too caught up in it to see clearly. But she was right. The book that I'd poured heart and soul into for five years had recently come out. The reviews were good. The sales were not. It was hard to say which took the bigger hit, my pride or my bank account.

The best thing I had going was that Michelle and I, after three years of a commuting relationship, were getting married and buying a house together. But even this had its downsides. The therapist that my ex, Jane, and I had been seeing about our daughter, Emma, now thirteen, had recently told us that the fifty-fifty custody arrangement we'd had for two years wasn't the best thing for Emma. The transitions between households were hard on her. She needed the stability of a home base and a primary parent. The shrink said that either of us was qualified for the job, but it was clear that Jane expected to be the primary parent.

Another painful truth was that Emma and I butted heads too often for me to believe that my house was the best place for her. Sitting in the guy's office, I'd reluctantly agreed to the new arrangement: Jane would keep Emma during the week. I'd have alternate weekends and Thursdays from after school until 8:30, when I'd drop her back at Jane's.

As soon as the words left my mouth, I broke down. It was as if I'd just had a hole installed in my heart. I felt like I was abandoning my daughter. Of the four parents involved in Michelle's and my situation, only one was giving up time with a child. Me.

Even as I toted up my grievances, I could hear the voice of my friend Paula Smith. "There are no victims, honey," she'd once told me. "There are only willing volunteers." She was right, of course. It wasn't the world that was screwed up. The thing was, I didn't know how to unscrew myself. But Michelle had been right, too. If there was any setting in which I might get a new perspective, it was away from the rest of the world, paddling a canoe and fishing for my supper.

Just a Little Turned Around

If anyone could understand how I felt, it was Steve. He's a former New York wheeler-dealer, a guy on his third marriage and at least his third career. A few years back he'd left the city to turn gentleman farmer in upstate New York. He tells me the neighboring farmers refer to him as "the citidiot." In all of Delaware County—prime dairy country since the 1700s—he is the only farmer attempting to grow vegetables instead of cows. And now, as the rest of us pack the canoes, he has already tied on a Mepps and cast out, hoping to snag first-fish bragging rights. A husky smallmouth—obviously placed there by the Ontario Tourism Bureau—nails his first cast. "Fish on!" Steve cackles as the rest of us cry foul. I watch him play the fish and try to decide which brings him the greater pleasure: catching the bass or pissing off his own relatives. I don't even want to speculate what it says about me that he's one of my closest friends.

These three members of the Burnett clan have all done monthlong Outward Bound canoe courses here, each including a three-day solo. They ought to know what they're doing. And yet, two hours after launching, we are literally paddling in circles. We have just circumnavigated a large island that is not shown on our map of Birch Lake. Doug, after stopping three times to reconcile map and compass, announces that his compass must be broken. A quick check against two other compasses dashes this notion. Now, as we round the island's last point, we see dead ahead the ranger station and beach from which we departed. According to the map, they lie to the south. According to three compasses and the sun, they are directly to the north. Irrefutable evidence of our cluelessness in no way slows us down. Instead—in the particularly haughty manner of college-educated men ignoring inconvenient facts—we turn right and continue to explore the lake, as if confident that around the next point there will be something—a landmark, a passage, a floating mental health facility—that will set everything to rights.

For once, I'm the one to unravel the knot. "Guys," I call, "is it possible that we were supposed to put in on the lake where we got dropped off rather than portaging down to this one?" A profound silence ensues. Doug lets out a groan and slaps his forehead. But since he's wearing a big hat, there's no noise. He just kind of crushes the brim against his head.

"Oh, man," he says. "Tell me you're not gonna tell this to anyone."

"Of course not," I say. "Could've happened to anybody." Not being the one responsible for this kind of screwup is so novel an experience that I'm savoring it.

Half an hour later and two trips each way hauling gear back to where we were first let off, we're leaning into a brisk headwind on Birch Lake. After a few minutes, Doug motions us alongside. "I brought maps for you guys, too," he says, handing me the chart in a waterproof case. He points to our location, then casually says, "I strongly suggest you wear your PFD." Something in his voice jolts me into the moment. There's no immediate danger, of course. But we're on the other side of the guardrail now. It's not that wild places are hostile, just unforgiving. I put on my PFD.

Pure Wilderness

We've lost a good bit of time, but Doug seems intent on reaching the campsite we'd originally planned on. This involves two more portages and about three hours of paddling. I don't mind. It feels good to be reacquainting myself with the old machinery of my body, stabbing the water and pulling the boat along, rolling my shoulders and hips into each stroke. Our canoes are so heavily laden that they present little profile to the headwind. It feels like we're making good time.

At 6 feet and 170 pounds, I'm the midget on this trip and in the bow. Steve, 6-foot-4, 210 pounds, has the stern of our 17-foot Wenonah. Doug and Matt are paddling an 18-footer, mostly because they're giants. Doug is 6-foot-10 and 280; Matt, a mere 6-foot-8 and 240. Neither is a particularly efficient paddler. They sit too far back in their seats, insert their paddles at 45-degree angles rather than close to vertical, and engage little more than their arms for each stroke. Worse, they pull well past their hips before taking their paddles out, wasting half of each stroke lifting water rather than propelling the boat forward. What's maddening about all this is that they're still moving faster than we are. They're so strong that they don't need to be particularly efficient paddlers.

I can't get over how pretty this place is. There are dramatic granite faces and boreal forests, bald eagles teetering on the transparent air, and loons lying low in the water that dive when the boat is just feet away. It's all so scenic that it looks photoshopped, a postcard vista everywhere you look. The glaciers that moved through here from the northeast millions of years ago gouged out the softer rock, creating what would become about two thousand lakes. When the earth warmed and the glaciers retreated, they dropped their rock debris, which would become beds for the streams connecting the lakes like beads on a necklace. The streams and the portages along them can be hard to spot. Sometimes all you see is a tiny opening in the shoreline pines, spruce, and cedar. In some spots the beaches can accommodate only one canoe at a time. We've decided to hold off on fishing until we're on the lake where we'll be camping so that we don't have to carry fish. But at one portage, waiting alongside a rock face while Doug and Matt unload, I can't resist dropping a 3-inch white twistertail on a leadhead. I open the bail and watch the jig flutter down for what feels like forever. I'm still following it when it touches bottom. I count ten cranks to bring it up, meaning the water is twenty feet deep. It's the clearest freshwater I've ever seen, home to smallmouth bass, pike, walleyes, and lake trout. I want to hurry up and make camp so I can get on some.

We finally drop our gear on a point with enough flat and smooth ground for two tents. We make camp and head back out into the early evening. Lacking charts or a depthfinder, Steve and I decide to target points first. His Mepps connects with a couple of smallies holding tight to rocks. I tie on a slightly larger version of the same lure—a No. 3 with bronze blades—and boat a few myself. On the rivers I'm used to fishing, you usually have to catch somewhere between ten and fifty little smallmouths before you get a 12-incher. That's not the deal here. They're almost all decent fish and in fantastic condition, fatter and healthier-looking than any bronzebacks I've seen before. The biggest we manage this evening is 14 inches—no monster, but a good fighter even by smallmouth standards.

We push on, now casting to the larger rock faces. In some places, with the boat tight against the bluff, we're fishing in thirty-two feet of water. The bigger fish are on the bottom and we soon discover that jigging, not cranking, is the ticket. I've brought mostly spinners, spoons, and Rapalas. I'm not well stocked for vertical fishing. I look through the few plastics I did bring and rig a root beer Hula grub on a quarter-ounce leadhead. It's my heaviest jig, and I wish I'd brought more and heavier ones. The moment it touches down, I'm doing battle with a big-shouldered smallmouth. I try to bring the fish in with slow, steady pressure. I want to keep it buttoned to my barbless hook and tire it out so it doesn't throw that hook during a big jump. I obviously don't have the hang of it yet, because throwing the hook on its first leap is exactly what it does. As if to add insult to injury, the leadhead lands right in my lap. "Dude!" Steve crows. "That thing was a monster! Eighteen inches easy!" The real disappointment comes when I realize that he took one of the Hula grub's twin tails. And the remaining parts of the lure aren't looking too perky, either. I have only a handful of Hula grubs—the best match for the abundant crayfish here—for the rest of the week. I'm going to have to ration them.

By the time we head in, we've got enough fish for dinner. We stop to clean them on an island to avoid attracting bears to camp. Just inside the trees we find a tiny glen with a flat log by the water. It's the ideal fish-cleaning station. But it's more than that. The ground is a carpet of thick green moss and artfully placed tufts of tall, flowering grasses. The rocks almost seem to glow in the twilight. Steve and I look at each other and say nothing, but we're both aware of a palpable magic here, a kind of power. If two hardened cynics like us can feel it, it's got to be strong. But it's the kind of thing you don't want to offend by breaking its silence, so we don't speak until we're back on the lake. "Did you feel that place?" Steve says. "It was like it knew we were coming! And I don't even believe in that crap!"

"I know," I call over my shoulder, still sorting through a minor kind of awe. "Shut up and paddle."

Eat. Paddle. Camp. Fish. Repeat.

Our days settle into a satisfying rhythm. We wake, make breakfast, strike camp, and paddle through a few lakes until we find a campsite we like. The average portage between lakes is around two hundred yards, but there's one that's the better part of a mile, with steep uphill parts over slippery rock. This, unfortunately, is the one on which I unwisely opt to shoulder the heaviest Duluth pack, all eighty pounds of it. I'm soon bent over like a beetle, sweat soaking my clothes and dripping off my brow, cursing myself for not finding a walking stick before setting out, but afraid I won't be able to get up again if I stop to cut one now. I look for trees to grab on to as I pull myself along. At one point, hearing someone coming up behind me, I step to the side. Matt passes me carrying a canoe on his head and a pack on his back, at least half again as much weight as I'm carrying. And the guy moves like a man strolling out to his mailbox.

After setting up camp, we fish for a few hours, come back, and review the day over a cocktail as we cook dinner. Later we sit around the fire, sometimes talking, sometimes silently watching the face of a log transform itself into a glowing orange wall of coals, and then wander off to our bags. Most nights, I wake a few times to the ghostly giggle of loons, a sound that isn't loud but seems as if it must carry for miles. When I go out to pee, the night sky's clarity feels almost like a rebuke. Why are we so afraid of the dark that we light up our neighborhoods until nobody even bothers to learn the names of stars anymore?

On our last full day before starting back, we decide to stay put and fish hard. We've had good smallmouth action and fresh fish almost every night but have caught only one walleye and one pike. Our camp sits beside a channel connecting two good-size lakes. Steve and I try the lower lake first. We get some hard bumps at one rock face but neither of us lands anything, and Steve's game when I suggest we paddle to the upper lake. The surrounding hills are higher here, suggesting equally deeper drop-offs. I'm betting this might be where bigger fish hang, maybe a bigger pike or even a lake trout, a fish I've never caught.

A half mile straight ahead, a steep-sided island rises in the middle of the lake, like a small Gibraltar. I suggest we try there. As we near the island, I break out a heavy jig I borrowed from Doug, a 2½-ounce chartreuse bucktail that looks like it might be a good lake trout lure. Even on a 7-foot, medium-heavy rod, however, it's a lot of weight to be working, and soon my wrist and forearm are sore.

As we near the rock, I sigh. The damn Hula grub is still the lure I have the most confidence in, even though I'm down to my last one, which has lost both tails. The thing is nothing more than three-quarters of an inch of body and the little skirt of tentacles at the collar of the lure. I run a bare 3/0 hook through it, glad that I have super glue to keep the body and hook together. I cast, bouncing the lure off the rock face so it falls into the water like something edible that lost its balance.

When it's about fifteen feet deep, something takes it and heads south. The rod arcs deeply. "Holy crap!" Steve yells. "What is that thing?" I have no idea, only that it's not swimming like a smallmouth. It takes me three or four minutes to bring the mystery fish in, by which time it has wrapped itself in the line. This turns out to be a good thing. "Lake trout!" yells Steve as he nets it. The hook is out of the fish's mouth, dangling from the net. If it weren't for the tangle, I wouldn't have caught this fish. My first ever laker is a fat 26-incher. I guess its weight at somewhere around 6 pounds as I heft the great fish up for Steve to snap a picture.

"I wish you could see your face," Steve tells me.

"Why?"

"You have this look of absolutely childlike delight. Really. Gotta say, man, I wasn't sure you still had that in you."

"I wasn't, either." I stop, letting that feeling wash over me. It's like the return of an old friend, somebody who disappeared along the way, and you only realize how much you missed him by your pleasure when he resurfaces. I'm quiet for a few minutes, trying to calm down, admiring my first lake trout, thinking what a good dinner he'll make. This is the biggest fish of the trip. And he wasn't deep, where lakers are supposed to be. He was hanging out in fifteen feet. It's a surprise and also not a surprise. Nothing, after all, is more natural than for a fish—or a man for that matter—to act in a manner other than as expected. Or for a familiar act to take on new meaning.

The world hasn't changed, but somehow I have. I don't know how this works, only that I can feel it. I'm no longer aggrieved. I see life again for the temporary and mysterious thing it is, full of terror and wonder, success and failure, but always—whether hidden in the background or blazing away right in front of me—a thing so mysterious and miraculous that it's almost more than I can bear.

How to Be a Winner

Somebody at the Camp Fire Club of America invited my friend Steve Burnett to its 2015 Spring Encampment, an annual outdoor-skills competition at the club's 233-acre preserve, and he invited me. Steve had been a member of the club but dropped out some years back. I figure he jumped before he was pushed. This is because the club, founded in 1897, was supposed to be a place where "neither wealth, power, nor social standing counted; only proven manhood in the outdoors." If that's the standard, Steve, who is six kinds of strange and one of my best friends, is not your man. David E. Petzal told me that Steve once stabbed himself in the leg on a caribou hunt just to get attention. That may not be accurate. Then again, neither is Steve. On a hunt on Anticosti Island in Quebec, I saw him miss a deer broadside at thirty yards with a .270. Our French-speaking guide turned his gaze heavenward and asked God to transform his client into a "fongus." There are times when I think God was listening.

Anyway, I quickly realized that Steve was concerned about his lack of woods skills and had asked me along as his wingman in failure. I was happy to oblige. He and I would be part of a five-man team competing in shooting firearms (.22 rifle, hunting rifle, pistol, shotgun), as well as making a bow and cordage to string it, building a fire, telling a story, and concocting dinner from whatever foodstuffs the judges doled out.

Even with me as company, Steve was anxious. An intervention by someone skilled in the art of failure was in order. "You dumbass," I said kindly, "have you learned nothing from our outings? Skills are wonderful things to have, but they aren't the point. Having fun is the point. Stop playing with your zipper. Instead of trying to be first, we should shoot for last."

Steve brightened at this. "That's twisted. I'm in. Last place or bust." We shook on it. When the teams were announced and Steve was named captain of ours, we informed the other three guys of our goal. We weren't going to intentionally screw up. We just weren't going to get all wound up if we didn't do well. One guy, Linc, seemed to be on board. Jeff and John were less keen. But once they saw Steve hacking away with his ax on our bow and me attempting to make cordage (which wouldn't have harnessed a pair of gerbils), they started leaning our way.

Highlights from the competition:

- Our bow snapped a limb when we tried to string it. Jeff, who is not on intimate terms with failure, found this unacceptable. Using the better part of a roll of duct tape, he reinforced it until the bow was capable of propelling a bamboo arrow ten yards if you aimed fifteen feet above your target.
- One of the events was shooting a .22 rifle with open sights at a steel plate seventy-five yards away. Doing my level best, I missed it ten times in a row. This was humbling. I might have done better with my eyes shut. As I walked back to the group, Steve showed why he should never be put in charge of anything. "There he goes, gentlemen," he crowed. "The poster boy for the PETA hunting team!" I smiled and—just as I passed my good friend—gave him a sharp knuckle-rap in a sensitive area. He yelped, doubled over, and became very quiet. The elder running the event smiled for the first time in the competition. "Well, you went oh-for-ten in the shooting, but I'd say you nailed the bonus round."
- Just minutes later, Steve had his own moment of glory, going 0-for-24 in the Grouse Walk, a shotgun event in which you walk among obstacles, never knowing when two clays will zing out of the trap house. Each of us went through it a dozen times. I surprised myself by hitting one of each pair, at least when I remembered to disengage

the safety. Steve got tenser and more frustrated with each miss. He cared too much about hitting that bird and it undid him.

- Steve did well in the cooking and storytelling parts. He didn't actually cook anything, but he carved a pigeon out of a potato and some kind of a caribou or something out of a carrot. "Garnishes," he said. "Presentation is key." During the storytelling around the fire, he put on a grass skirt and beer-cup boobs to play an Indian maiden. He stayed in costume for a good part of the night. Cross-dressing seemed to be therapeutic for him.

After it was all over on Sunday, the results were announced. To our shock, we came in half a point ahead of the lowest-scoring team. Steve looked like a kid who'd just had his Popsicle fall in the dirt. "We set our sights on failing and somehow even screwed that up," he said.

I shook my head. "You still don't understand the Zen of failure, do you? We have succeeded beyond all imagining. We set a goal of coming in last and failed. We failed to fail. Tell me, Grasshopper, what more complete failure can a man attain?"

I could almost hear the rusty gears of his brain processing this. "Whoa," he said, his eyes widening. "That is some seriously twisted $#*+. But you're right. We failed to fail!" He looked like a new man.

Flats Fever

The terrible primacy of fishing in the human psyche—okay, in mine—was recently brought home to me for the millionth time. It began when Michelle called, excited at having found a last-minute deal to Cancun. I didn't have the money. I was also on deadline—these columns don't make this stuff up all by themselves. I resented both my poverty and the need to maintain it. "Hell yeah," I heard myself say. I was already thinking about fishing.

Six hours after nearly missing the plane due to sleet and traffic, we found ourselves dodging coconuts in the road as we fled Cancún, driving south along the coastal highway in a rented Jeep. I've always loved the Yucatán. It's as weird and unpredictable as the rest of Mexico, but somehow that stuff bothers me less here.

Michelle lamented all the coconut water going to waste. She pays two dollars for the canned stuff at home and here we were passing up fresh. "I wish I knew how to open them," she said. I pulled over at the next *ferreteria*, pantomimed certain parts of *Friday the 13th Part IV*, and was immediately sold a machete. But you can't buy a sharpened machete in Mexico—I guess it's their version of a waiting period—so I also bought a small file. Although I'm easily overwhelmed by complex tasks like buying groceries, give me a blade to sharpen and I'm a happy camper. A while later we stopped to collect and behead six coconuts, drinking the slightly sweet, electrolyte-rich juice straight from the shell. "I love that you're insane," Michelle said amiably.

Googling fishing possibilities on my phone, I'd found Boca Paila Lodge, a flats fisherman's dream destination that *averages* a hefty forty grand slams—bonefish, permit, and tarpon in the same day—each year. Unknown to Michelle, our vacation had become a mission.

The flats-fishing porn I'd seen on bocapaila.com was such that when we arrived, I promised the manager, on my honor as a journalist, a sixteen-page spread if he would comp us a couple of nights. He bit. The only problem was that a group of fly-fishing Danes had engaged all the guides. Our only option was Edilberto, the maintenance man and a guide-in-training who spoke little English. "Not a problem," I told the manager. "I can speak English really loud." The fellow looked bewildered. Michelle kicked me under the table. "Sorry," I said. "Haven't been on vacation for a while."

Edilberto Noh Mis spoke about as much English as I did Spanish. He was a short, dark, barefoot man in tortoiseshell shades. These lent him a distinguished air—like a Mayan Aristotle Onassis. Compared to the other guides' tricked-out boats, his was short and lacking paint, decals, upholstery, and a poling platform. But he knew how to find fish. I'd had the foresight to bring a 9-weight fly rod and a reel with a 5-weight line, but it was blowing too hard to fly-fish anyway. Even on spinning gear, bonefish lived up to their reputation: skittish as turkeys, fast as NFL backs when hooked, stronger than anything their size had a right to be. And when the fish finally saw the boat, the fight began all over again. Mine averaged 2 to 4 pounds, and I was actually thankful they weren't any bigger. I caught ten before my arm started hurting and I stopped counting. Then I started catching bigger fish. A 5-pound jack crevalle, its body compressed as if it had escaped from a George Foreman Grill. Then something with shoulders. I fought it for ten minutes before it took off in a straight line. I was relieved when it bit the leader, because otherwise it would have spooled me. I landed back-to-back snook of 6 and 7 pounds. We kept one for dinner and gave the other to Eddie.

Finally, with the light going, Eddie showed us the ruins of a Mayan temple in the water. Behind it was an island where pelicans, frigate birds, and parrots were arriving to roost for the night. "This is amazing," Michelle said. Eddie spoke and she translated. "He wants to know whether we want more fishing or to see the sights." My girlfriend had just watched me fish for eight hours without complaint. I'd caught more fish and tougher fish than in any single day of my life. I should have been satisfied. (Also, my forearms were in agony. I'd forgotten to frontload the ibuprofen and had put everything I had into every single cast.) This was my moment to step up, show some chivalry. "Up to you, babe," she said brightly.

I knew the right thing to do. I wanted to do it. But my higher brain had checked out hours ago. Maybe it couldn't take the sun. My reptilian brain, which wants what it wants, had taken over. I looked at my girl. I looked at Eddie.

"Fish," I said.

Faced with an Anti

Don't take this the wrong way, but you're a moron. It's okay, I'm a moron, too. That's because we hunt. And while surveys say that public acceptance of hunting has risen in recent years, there are still tens of millions of Americans for whom hunting is nothing less than the murder of innocent wild creatures by bloodthirsty rednecks. After reading part of my book *It's Only Slow Food Until You Try to Eat It,* one woman wrote me: "That you call killing an innocent deer 'awesome' and then thank the poor, dead, innocent animal whose life you snuffed out to make yourself feel competent, makes you sound even more nauseating." I thanked her for writing and suggested Tums for her stomach.

It's hard to think of a group more misunderstood than hunters. To many nonhunters, we all drive pickups and wear just two kinds of shirts, camo or plaid, depending on the occasion. We have the manners of warthogs and the sensitivity of toilet seats. And we mourn the passing of any day devoid of bloodshed.

To me, hunting can be like the passionate lovemaking of two fat people. It feels wonderful for those involved, but I don't want to see pictures of it. In the same way, the experience of hunting is vastly different from how it appears to an outsider. This is why the typical hunting photo—smiling hunter, lifeless animal—can be mistaken for heartless bloodlust. (This is one reason I seldom pose for hero shots. The other is that I seldom kill anything with big antlers.)

While hunters are frequently misunderstood, we're not exactly blameless in this. Think about it: How many guys in your wider circle

228

are slob hunters? I'm talking about guys who bend the law or fail to respect and care for their kill. How many actually brag about being killers or delight in antagonizing antihunters? If I'm honest, maybe one in five hunters I know falls into this category. I hope you hunt with a better class of people than I do. But if you're honest, you might have to admit that you don't.

Want to blow an antihunter's mind and do something positive for all hunters? Next time you're confronted by an anti, don't confirm the stereotype. Don't dismiss them as easily as they dismiss us. Instead, acknowledge that they might have a point. Admit that you yourself have mixed feelings about the kill. Then watch what happens.

At a cookout last year, a woman who'd heard I was a hunter sought me out to inform me that hunting was a cruel sport in which slobs like me made ourselves feel manly by killing innocent animals.

I wanted to say, "Ma'am, my compliments. Not many people with their heads so far up their butts could've walked over here without spilling their drink." But I didn't.

Next I wanted to say, "Listen, that part about them being 'innocent' animals is a crock. Every November, countless whitetails violate the Mann Act by brazenly crossing state lines for immoral purposes. I prefer the term *bounty hunter*." But I didn't say that, either.

"Well?" she said, bristling, ready for battle. I swirled my drink and looked down at the ice cubes. Then I spoke as if I were talking to a friend.

"I think some of what you say is true," I said, still looking into my drink, wishing it were bigger. "I love hunting. But the older I get, the more conflicted I am about the killing part." She looked taken aback but wary, as if this might be a trap. I kept on. "A lot of people think it's all about 'the thrill of the kill.' But the longer I hunt, the more I dread the killing part. It's hard to explain. It's the hunt that's thrilling, that whole process—the waiting and expectation, the focus and heightened sense of awareness, how the woods suddenly seem so vivid and alive. I've had great hunts where I didn't kill a thing. But in order for that process to be real, you have to be willing to make the kill.

"The thing about killing is that it makes you recognize the reality of your own death, which is as inevitable as any animal's. And as inconsequential. In the grand scheme of things, I mean. It also brings home the fact that all life—from frog to man, robin to alligator—sustains itself at the cost of other life. And that there aren't any easy answers as to what's right and what's wrong." I stopped abruptly. I wondered whether I'd gone too far. I wondered if any of it made sense.

I looked up. Now she was the one staring into her drink. She was no longer bristling. "I still don't approve of hunting," she said, looking up. "But it's a relief to find a hunter who thinks this way."

I shrugged. "More think this way than people know. I just talk more than most."

I don't remember what else we said before she left. I do remember feeling that I'd changed one person's opinion about hunting and hunters. And that if we hunters ever do change the stereotype, maybe that's how it will happen—one person at a time.

The Lake Effect

Although my father bought me my first fishing rod, he had no interest in the sport himself. I picked up the habit at summer camps. I was mesmerized. I sat for hours watching my bobber ride the water's surface—that membrane between two worlds. Above, the known world of clock time, overdue books, and soap. Below, an unknown universe of wild things. I was sure there was something down there meant for me alone.

I listen with envy when friends recall boyhood days spent fishing or hunting with their fathers. I would have liked that. But I don't recall feeling cheated at the time. My father and I spent most of my youth locked in conflict, him determined to make me obey, me determined not to. My only power lay in rejecting him. Dad loved to sail and tried to teach me. He liked golf and bought me a set of clubs before I'd ever taken a swing. By then it was too late. If he'd really wanted me to like something, he would only have needed to forbid it.

Maybe he wasn't the greatest father. I probably wasn't the greatest son. But now that I'm learning how hard it is to share something you love with your kids, I have much more sympathy for my dad. We scattered his ashes seven years ago in Lake Champlain, where he'd learned to sail, and where I'd caught my first fish.

Emma showed promise early on as a bluegill specialist, happily fishing with me in my canoe. Then, almost overnight, all her focus shifted to her friends, who didn't fish. A few years back, she became obsessed with *The Hunger Games* and was manic to get her hands on a bow.

231

But shooting in real life is a good deal harder than Katniss Everdeen makes it look in the movies. We were both frustrated. I could feel my father's blood rising in me at the waste—two hundred dollars for an outfit she'd shot three times? I bit my tongue, wondering if it had been this hard for him when I'd turned up my nose at the golf clubs.

When I met Michelle, her older boy, Jack, was dying to catch a fish. The first time a bluegill hit, he set the hook so hard the fish sailed out of the water and over our heads. Then Jack discovered video games. The delayed gratification of fishing was defenseless against Minecraft and Roblox.

My last and best hope is Cole. He's eight, with an iron will and an IQ that dwarfs mine. Of all the kids, Cole has shown the most sustained interest in fishing. On a recent outing, he insisted on changing lures every few casts, convinced that the new one would do the trick. He still requires an attendant (me) to tie each knot, but he wants no advice about how to rig or fish any bait. He doesn't believe a jig should ever get anywhere near the bottom. He'll thread a tiny curly-tailed grub onto a 5/0 wide-gap worm hook. I know better than to enforce any rules. And when he wants to tie knots, he'll learn them in no time. The important thing now is to stoke the boy's natural predatory fire.

Later that week, we were fishing a local lake at dusk when a flock of geese and goslings came ashore. As Cole dropped his rod and approached them, two adult birds moved in to intercept. "Easy, bud," I called. "Geese can bite pretty hard." He gave no indication that he heard me. I started breaking down the rods and checked back two minutes later. Cole was now on his hands and knees, pretending to peck at the grass like a gosling. He even had the cadence down—peck, lift your head to confirm mama's presence, take a step, peck again. In this manner, he'd calmed the adult birds and moved to within a few feet of some goslings.

You can't teach that kind of woods smarts. It's a gift, a kind of intelligence that doesn't show up on standardized tests. At that moment, I was seized by the image of Cole as an Indian boy, playing under the watchful eye of me, his hunter-gatherer father. Michelle had by this time come down to help gather up the kids and towels. I touched her hand and tipped my chin toward Cole among the birds. In my best Tonto imitation, I said, "Ah, you see? The boy does well. We will not starve in our old age."

"Idiot," she murmured, but smiled. "C'mon, Coley. Time for s'mores." But then she saw and understood what I'd seen. She said nothing but tightened her grip on my hand. I returned the squeeze. I was thinking that my father had taught me better than he ever knew.

Out of Orbit

I'm a lousy rifle shot. I blame this on living two hours from anywhere I can shoot a firearm and on the side effects of a medication I take to keep from biting people in the leg when they gush about how the new iPhone has changed their lives. Recently, however, a sudden desire to improve sent me to North Boondock, Arizona, for two days at Gunsite, a serious shooting school that sits on two thousand acres of high desert. My teacher was Cory Trapp, who is the school's "gunsmithy," served in special forces, and tests rifles for the military. He was about my age, but smarter, harder, with clearer eyes and pressed clothes.

Within five minutes, I felt like I'd been sucked into a parallel universe of shooting, one in which everything I knew about firearms was wrong. It started with the first of the four cardinal safety rules, usually given as "Treat every gun as if it were loaded." Wrong, said Trapp. "There's no 'as if,' nothing conditional about it. It's a fact. *The gun is always loaded.* Accept that and you'll be better off."

Gunsite stresses "practical marksmanship"—how fast you can put two shots in an eight-inch pie plate from different distances and positions. In the real world, a good fast shot beats a perfect slow one. In that extra moment a game animal will vanish, while a bad guy may put a bullet in your pie plate.

Looking for a good argument about rifle brands? Wrong place. "There's not ten percent of the shooting public that can exploit the inherent accuracy of the rifle they're shooting," Trapp said. "You buy a gun and it already shoots better than you do." Shooting, he explained, is simplicity itself. "Align the sights, place them on the target, and press the trigger to the rear without moving anything." Those last three words, incidentally, are where most of us screw up. We don't follow through on the trigger pull. This is a pesky by-product of a strange fact: The human brain actually works faster than a rifle. We press and relax the trigger finger—breaking form and moving the rifle—before the bullet leaves the barrel. We do this because the "dwell time," the interval between the trigger being pressed and the bullet leaving the barrel, is far longer than we believe. The cure is simple but not easy: Continue pressing the trigger until the recoil impulse has subsided and you've regained your sight picture. That's when the shot is complete. Your next move, by the way, is to run the bolt, not to lift your head to admire your handiwork.

Outside at a muddy range, Trapp demonstrated assumption of the prone position while keeping both eyes on target. "Drop to both knees," he said. "With the rifle in your off hand, plant the strong hand. Then move forward onto your stomach." He lay flat, oblivious to his ruined duds. And something else had just happened. Trapp had gone away. He had sealed himself inside a force field of intent, a bubble of concentration. He stayed there even as he kept teaching, his voice saying that you press toes *and* heels flat for maximum stability.

I suddenly recognized I was in a one-on-one master class, which unleashed a host of other realizations. I sensed Trapp pressing every atom of his body into the earth to steady the rifle. I finally got the phrase *in the gun,* the mental state in which everything unrelated to the moment's shooting task ceases to exist. I understood that the shooter's task is mainly to get out of the rifle's way, to let it do its work. And I saw that Trapp had left behind distinctions of "practice" and "real." Mentally, he was where he would be in combat.

I returned to my universe knowing what to do to improve: daily dry-fire exercises to achieve a consistent mount, and lots of pellet gun practice. ("Excellent for trigger control," Trapp said. "A pellet gun's dwell time is even longer than a rifle's.") One afternoon, while I was putting my Gamo 440 away, the crazy squirrel that had been eating my attic insulation like it was cotton candy came hopping over the fence. Keeping both eyes on it, I dropped to my knees and slid forward to prone, then centered the crosshairs on its head. I had unloaded the gun and couldn't have shot legally anyway. But the real problem was that I couldn't hold steady. The crosshairs were doing big, loopy figure-eights over the rodent's head.

In my case, improved accuracy was going to require more than drills. It would mean going off the medication. It would mean not reacting to people who were content, even proud, to pay for apps with names like iFart, Pro Zombie Soccer, and Zit Picker.

If there's an instructor out there who can teach me this, please get in touch.

The Smallmouth Man

Harry Murray's stainless steel spatula zips five green pills at a time across the counting tray as he gives an animated tutorial on drift nymphing, his favorite smallmouth tactic. "What most fly fishermen don't understand, Bill, is that on a twenty-five-foot cast upstream, you burn up the first six or eight feet of drift just getting the darn thing down. Then, of course, you use the next six or eight feet getting the fly under control so it's where you want it and you can detect that strike. So, you're actually only fishing the nymph for about—"

The phone rings. As he cradles the receiver to his ear, his voice suddenly turns into that of a professional pharmacist. The pills keep sliding uninterrupted from right to left like a metronome, like a lifelong flycaster, like a man not easily distracted from his business.

"Okay, Doc, twice a day. Generic okay on this? Yep. Sounds good. You, too." He hangs up and instantly his voice regains its enthusiasm. "So, like I say, you're only fishing the nymph for about ten feet. But it can be fantastically productive, Bill, it really can. And there's this great mystique about nymphing, but it's really all just line control. You want to actually feel—" Seeing a customer waiting, he interrupts himself this time. "How're you and that doctor getting along, Mazy?" he asks cordially.

"Not too good, Harry."

"You want me to call him?"

She blushes. "No. He'll think I'm crazy."

"No, he won't. I'll just tell him I can't read his writing." She smiles. Without missing a beat, he picks up where he left off, explaining how with a little practice you can actually feel the nymph ticking the bottom and develop a sixth sense about when to strike. He pours the pills, shaped like little bow ties, into a brown plastic bottle, labels it, and sets it on the counter.

If he were never to pick up a rod again, at fifty-six Harry Murray has already earned his place in the fly-fishing pantheon. Rod companies throw equipment at him like a one-man R&D division. He literally wrote the book on fly fishing for smallmouth bass. He's also the author of the definitive guide to trout fishing in Shenandoah National Park. People from across the country call months in advance to reserve a space in the twenty smallmouth and trout classes he teaches a year.

At first glance, the combination drugstore and fly-fishing shop in Edinburg, Virginia, is an unlikely hybrid, sort of like the jackalope hanging over the door to his office in the back. You're looking at a rack of fifty top-of-the-line fly rods by Scott, Orvis, and Loomis, and in the next aisle over are Pepto-Bismol and No-Nonsense control-top pantyhose. The sink behind the pharmacy counter holds two gallon batches of Murray's Liquid Dry Fly Floatant that are just about ready for bottling. (Harry says it's the best on the market because it has no silicones to attract dirt and no paraffin to make your fly stiff.) While you're waiting for your prescription, you can peruse more than four hundred flies, including the ones Harry has made famous, the Mr. Rapidan, Murray's Hellgramite, and Murray's Strymph, which can be fished either as a streamer or a nymph. You can't figure out if you're in a fly shop or inside a pharmacy. After a while you stop trying. It is what it is.

In *Flyfishing for Smallmouth Bass* Harry writes that to understand the fish and how to catch them, you have to read the water where they live. He might as well have been writing about himself. The Shenandoah Valley is a 150-mile-long world unto itself between the Blue Ridge and Allegheny mountains. Edinburg sits in the heart of it, near where Stony Creek joins the North Fork of the Shenandoah, increasing the river's volume by a third. During the Civil War, when Stonewall Jackson was giving the Yankees fits, there were five hundred people here. Now the population is up to about 650. The Murrays have lived here for seven generations, and the white house Harry grew up in is visible from the front door of the store. He has some nineteenth-century fly rods on his wall, collections of early bass bugs, and a 1915 photo of his grandfather holding a 5-pound, 15-ounce North Fork smallmouth. He's wearing a straw boater and standing in front of a sign for King Cola.

Anglers seeking smallmouths in the two forks of the Shenandoah River or trout in the mountain streams of the park know Harry is not a hoarder of information. Whether you're coming in to pick up the $430 Scott Mountain Trout rod that bears his name or a Baby Ruth and some 2X tippet, he'll tell you everything he knows about what the fish are hitting, and where and how to get there. He wants you to catch fish—as long as you put most of them back.

The guy is a perpetual-motion machine; he's always busy. But he's never too busy to talk about fishing. As you head for the door, he calls, "Keep in touch."

He distributes thirty thousand copies of his forty-page mail-order catalogs a year, teaches fly-tying courses at a local college, and runs a guide service. Yet he insists he couldn't make it without the pharmacy, which accounts for half his business. Last year he considered getting an 800 number, renting a big mailing list, and sending out eighty thousand catalogs. Before he did, he ran the idea past his friend Leigh Perkins, the owner of Orvis. "Leigh told me there's a big difference between doing business and making money," Harry says. "And, boy, is that true. The other thing he told me is that if I put in an 800 number, I'd never get off the phone. I'd be too busy listening to everybody else's fishing stories." Harry put in a toll-free fax number instead.

He's not the kind to make a lot of noise about it, but it's plain that he doesn't like the elitism that has taken over fly fishing. He sees too many anglers who "evolve" technically as fishermen but never get the point. "Too often, the deal goes something like this," he says. "First, we want to catch A Lot of Fish. Then we want to catch Big Fish. If we get past that, we want to catch Difficult Fish, the ones that lesser anglers can neither locate nor fool. But if that's all you're after, then maybe you're the fool. Because the only real reason to fish is because it's fun, because you love being out there. And, if you have the antennae for it, to feel the hand of God at work in the rocks and the riffles and the wildness of the fish."

Talk to Harry's fishing buddies and you'll learn they agree that the guy has three main characteristics: insatiable curiosity, intensity, and the ability to have a good time. "Last time the two of us got out together, we drove south of Livingston to a stream I wanted to try," says Richard Parks, who owns a fly shop and guides in Yellowstone National Park. "And the fishing absolutely stunk, no two ways about it. We busted our humps all day for five, six fish. And at the end of the day, after having fished for eight hours and driven for four, Harry was grinning from ear to ear and telling me what a great time he'd had. You can't help but appreciate being around a guy like that."

Harry's smallmouth book is loaded with that rare commodity, common sense. Everything is broken down into simple components. Reading the water, for instance, is a three-step procedure: Where is the fish? Where do I cast my fly? Where do I need to be when I'm doing it? Of the three parts, casting the position may be the most important, since moving as little as five feet can often put you into fish you couldn't reach before. He writes of "doing justice" to the water, a kind of moral obligation not to waste it, to work every productive angle it offers.

You're not doing justice to a grass bed, for example, unless you're fifty feet away from it and probing not only the edges, but the tiny pockets inside the bed and the open water near it where fish may be cruising or resting. Should you hook a big fish on a light leader and have it head for the grass, he even offers a strategy for you—if you've got the nerve. Just release all tension on the line. "In some cases, the bass, feeling nothing forcing him in a direction he does not want to go, will stop his run short of the grass bed." In the next paragraph, the fisherman's fisherman admits that he wasn't brave enough to try it the last time he hooked a big one. You can't help but appreciate a guy so devoid of vanity.

A typical Murray lesson in the book begins when nothing's going his way. After half a hot summer day spent throwing nymphs, streamers, hair bugs, and hard poppers, he confesses, "I was disappointed, but more than this I was curious," in this case, it's because even though the bass refuse his offerings they're leaping—usually without success—after dragonflies buzzing along the surface. Harry remembered how Ed Hewett used to fish for trout on the Neversink River in New York using a dry fly with a great oversize hackle on a tight line to impart a skating action. He proceeds to dress his fly with extra silicone, casts down and across, and retrieves all slack out of his line, bringing the big fly up on its toes in 6-inch darts. The fish slam it.

Most guys would pat themselves on the back and keep catching fish. But Harry's true quarry is knowledge, not numbers. He switches back to the nonproductive flies he was using to satisfy himself that it's not just a case of the fish having suddenly gotten their appetites back. He continues fishing it in a variety of situations to verify his theory.

Sitting in his little office in the back of the store, he looks out over Stony Creek. "I seined minnows and hellgrammites in those riffles right there when I was a kid," he says, motioning with his chin. "And one of my best friends caught the biggest smallmouth of his life in that pool just above it. Someday I'm gonna cast from in here just so I can tell people I fished out my office window."

Asked about the future, he says he just wants to keep doing what he's doing for as long as he can. His publisher has just accepted another book, this one about his reminiscences of growing up fishing in the Shenandoah. He likes running the pharmacy and has inserted himself into the lives of so many of the townspeople that a sense of obligation alone would probably keep him in the business. And he fishes not only in Virginia, but pretty much anywhere in the world he wants. Not long ago, a young fellow from a paper in Richmond came up to do a story on him and ended a long interview by asking him what his dream was. "I told him I'm already living my dream," he says. He smiles for a moment, remembering the encounter. Then he stands up to go back to work.

Tackle Underworld

About every ten years, I organize my fishing tackle. Before entering my basement, I should don a safety harness, leave a note stating my intentions, and stamp a footprint in aluminum foil. Instead, I just wear heavy shoes and a headlamp. And then I go down into damp and dim Deal-With-That-Later Land. Stick to the narrow path to the washer and dryer and you'll be okay. Off-trail, you'll encounter strings of pre-LED Christmas lights that make the neighbors' flicker and dim when plugged in, ammo dating from the Spanish-American War, or my three vacuum cleaners, one of which still works.

Fishing tackle is in the Area 51 of the basement. Lure, hook, weight, bead, or swivel—if you can tie it to a fishing line, it's down here somewhere. Undifferentiated gear chokes the mouths of four tackle bags, overflows two forty-gallon Rubbermaid totes, and lies in loose mounds on the cement floor. All of it is guarded by blind crickets the size of cupcakes.

If you can tell a man by his tackle, mine bespeaks a gullible and easily confused angler. But also a stubborn guy who goes his own way, mostly because he can't keep up. The cubic footage is staggering.

I have, for example, three hundred miles of fishing line. There must have been a time when I feared they'd make it illegal. I have it in tests from 4- to 30-pound and in spools from 330 to 1,500 yards. I've got Stren LoVis Green mono, Magnathin, and Super Braid. I have Trilene TransOptic, FireLine, and Spiderwire EZ Braid. I have Berkley 4-pound Micro Ice. Which is strange because I can't remember ever going ice fishing. I have fluorocarbon and steel leaders. With two soup cans and a hole punch, I could set up a secure link to North Carolina.

Here's a strange thing. For years, I must have believed that my success and that of Gary Yamamoto Custom Baits were one and the same. How else to explain twenty-plus pounds of Yamamoto plastic? It's mostly Senkos: regular Senkos, Pro Senkos, Swim Senkos, and Slim Senkos. If they'd made a Sin Senko, I'd have bought that, too. They come in more shades than Sherwin-Williams paint, and I own most. With a five-pack of 6-inchers running six or seven bucks, I've got Emma's first year of college at my feet, all tied up in soft, salty fishing pencils with the structural integrity of soap bubbles. One good hit from a largemouth and it's lights-out for a Senko. But the bass that takes one will hold on to it like a fat man to a bag of Cheetos.

The Senko is, famously, a do-nothing lure. Which is why reeling in a Senko-caught bass always feels like a mixed blessing. Sure, I caught that bass. But it's like being a kid at a bowling birthday party with gutter bumpers. You roll the ball, walk back for more cake, and hear a cheer when it's a strike. But you're not sure how much you had to do with it.

Look, a tray of old spinnerbaits, some still in packaging touting a Lifelike Silicone Skirt! Thing is, the latex band securing each skirt rotted ages ago. I discover this by picking one up and finding myself inside a cloud of almost weightless strands—blue, black, and chartreuse—that waft slowly down. I'm transfixed by the odd, unexpected beauty. For a moment, I'm inside a spinnerbait snow globe. I vow to get replacement bands, knowing I won't. And then I carefully shut the tray.

In a shoe box I find my Lauri Rapala Memorial Hospital, home to old soldiers that lost an eye or a lip or were gouged by something with teeth. I touch each and remember: a barracuda in Panama, a northern in Wisconsin, something I never did see in Lake Nicaragua. They're old comrades. The odds that I'll actually fix them are zilch, but that's not important. I've never had a bad Rapala. It's as if they know what's expected and don't want to let you down. How do you throw that away?

243

My stomach growls. It's been four hours. The chaos level is unchanged, but it is reconfigured. And it's not a total loss. I've reconnected with some old friends. I've established that I don't need line. I do wish I'd funded my retirement plan half as well as I did Gary Yamamoto's.

From above comes the Emma-slam of the front door, the familiar tread. "I'm home!" she announces. "Daddy?"

"Downstairs," I call. "Coming up." A cupcake cricket, one of the ancients, with serrated back legs and antennae four inches long, twitches one of its feelers. Summoned, I bend down as to an old man. Wordlessly, the cricket says that it knows everything and will keep my secrets.

What the Horse Saw

As a twenty-first-century outdoorsman, I'm constantly redefining what it means to be manly. Frequently, it involves using products originally developed for women. On a late duck hunt some years back, my lips got so chapped it felt as if they'd been attacked by an orbital sander. The day was cold, with winds gusting to thirty miles per hour. If I pressed my lips together, I could practically hear them cracking. One of the men in the blind had brought his wife along. I asked if she happened to have any lip balm. She didn't. But she volunteered that she did have lipstick.

"That'll work," I managed to croak. "Pass it down." The lipstick came in a little gold tube about the size of a 28-gauge shell, something you wouldn't expect to be a cause of discomfort. I guess context really is everything, however, because these guys looked like they'd rather have been handling a water moccasin. When the lipstick reached me, I smeared some on. The relief was instantaneous and complete. I was back in the game, scanning the sky for birds. I still don't know what was in that lipstick, but it beat anything I'd ever used on chapped skin. Meanwhile, the other guys looked at me and howled. One asked if I was free Saturday night. Out of curiosity, I asked my benefactress the particular shade of the lipstick.

"It's called Pink Voltage," she said.

In a photo from the hunt, I'm the smiling guy in muddy camo, a three-day beard, and pink-voltage lips. The picture explains why the guys laughed, of course, but it also validates my decision. In it I'm smiling, and that's because the lipstick worked. And maybe it's just me, but I think I looked like the kind of bald, outdoorsy transvestite that any guy would be happy to introduce to his parents.

My latest foray into repurposing girl stuff came on a fishing trip— described earlier in this book—where I found myself buying pantyhose in Lander, Wyoming. The day before we rode horses up into the Wind River Range to go trout fishing, our outfitter, George Hunker, warned that our legs could get badly chafed if our jeans didn't fit right. I hadn't been on a horse in so long that I couldn't remember what constituted the right fit. George said that the best insurance was a pair of pantyhose. At first, I thought he was kidding. He wasn't. "Heck, enough guys buy them that we sometimes call 'em mantyhose," he said. While you probably wouldn't guess it from my appearance, I'm as proud as the next guy. On the other hand, I'm strongly opposed to physical discomfort. If the choice is between five hours of pain and feeling silly, my priorities are clear.

Back at the motel, I asked Michelle if she was considering buying pantyhose. "No, I've got those SmartWool long johns of yours," she said. "I'm good." I had lent her those to hunt deer in last winter. Unfortunately, she'd loved them. By the unwritten-but-universal rules of Lending Gear to Your Girlfriend, they had become hers. She was kind enough to offer to purchase pantyhose on my behalf.

We'd been in Lander for less than twenty-four hours, but it's an honest-to-God western town, a place where cowpokes still sometimes ride their horses into the local bar to order a beer. Either the atmosphere was already rubbing off on me or it was the altitude. In any case, I decided that there were some errands a real man didn't farm out. And buying pantyhose was one of them.

Striding across the sun-blasted asphalt between the motel and a nearby dollar store, I flashed on Gary Cooper in *High Noon*. Like him, I was alone and headed into a potentially hazardous situation. Like him, I had no option but to see it through. I pushed my way in and found a saleslady.

"Need a pair of pantyhose," I boomed. I had two reasons for speaking loudly. One was that I didn't want to seem embarrassed. The other was that I didn't want to have to say *pantyhose* twice.

"What size would you be wanting those in, sir?" she asked.

"XL," I said.

"And the color?"

"Taupe." I managed to pronounce the word as if it were a brand of whiskey rather than a color.

"Control top or regular?"

"Reg'lar," I said, dropping the middle syllable. (*What's with you? I wondered. You're buying pantyhose, not a new set of spurs.*)

"Sheer or opaque?" she asked.

I gave her a weary smile. I could see exactly where this little game was headed. We both knew that no real man would be caught dead in sheer pantyhose. "Opaque'll do just fine," I said. My purchase folded under one arm, I strode back out into the afternoon sun.

The pantyhose worked like a charm and turned out to be one of the smartest moves I've ever made. Just remember that you don't want control top and you do want opaque. Otherwise some people might question your masculinity.

Bull's Eye

As a civic-minded fisherman, I feel I have a duty to tell other anglers about places they should visit and places to avoid. And I'm telling you right now: Do not go fishing in Louisiana. Specifically, do not go fishing down in the Mississippi River delta out of Venice, the last outpost, the place where the pavement ends and thousands of square miles of endangered wetlands begin. The fishing here is so good that when it's time to go home they may have to force you out at the point of a fillet knife.

Captain Brent Ballay of Venice Sport Fishing cuts the engine of a 23-foot Hydra Sport twenty minutes out of the marina and hands me a medium-heavy spinning rod. It's rigged with a D.O.A. Shrimp jig tipped with a piece of the real thing. Just above the baited lure rides a tennis-ball-size cupped bobber, through which runs a heavy wire strung with red plastic beads. That, it turns out, is Cajun Thunder, a slice of Las Vegas tied to your line. Popped back after the cast, the cupped face *bloops* like a surface-feeding fish, while the clacking beads mimic, well, I have no idea what. But I'm a tourist and accustomed to making a fool of myself, so I give it a try. After a few hitless casts, I find myself mesmerized by the scenery. In the middle distance, a flock of glossy ibis lifts, iridescent purple confetti falling the wrong way. Two members of the Brown Pelican Flight Team appear, rolling out low and slow, one inch off the deck, on patrol for any mullet fool enough to surface. The sun glints off gas pipelines straight as rifle barrels, which run past an ancient-looking lighthouse returning brick by brick to the mud from which it rose. I'm wondering at the strangeness of such a place when a voice interrupts. "Set the hook! Set the damn *hook,* cuz!" I do, and a redfish splashes twenty-five yards out. It surges, heads for the weeds, turns back the way it came, turns back toward me, then surges harder yet when it spots the boat. Finally lifted into the air, it is impossibly vivid, a hammered copper torpedo. Nothing I've ever hooked in skinny water has fought like this. It has white flanks and distinctive black eyes along its tail and looks as if it would happily amputate my hand. Ballay says it'll go 34 inches, maybe 16 pounds. The big ones aren't for eating, though. Back he goes.

Ballay grew up on the river, crossing it to reach school each day. "Except when it was foggy," he says. "Mama didn't believe in radar." His parents started the marina in 1985. He tells me his dad violated every child labor law on the books, having both sons working the slips, dock, and register whenever possible. He tells me he was tarpon fishing at three; that in high school, while his buddies were getting in scrapes on Bourbon Street, all he wanted to do was fish and guide; that he was sitting in a math class at Southeastern University toting up how much money he was losing by not guiding when he finally gave up trying to live any other kind of life. He tells me that his mama can still whip his behind when it comes to putting fish in the boat. "I'm just glad I never had to face her in a tournament."

Everything is a little different here. Distances are measured in a commodity never far from hand: beer. As in, "We got into 'em yesterday not half a beer from the dock." The names for fish themselves are different, too. Red drum are either "bulls" (big) or "rats" (little), speckled trout are "mules" or "cigars," largemouths are "green trout," and flounder are "doormats." It's not unusual to pull a bull, a mule, and a green trout from the same cove.

Ballay spies schooling reds working over some shrimp and moves us into position. I cast just ahead of the fray and hook up five seconds later, only to watch another fish immediately slash at the Cajun Thunder itself, breaking the first fish off. The whole school, alarmed, streaks away. We retie, fishing for our dinner now, keeping a few reds, a black drum, and a speckled trout. Katrina tore right through here,

Ballay says, devastating the marina, the town, and countless other delta communities. Many, if not most, people rebuilt because they couldn't imagine leaving. He says the fishing is as good as or better than ever, and when he apologizes that today was slow, it takes me a while to realize he's serious.

We ride back to the dock and unload at the cleaning station, where Joe Adams, a sunburned guy in a Harley bandanna, deftly zips out fillets with an electric knife. He buys them by the case. "Damn knives have plastic gears," he says. He goes through a hundred a year.

The next morning, taking a final stroll along the docks, I see a boy on the deck of a houseboat. He picks up a rod and idly starts working nearby pilings with a bass jig. On his third cast, the rod arcs. I find myself wondering how much it would cost to catch a later flight.

Hoofing It for Caribou

How would a middle-aged bowhunter (gasp!) from the leafy Virginia suburbs (where am I?) fare without a guide (help!) in the tundra wilderness of northern Quebec?

For the past forty minutes, ever since the floatplane lifted off the lake in Schefferville, the scenery below has been singularly constant. It's a land of glacier-smoothed hills, little lakes, stunted shrubs, and spruce. Each piece of water, with its surrounding hills and tundra, is a carbon copy of the last and the next. It must be how a wet beach towel looks to a sand flea.

This is partly because Quebec is a big place, three times the size of France. Unlike that country, it is almost devoid of human presence, since practically all the population resides in the cities of the south. Get lost here and there's a very good chance nobody will find you until the ravens and wolves pick your bones so white that they show up like a signal mirror against the dark lichens.

The pilot cuts the de Havilland Beaver's airspeed to 60 knots, touches down on a small lake, and coasts to a stop by a tiny gravel beach just past three walled tents. Waiting onshore by the little wooden trucking pallet that passes for a dock are four hunters from Michigan. They're headed out with impossibly wide caribou antlers still in velvet, green plastic meat boxes, gun cases, and duffels.

The pilot unloads propane and cooking oil, then passes out my duffel and the SKS double bow case that allowed me to bring both a bow and a .270 without violating the airline's two-bag limit. The Michigan boys cram inside, laughing and joking. The absurdly big, complicated antlers only fit by being stowed at crazy angles on their laps. One bad air pocket and some caribou will take his revenge on the hunter who shot him. The plane whines out into the lake, lifts itself into the sky, makes a half circle, and disappears over the trees. This marks the end of the officially supervised part of my hunt.

A strange confluence of factors has induced me to book an unguided hunt. Number one—and the trump card for all of us in the Brotherhood of Skinflints—it's cheaper. Number two, I wanted to see how I, an eastern hardwoods whitetail guy who mostly hunts small farms and patches of woods, would fare chasing big deer in even bigger country. Number three, the editors of this magazine, fully aware that I'm the kind of guy who leaps before he looks, have apparently decided that sending me up here without adult supervision could be a discreet way of reducing payroll without having to shell out unemployment.

I stow my gear and take a practice shot at a stump with a judo point. The guides, waiting for a party of four due in the next day, are instantly intrigued by my bow, a slick new Mathews LX with a Trophy Ridge fiber-optic sight, a Whisker Biscuit arrow rest, and LimbSaver dampeners. I tell them my plan is to hunt three days with the bow and the final two with a .270 if I haven't gotten anything by then. "She's a fine one, all right," says Sam, hefting the bow. He's a sinewy Newfoundlander with a whiskey brogue and a red beard you could hide a set of cutlery in. "But I wouldn't take her myself." I ask why the hell not. "Bow like that, you got no excuse if you miss." He hands it back and winks.

There are about three hours of sunlight left, and I want to get the lay of the land before dinner. Sam tells me to head up the narrow trail that winds a third of a mile up from camp to another small lake and the big bowl surrounding it. "Stay on the trail and you can't get lost. There's a rock up there, good place to sit and glass for 'em." Sam is obviously overestimating my navigational skills. I can get lost in my own laundry room. I pull out my GPS, calibrate the compass by turning slowly around twice like some nutcase monk in prayer, then lock

252

in the camp's location as a waypoint. Because of the tendency of high technology to transform itself into junk at the slightest excuse, I'm also packing a compass and a roll of orange flagging tape. And two butane lighters, waterproof matches, fire paste, a candle, a plastic bag big enough for me and a caribou to spend the night in. Plus fifty feet of parachute cord, a water bottle, a Mini Mag flashlight, and energy bars.

The bowl is several miles across, and I glass it for a half hour, seeing nothing, though there are prints in the mud all around me. Any whitetail hunter would quickly identify ten good rifle stands: saddles, bench overlooks, points of timber, transition zones from one kind of cover to another. The guides have told me that a lot of good bulls have been taken right where I'm sitting, a small gap between two hills.

I decide to move, crossing a stream and heading up through the woods, keeping the bowl's lake in sight. There are blueberries everywhere, and I stop to pick them, feeling like a boy back at summer camp in North Carolina. I take up a position downwind of where a caribou trail leaves the woods and settle in. After ninety minutes, just as I am about to leave, I spot them through my binocs: six antlike silhouettes on the far rim of the bowl, at least three miles off and one thousand feet above me. They're here, all right. I just need to close the distance a little.

Caribou Everywhere—and Nowhere

The next morning, the plane returns and disgorges four hunters. I head up the trail as they're storing their gear. It's chilly and spitting rain under gray skies. I station myself on a bench halfway up the bowl, where a draw full of timber runs down to the lake. I stand behind a clump of stunted trees that break the ever-present wind and glass constantly, though I can only do so downwind. The moment you turn into the rain, your binocs fog over and you spend the next twenty minutes trying to wipe them dry. After about an hour, I notice two antlered animals with young slowly grazing their way over the open ground three hundred yards above me. Caribou are the only deer in which animals of both sexes sport antlers, but the females' are much smaller. These are two cows with calves. You can take cows, but I move deeper into the cover to let them pass upwind.

The deal with caribou, I know from doing a little pre-trip research, is finding them. At last count, the George River herd in Quebec numbered somewhere around 700,000 animals. That's a lot of caribou. Quebec covers 700,000 square kilometers, however, which is a considerable hunk of real estate. Caribou are migratory beasts, with wintering grounds, calving grounds, and extensive ranges in between. An animal may move twenty miles a day, especially while heading to wintering grounds in early fall. The enduring campfire tale among hunters is of emerging from a tent to take a leak and finding yourself surrounded by thousands of 'bou streaming past in an hours-long parade. This indeed happens, but it is fairly rare. (I find out later that none of the four guides in camp, with nearly a century of combined experience, has ever seen it during the hunting season.) Much of the time, the animals are widely dispersed. Now, in early fall, it's common to see groups of bulls traveling together. This presents the hunter with a choice based on his inclination and endurance. You can walk around looking for them, but you have to be sneaky because they are adept at picking up movement at great distances. Or you can do as most hunters do: spot and stalk or simply wait by a likely saddle, river crossing, or other travel corridor, and ambush them as they walk by. Your hunt may end the same day you arrive in camp, or you may still be at it when you hear the whine of the plane coming to pick you up.

Two hours later, my bones stiff from standing motionless in raw weather, I spy two bulls making their way along a ridge a thousand yards up from me. There's no hope of a stalk; everything between them and me is less than eighteen inches tall, a long way to belly-crawl, and they're moving fast, as though they've got someplace to be. I watch them hoof it out of sight and over into the next drainage, taking a piece of my heart with them.

In the afternoon, the skies clear and I run into Sam, who has jogged ahead of his new clients coming up the trail, for a quick look by the glassing rock. Silently, he points to the bench I just left half an hour ago. Through my binocs I see two bulls there now, one with white antlers, another, bigger, with a chocolate brown rack still in velvet. They are feeding along slowly. If I'd stayed where I was another forty-five minutes, I'd be drawing on them now.

At this point, I have no real idea whether a given animal is one to pass up or a trophy. Caribou antlers are notoriously complicated. You have all the normal measurements to consider—main-beam length, inside spread, mass and length of various points. But on a caribou you're doing it for the shovel (which may be single or double), the bez (the secondary mass of antler halfway up the rack), the size of the top palm and its points, whether there are rear points behind that, and if so how long. It takes practice to judge them, something I am very short on.

"Both nice animals," Sam says casually. "They've got it all." I stand there like a doofus for a few minutes, watching the caribou as if they were lobsters in the tank at my local supermarket. Finally, I ask Sam what he'd do. "I'd get my ass back over there fast," he replies.

I take off on a headlong run through the mud and bushes and trees. "Get below 'em and use that seam of shrub to sneak up," he calls after me. I arrive twenty minutes later, sweating and sucking wind, and stalk up to the bench. The bulls are no longer there. I theorize that they've headed upwind if I haven't already busted them. I parallel the bench from below, occasionally creeping up the ridge for a look. Still no bulls. They might be just over a little ridge in the swale between the lake I'm hunting and the one above it. I creep down to where I can see if that's where they went. It's a risky move: I'm traveling crosswind, and the wind probably swirls once it hits the swale.

But it pays off. There below me are both bulls and eight cows and their young, all feeding contentedly. I guess the distance at 150 yards, though with almost nothing for reference between them and me, it's hard to say. With a rifle, I could limit out now with two well-placed shots and spend the rest of the week patting myself on the back. With a bow, my only hope is a wide backtrack to station myself in the thick stuff by the lake's edge in the hope that they will graze that way and offer a shot. By the time I have the group of caribou back in sight, all I see are cows. The bulls have vanished. Suddenly I hear loud scraping sounds. High above me on a ridge I see the rears of the two bulls, side by side, walking fast. They saw or heard me and left the belt of trees to walk straight up the loose shale toward safety, setting off mini rockslides with each step. The cows are still there, so I probably wasn't scented, but it doesn't matter. The bulls ascend the steep ridge, silhouette themselves vividly for a moment at the crest, and are gone forever.

Agony on the Tundra

Although I'm here as a single hunter I've somehow managed to attach myself to the gravy train being prepared for the other clients. The bottle of Scotch I gave to Lloyd, the cook, hasn't hurt. (I notice that he's slipping me turkey sandwiches to take for lunch while the other guys are getting peanut butter.) And I pass out plenty of Labatt's Blue to the guides, deceptively small men from dying fishing villages in Labrador and Newfoundland who can carry half their weight in caribou meat all day and leave you eating their mud.

The next afternoon, I find myself pinned down by two fairly small bulls—either of which I would happily shoot—that come feeding toward me and bed down in the open. I take their range at 142 yards. Once again, there is no cover over six inches high between us. I am crouched behind a rock, back and knees getting tighter all the time, trying to come up with a strategy. Finally I leave all my gear except for my bow and, keeping the rock between us, start to crab-crawl backward one hundred yards to a line of shrubs. Meanwhile, the rain starts. I am wet, dirty, scratched, and bleeding slightly in two places when I make the shrubbery. Gloves might have been a good idea. I crawl around to the continuation of the path they were taking when they had bedded down and set up twenty yards downwind of it. The sweat I worked up now chills me. After an eternity, the bulls rise and mosey back the way they came.

I don't want to kill them now. I just want to punish them, tie them up, and make them watch early Madonna videos until their caribou minds are mush. It is now dusk. I head back to camp and ask Lloyd if he can spare some Scotch.

On my last day of bowhunting I set up in the faintest of saddles set in a high ridge, a place where I've spotted animals crossing fairly regularly. It's all loose dark rock around me, no boulders, and I am tucked into the lone clump of bushes for two hundred yards in any direction. At 10 a.m., I'm sitting there on my knees and heels when a group of cows and a few yearling bulls comes plodding over the saddle. Just as they're nearly in my lap, the wind shifts and they catch my scent but can't quite unravel it. They mill about nervously. One good-size cow turns broadside and stops long enough for me to laser the distance at twenty-nine yards. It's an eminently makable shot, but I let her walk. I'm still holding out for bulls.

Ground Work

On day four, I come over to the dark side, increasing my range from forty yards to 250, thanks to the Winchester division of the Olin Corporation. I set up above the same saddle. The reality of the situation has dawned on me: two days left, nothing on the ground, a yawning freezer at home. I resolve to drop the first legal bull I see. A few minutes later, I spot two cows with fawns in tow crossing 150 yards below me, stopping to nibble lichens. Then a young bull appears. I already have my pack in front of me to use as a rest. I put the crosshairs of the .270 just behind his shoulder and squeeze. He goes down, hooves in the air, legs churning. I fire again and he goes down for good.

You have to clean caribou quickly because a diet of lichen causes their stomachs to bloat within minutes. Wait too long, and they actually explode. I get the animal gutted pretty fast. In another hour, I manage to cut, hack, and saw it into pieces that might loosely be called quarters. Fortunately, I'm only half a mile from camp, almost all of it downhill. It takes me four trips to get it all into the screened meat house by the dock. There is a surprising sense of satisfaction in packing your own meat out instead of following a guide who is doing it for you. Sure, after my amateur cutting job, a lot of the meat is only fit to be ground into burger. But it's mine. I'm the one who stalked it, killed it, and carried it out. On the last trip down, I run into one of the other rifle hunters with his guide heading out for the afternoon. "You packing one out?" he asks. "Yep," I say. There is something very much like envy in his face.

That night, I discover that only one of the four other hunters has scored. Two of them are bowhunters; one missed an animal at forty yards. It seems as if I'm not doing too badly on my own.

My last full day of hunting brings a 30-knot west wind and a cold, steady drizzle. I choose a spot along a path connecting two lakes. By sitting with my knees bunched up close to my chest, I can get much of my body behind a small boulder and blunt the wind and rain. Every half hour, when I start to hear my own teeth clicking, I get up and slowly climb a hundred yards farther up the ridge to get some blood moving. Lloyd sees the look on my face as I trudge into camp that night, wipes his hands on his apron, and reappears with a coffee cup half full of 80-proof muscle warmer.

The plane is due to pick me up early the next morning. During the night, the weather turns. I rise to a rarity on this trip: sunshine and bluebird skies. I pack reluctantly, sure that today would have brought a big bull my way. I put on blue jeans instead of camo and settle down with coffee and a novel in a chair facing the sun. Then one of the guides tells me he just heard on the radio that the plane will be a couple of hours late. Something about extra propane needed in another camp. I drop the book and get out my rifle, a handful of shells, and binoculars. I jog up to the saddle by the lake where Sam told me to glass from the first evening. Two hours later, when I hear the whine of the floatplane coming to take me away, I'm still there, convinced that at any moment a big one's going to emerge from the trees and give himself to me.

Wishful Thinking

I just turned sixty. Or, as Michelle puts it, "More like fifteen for the fourth time." Having just spent a year being fifty-nine, I had a pretty good idea which number was coming next. So I shouldn't have been surprised when the day came around. Some part of my brain hadn't gotten the word. It felt like I'd just been clobbered by a sack of potatoes. This, obviously, was absurd. Sixty, in itself, isn't all that scary. It's just a number. On the other hand, I suspect that anybody who ever survived being run over by a bus would tell you that it looked like a normal bus—right up until the moment it didn't.

There's a bunch of hogwash out there about the blessings of aging. I've read stuff about how people discover that they're more patient, more tolerant. They see the good in people more readily. They're more comfortable in their own skin. It's like their only regret is that they couldn't turn sixty a long time ago.

None of this is true in my case. Especially the skin part. My neck, for example, used to be a smooth, one-piece unit. Now, when shaving, I get a closer look than I really need at all the ligaments and muscles that make up my neck. I have the neck of a fairly attractive snapping turtle.

Patience? I have less than ever. Take, for example, a child who gives me a limp handshake. It's the nonverbal equivalent of the child declaring, "I'm headed for a life of mediocrity at full speed, and my parents are buying the gas." I'll ask the child, have I just made the acquaintance of a dead fish? No? Then shake hands like you mean it. There, that's the stuff.

I regard this form of intolerance as a public service. I've noticed that not everyone thinks the same. This no longer bothers me. Caring less about what others think may be the one genuine payoff of aging.

Experience has, however, helped me make peace with certain things. I'll never be a good offhand rifle shot. I'll also never be a threat to fish with a fly rod. This awareness doesn't stop me from trying anyway. For my fly-fishing efforts I have awarded myself an imaginary citation—Advanced Beginner with Oak Leaf Cluster for Persistence in the Face of Overwhelming Lack of Skill.

I'll never be able to do that piercing two-fingers-in-the-mouth whistle. It's sort of a kee-kee run for humans and would have saved me a lot of shouting trying to locate friends in the woods and Walmart parking lots. I'll never master the Bimini twist or that trick where you pop the top off a beer bottle with a plastic lighter. Four people have shown me how it's done. I still can't do it. Fortunately, I am stubborn. If there's beer inside, I'll find a way.

Another of the supposed benefits of aging is that, over the accumulating decades of experience, you eventually learn *how* to learn from your mistakes. Once again, this is patently untrue. I still routinely show up at the wrong airport on the right day, and the right airport on the wrong day. The same has happened with bodies of water and fishing dates with buddies. I won't go into detail. Except to note that this magazine does not always reimburse me for the full cost of being me.

You'd think that after a great deal of travel, I'd have a procedure to follow when packing. I do. I wait until the night before, then panic. I make piles of the stuff I'm considering in different rooms and run back and forth between them like a deranged retriever. I know that wherever I'm going, it will be hotter and colder, wetter and drier than I expect. But I am incapable of putting this knowledge to good use. On a recent five-day turkey road trip, I wore my good "travel shoes" afield every day and never once donned the boots I'd brought. By the end, the boots were far more presentable than my travel shoes. So I wore them on the plane.

There is one bit of wisdom I have been able to claim and, more important, retain. I will now pass it along in this column, in the interest of educating younger readers with my hard-won experience. It is this: Attach your release to your bow as soon as you take it off. That way, if you have a bow, you have a release. I learned this from a guy I met at a lunch counter after a public-land hunt in Ohio. At the time, I'd recently spent an afternoon without a release in a ground blind in Texas. I couldn't leave to go get it because I was hunting with another guy and didn't want to hurt his chances. That was a long afternoon.

One more thing: Never shy away from having your photograph taken because you don't like the way you look. You look as good right now as you ever will.

Acknowledgments

You would at this moment be holding empty air in your hands and receiving strange looks from the people around you were it not for the many people who helped put this thing together. Jean McKenna, who edits my column at *Field & Stream*, worked tirelessly to make material available to Grove Press. She was also amazingly patient with my frequent and generalized cluelessness. Michelle Gienow was invaluable in helping me make selections to include here. (Some writers are good at recognizing their best stuff, others not so much. I still don't know which category I belong in.) She was also unstintingly supportive and encouraging. I'm immensely grateful to artist John Cuneo for doing the cover art, for all the editors at *Field & Stream* who put up with me, and for everyone at Grove, especially Morgan Entrekin and George Gibson.